U-48

U-48

The Most Successful U-Boat of the Second World War

Franz Kurowski

FRONTLINE
BOOKS

First published by Verlagshaus in Germany in 2007
Republished in Great Britain in 2012 by
Frontline Books

an imprint of
Pen & Sword Books Ltd
47 Church Street
Barnsley
South Yorkshire
S70 2AS

Copyright © Franz Kurowski, 2007
Foreword copyright © Charles Messenger, 2012

ISBN 978 1 84832 606 4

The right of Franz Kurowski to be identified as the
author of this work has been asserted by him in accordance
with the Copyright, Designs and Patents Act 1988

A CIP catalogue record for this book is
available from the British Library

All rights reserved. No part of this book may be reproduced or
transmitted in any form or by any means, electronic or mechanical
including photocopying, recording or by any information storage and
retrieval system, without permission from the Publisher in writing.

Typeset in Times New Roman
by Chic Media Ltd

Printed and bound in England
by CPI Group (UK) Ltd, Croydon, CR0 4YY

For a complete list of Pen & Sword titles please contact
PEN & SWORD BOOKS LIMITED
47 Church Street, Barnsley, South Yorkshire, S70 2AS, England
E-mail: enquiries@pen-and-sword.co.uk
Website: www.pen-and-sword.co.uk

Contents

Foreword vi

Chapter 1   The German U-Boat Arm: Development and Command 1

Chapter 2   The U-Boat War Begins: The First War Patrol of *U-48* 7

Chapter 3   The Second World War Patrol of *U-48*: Five Days –
                  Five Sinkings 20

Chapter 4   The Third War Patrol of *U-48*: Cruiser in Sight!...................47

Chapter 5   The Fourth War Patrol of *U-48*: General Observations 64

Chapter 6   Wooden Swords: The Fifth War Patrol of *U-48*:
                  Preparations for *Hartmut*..80

Chapter 7   The Battle of the Atlantic: *U-48* under New Command –
                  Sixth War Patrol..89

Chapter 8   The Seventh War Patrol: Summer Duel 98

Chapter 9   The Biscay Front 112

Chapter 10   *U-48* and Her New Commander: Convoy SC3....................115

Chapter 11   The Duel with Convoy SC7 – 'The Night of the
                  Long Knives'..127

Chapter 12   British Anti-Submarine Developments 138

Chapter 13   The Grand Finale – *U-48*'s Tenth War Patrol......................144

Chapter 14   The Eleventh War Patrol – Rapid Fire 148

Chapter 15   The Last Tanker Attacks: The Loss of the *Bismarck* 153

Appendices 160
Notes 168
Bibliography...170
Index 175

Foreword

U-48, a Type VII B, was the most successful U-boat of the Second World War, carrying out twelve patrols and accounting for 57 vessels, including a Royal Navy sloop, with a total gross tonnage of just under 322,500. Yet her active war ended in June 1941 and thereafter she was used as a training boat. Thus her story is very much one of the early phases of the Battle of the Atlantic, with both the German and Royal Navies suffering from shortages, especially in numbers of U-boats and convoy escort vessels.

Both sides set out to observe the terms of the 1930 London Naval Treaty, which had been signed by all the naval powers, including Germany. This stressed the need for the crews of merchant vessels to have the means to reach land or another ship before their own was sunk. Admiral Karl Dönitz's U-boat skippers were initially very careful to follow this rule. As the author describes, the usual practice was to halt a vessel by firing a shot across its bows, summon the captain across and inspect his papers. If it was a neutral vessel, sailing to a neutral port, it would be sent on its way unharmed. If it had contraband goods and was bound for an enemy port the crew would be ordered to take to their boats and once this had been done their ship sunk. Because the U-boat was on the surface throughout, it was vulnerable. Yet because convoying only applied to ships able to steam at certain speeds, there many sailing alone and unescorted during the early months of the war and so the danger to the U-boat was not nearly as great as it might have been.

In spite of this, the sinking of the liner *Athenia* by *U-30* on 3 September 1939 caused the British to believe that the Germans had embarked on unrestricted submarine warfare. Furthermore, Winston Churchill, occupying the same position of First Lord of the Admiralty as he had done in 1914, insisted on taking the war to the U-boats. One of the measures he took was to begin arming merchant vessels and once the Germans became aware of this they considered themselves entitled not to abide by the London Treaty, as they did ships sailing under escort.

Dönitz and his crews did, however, suffer other frustrations. First was the problem of having too few U-boats to make a significant impression at the outbreak of the war, and this in spite of the sinking of the aircraft carrier *Courageous* and the elderly battleship *Royal Oak*. At root lay Hitler's Plan

Foreword

Z expansion programme for his navy, with its emphasis on surface ships and initially not due to be completed until 1948. It meant that it was only possible to have up to some ten boats on patrol and while he did at times attempt to form wolf packs to intercept convoys, their small size meant that they could only cover a very limited part of the ocean.

The other major frustration was torpedoes, many of which malfunctioned. Franz Kurowski makes more than clear the intense frustration of the U-boat crews, not least that of *U-48*. The fault lay firmly with the Torpedo Research Institute and the Torpedo Inspectorate, which consistently ignored the fact that there was a problem. Matters reached a head during the Norwegian campaign, when few torpedoes worked and a significant number of British warships lived to fight another day as a result. Only after this was urgent action taken and torpedo reliability improved.

The fall of France in June 1940 and the subsequent deployment of U-boats to the French Alantic ports marked the beginning of what the U-boat crews called the First Happy Time. By drastically cutting the time needed to deploy from port to operational areas more U-boats could remain on station and wolf packs now really began to come into their own. This is graphically illustrated by the major successes against Convoys SC7 and HX79 in autumn 1940, in which *U-48* played a major part. Indeed, Allied shipping losses for September and October rose to over 400,000 tons per month.

By the early summer of 1941 the U-boat fortunes were on the wane. Increasing numbers of escorts, more maritime patrol aircraft, better anti-submarine detection equipment and improved escort tactics all helped to swing the pendulum the other way. An indication of this came on 25 March, when Doenitz's HQ war diary noted that five U-boats with veteran crews were no longer answering radio messages; they had all been sunk. Perhaps it was symbolic that *U-48*'s last patrol would involve supporting the wounded *Bismarck* as she attempted to seek haven at Brest. She never made it and the U-boats in the area were then involved in looking for survivors of her crew. Then, *U-48* moved towards the Azores, as part of Dönitz's tactic of turning his attention to the West African coast, where convoys were less well guarded.

Not mentioned in the book is the effect of Ultra on the Battle of the Atlantic. True, this was very limited during the period at *U-48* was operational, but the seizure of Enigma rotors from the trawler *Krebs* in February 1941 and the capture of a complete Enigma machine from *U-110* in May meant that the Submarine Tracking Room in the Admiralty began to have a much clearer idea of the German tactics. This enabled some convoys to be rerouted so as to avoid wolf packs.

There would be a Second Happy Time, when the U-boats were able to wreak havoc off the US Eastern Seaboard during the six months after the United States entered the war. Another grim time for the Allies occurred during the first months of 1943, largely because the Germans had installed an extra rotor in the Enigmas use by the U-boats. The decisive time came after the Allies finally managed to close the Black Gap, that area of the North Atlantic which was devoid of air cover. Thereafter the Battle of the Atlantic swung increasingly in their favour, although the U-boats would continue to operate right up until the bitter end.

As for the story of *U-48*, it illustrates all too clearly that war boils down in the end to the performance of human beings operating under enormous stress. This U-boat was blessed with three highly professional skippers and an exceedingly well trained crew. Thus, it was able to rise to every challenge, not least because of the entire confidence felt by the crew in their captain.

Charles Messenger

CHAPTER 1

The German U-Boat Arm: Development and Command

When the representatives of the German Reich and Great Britain signed the Anglo-German Naval Treaty on 18 June 1935, they agreed that Germany would limit her fleet of naval vessels to 35 per cent of British numbers except in submarines, where the limit would be 45 per cent. The treaty even went so far as to allow the U-boat fleet to equal the British in numbers if approved following bilateral discussions.

The British concession no doubt had regard to the small number of British submarines, only fifty-four boats at the time when the agreement was signed. Even in 1939 Britain had only fifty-seven submarines. The situation was accurately described in the House of Lords by Admiral of the Fleet Lord Beatty when he said: 'I am of the opinion that we owe Germany a debt of gratitude. The Germans came to us with outstretched hands and declared they agreed to a ratio of 35 to 100 in submarine construction. It they had made alternative proposals we would have met them. It is truly a thing for which we must be thankful that we have at least one country in the world from whom we may fear no arms race.'

A year later the Submarine Protocol between Britain and Germany was signed in London. This document introduced a number of difficulties for the prosecution of U-boat warfare. One of its clauses stipulated that in stopping and sinking a merchant ship, a U-boat had to act as would a regular surface warship. Guns 'installed aboard merchant vessels for defence' did not transform merchant ships into another category of vessel, and the protection they enjoyed under international law was unchanged unless they used the gun to fire at the submarine. Accordingly, in an armed encounter, U-boats had to proceed according to the Prize Regulations. This required that once stopped, a merchant ship had to be searched for contraband (specified merchandise or materials appearing on an arbitrary list declared by the belligerent nation to be contraband, but depending upon its destination). Only if this were found could the ship be sunk.

U-48

On the high seas, lifeboats were not considered to be places of safety for the crews of sunken merchant ships. U-boats would therefore have to leave the crew aboard ship, which would not be sunk, or bring them aboard the submarine, or search for some other vessel to take them. This made sinking a merchant ship on the high seas a very complicated affair. Nevertheless, on 23 November 1936 the German Reich signed the U-boat Protocol, and this almost nullified the military value of the U-boat in a war against merchant shipping.

Because Germany had declared her military sovereignty on 16 March 1935, Britain wanted the Reich to participate in the naval conference that year, since by its declaration the Reich now declared itself to be a Naval Power. The purpose of the naval conference was to draft a new agreement replacing the 1921-2 Washington naval treaties at their expiry. France opposed the British proposal and urged Britain and Germany to negotiate separately, which they did in November 1936.

Coinciding with the announcement of the Kriegsmarine naval building plan, the German public learned of the commissioning of the first U-boat on 9 July 1935. The declaration explained that: 'For the expansion of the Kriegsmarine, the following new vessels have either been laid down or will be so during the year in accordance with the prescribed basis of 35 per cent of the British displacement set out in the Naval Treaty with Britain – (a) twenty U-boats of 250 tonnes, (b) six U-boats of 500 tonnes, and (c) two U-boats of 750 tonnes. This was the first Press notice admitting the construction of new U-boats, although the building-up of the U-boat arm had begun much earlier.

In 1930 and 1931, Reichsmarine officers had sailed aboard submarines from the Finnish port of Abo, and Cadiz in southern Spain, and also on U-boats built by German staff to German designs in Dutch yards. Led by the veterans Bräutigam and Papenberg, many Great War commanders and technicians were involved in these voyages and learned to master the new technologies. Reichsmarine Command had been planning for the domestic construction of U-boats from 1932, and on 1 October 1933 the Anti-Submarine School had been established at Kiel-Wik. Here the core personnel of the first U-boats received their theoretical training, completed in submarine voyages from Abo in 1934.

At the same time initial preparations were set in train at Germania Werft Kiel for a U-boat building programme, and by the end of September 1934 the first half-dozen boats, *U-1* to *U-6* were accepted by the U-boat School (Flotilla Chief, Fregattenkapitän Slevogt).

The German U-Boat Arm: Development and Command

The First U-boat Flotilla

1.U-boat Flotille *Weddigen*, named after the famous U-boat commander of the First World War, was established on 27 September 1935. The flotilla-chief was Fregattenkapitän Karl Dönitz, who had been a U-boat commander in the Great War and was appointed immediately after his return from a training cruise commanding the light cruiser *Emden*.[1]

The flotilla consisted of six boats: *U-7* (Kapitänleutnant Freiwald), *U-8* (Kapitänleutnant Grosse), *U-9* (Kapitänleutnant Looff,) *U-10* (Oberleutnant-zur-See Scheringer), *U-11* (Kapitänleutnant Rösing) and *U-12* (Oberleutnant-zur-See von Schmidt). These six small boats formed the nucleus of the flotilla which included Slevogt's special unit at the U-boat School. The six training boats were: *U-1* (Kapitänleutnant Ewerth), *U-2* (Oberleutnant-zur-See Michahelles), *U-3* (Oberleutnant-zur-See Meckel), *U-4* (Oberleutnant- zur-See Weingärtner), *U-5* (Oberleutnant-zur-See Dau) and *U-6* (Oberleutnant-zur-See Mathes).

The Testing Committee for New U-boat Construction was set up on 1 June 1935, and had a chairman with technical experience in Korvettenkäpitan Bräutigam. This committee was attached to the Testing Command for New Warships under the title 'Testing Group U-boats'.

More U-boats were added in subsequent months, and on 1 January 1936 the new German U-boat arm was constituted as follows:

FdU (Führer der U-boote): Kapitän-zur-See (Kommodore) Dönitz

1.U-Flotille *Weddigen*: Kapitän-zur-See Loycke

U-7 (Freiwald), *U-9* (Looff), *U-11* (Rösing), *U-13* (von Stockhausen), *U-14* (Oehrn), *U-15* (von Schmidt), *U-16* (Beduhn), *U-17* (Fresdorf), *U-18* (Pauckstadt), *U-19* (Schütze), *U-20* (Eckermann), *U-22* (Grosse): all these commanders held the rank of Kapitänleutnant. Reserve boats without commanders were *U-8*, *U-10*, *U-12*, *U-21*, *U-23* and *U-24*.

The following units were attached for instruction and torpedo training:

Torpedo boat *Albatros*: FdU flag boat.

Torpedo retrieval boats *T-155* (Kapitänleutnant Barsch) *T-156* (Oberleutnant-zur-See Huber), *T-157* (Oberleutnant-zur-See Hänig) and *T-23* (Oberleutnant-zur-See Bening). The U-boat tender *Saar* (Korvettenkapitän Schönermark) was also available. U-Flotille *Weddigen* and its units were based at Kiel. On 1 September 1936 2.U-

Flotille *Saltzwedel* (Fregattenkapitän Scheer) was formed at Kiel with twelve boats, *U-25* to *U-36*.

The tried and tested 'wolf-pack tactics' formulated by Dönitz made the involvement of the greatest possible number of U-boats essential. For this reason he forced through the construction of further U-boats, although nobody shared his view on how tactics would be directed in a future war. At the highest level of Reichsmarine Command it was thought that in the next war U-boats would operate over long ranges and independently. Dönitz held the direct opposite opinion and required a manoeuvrable, powerful U-boat of medium size because only these, so he argued, would place him in the position 'to attack enemy convoys, which would certainly reappear, with whole U-boat packs and so sink ships from them'. Eventually he got his way but without managing to create the preconditions for wolf-pack attacks on enemy convoys using large numbers of powerful U-boats.

Britain as Possible Foe!
At the end of May 1938 Adolf Hitler informed the Commander-in-Chief Kriegsmarine, Generaladmiral Raeder, that in a future war he should *even* reckon with Britain as a possible enemy, although such a clash was not imminent. In October that year Raeder formed a planning committee to examine possible tasks for the Navy and the requirements arising as a result of Hitler's cautionary statement. The result of the meetings of the Commission was a new Ten-Year Fleet Plan based on a powerful surface fleet, although 233 new U-boats were provided for by 1948(!), amongst them a number of U-cruisers, very large submarines due for completion in 1943.

In the case of an unexpected early war against Britain, Dönitz saw a danger that the burden of naval operations would fall on the U-boat arm because there was no alternative way to engage Britain, an island power. He asked Raeder to report his fears to Hitler. On 22 July 1939 aboard the State Yacht *Grille* at a conference with the officer corps of the U-boat arm, Raeder advised them of Hitler's answer: 'The Führer will take steps to ensure that under no circumstances will there be war with Germany. That would be *"finis Germaniae"*. You, gentlemen, may rest assured.'[2]

Less than a month later, on 15 August 1939, Dönitz was recalled from leave and given the task of 'preparing the U-boats for the possibility of mobilisation'. At this, Dönitz gave Raeder another memorandum, *Gedanken des Aufbaues der Uboot-Waffe* ('Thoughts on Expanding the U-boat Arm') in which he advised the Commander-in-Chief that the U-boat arm was not

The German U-Boat Arm: Development and Command

yet in a position to carry out its role should war come. He requested that the arm be built up as quickly as possible, emphasising that the brunt in the Atlantic would fall on the Type VII boats. He would need 300 boats if he was to have 100 constantly at the enemy's throat: another 100 would be either sailing out or returning to port and the other 100 refitting or re-equipping. 'With the U-boats available to date, our war on commerce can only achieve pin-pricks against the British merchant fleet,' he declared and concluded his memorandum by saying: 'The U-boat arm must be enabled to resolve its main objective of defeating Britain in war by all means, including those outside the normal framework.'

On Standby Alert

On 19 August 1939 the operational U-boats of the U-boat arm were sent to waiting positions in the Atlantic. Of the fifty-seven submarines in commission, only forty-nine were operational. These were:

In the Atlantic, eighteen boats:
2.U-Flot: *U-26, U-27, U-28, U-29, U-30, U-33, U-34*.
6.U-Flot: *U-37* to *U-41* inclusive.
7.U-Flot: *U-45, U-46, U-47, U-48, U-52, U-53*.
Gruppe West, twenty-one boats:
1.U-Flot: *U-9, U-13, U-15, U-17, U-19, U-21, U-23*.
3.U-Flot: *U-12, U-16, U-20, U-24*.
5.U-Flot: *U-56, U-58, U-59*.
U. School-Flot: *U-1, U-3, U-4, U-36*, and after further working up from 3 September, *U-2, U-8, U-10*.
Gruppe Ost, ten boats:
2.U-Flot: *U-31, U-32, U-35*.
3.U-Flot: *U-14, U-18, U-22*.
5.U-Flot: *U-5, U-6, U-57*.
U. School-Flot: *U-7*.

Eight boats were not operational: *U-25, U-51* and *U-42*, yard-work on frames. Remaining work scheduled to conclude 17 September 1939. Still at training stage or working-up: *U-43* (commissioned 26 August 1939), *U-49* (commissioned 12 August 1939), *U-60* (commissioned 22 July 1939), *U-61* (commissioned 12 August 1939).
Summary: Operational forty-nine boats, non-operational eight boats, total in commission: fifty-seven boats.[3]

U-48

On 22 August 1939 FdU Ost was created within Kriegsmarine Gruppe Ost at Swinemünde. Its Command Staff was composed as follows:

C (Operations) Fregattenkapitän Schomburg
A1 Korvettenkapitän Godt
A2 Kapitänleutnant von Stockhausen
A3 Kapitänleutnant Oehrn
V (Engineers) Kapitänleutnant Zerpka
Radio Comms Leutnant-zur-See Kuhnt

This temporary arrangement lasted until 19 September 1939 and was disbanded at the end of the Polish campaign.[4]

CHAPTER 2

The U-Boat War Begins: The First War Patrol of *U-48*

On 19 August 1939 a total of seventeen Type VII U-boats cast off and ran northwards from their bases at Kiel and Wilhelmshaven, bound for assigned waiting positions stretching from the southern tip of Iceland to the Bay of Biscay. Eight days later six 250-tonne boats sailed for their operational areas in the North Sea and off the British East coast: on 29 August ten 'dug-out canoes' (as the smallest U-boats were known) joined them. Finally, five of the large boats left Germany in the period up to 30 August for the Narrows between the Orkneys and Iceland: all then lay in wait for orders.

On 1 September these boats received the radio signal advising of the outbreak of war with Poland. It was not yet clear whether Britain and France would enter the war by coming to Poland's aid as they had obliged themselves to do under a recent treaty. A few weeks before, Generaladmiral Raeder had said that Britain would not become involved, and if they did it would eventually mean 'finis Germaniae'.

* * *

U-48 was a boat of 7.U-Flotilla of the Atlantic group. She had been commissioned by Oberleutnant-zur-See Herbert Schultze on 22 April 1939. Schultze had joined the Reichsmarine in 1930 and commanded *U-48* on this her first war patrol. Now Kapitänleutnant Schultze, his crew considered him an experienced officer who had passed the rigours of U-boat Training School and trained aboard *U-2*. 'Vaddi', as the crew called him when he was out of earshot, was trusted by them completely and wholeheartedly, and this trust was not to prove misplaced.

U-48 had reached the appointed operational zone undetected and made a leisurely patrol. On 26 August 1939 Schultze had written in the war diary (KTB): 'Signals from home are very thin. The image of the political situation is hazy. I am trying to build an approximate picture of the situation by intercepts from the Nauen Press agency and monitoring signals from Zeesen and London as well as other transmitters. I expect an outbreak of war and the opening of hostilities with Britain and France next week, since Britain's stance appears to be certain. On the other hand it seems that negotiations are continuing and that our leadership is walking a tight-rope following the principle "Let us see who has the better nerves" and will eventually come round.'

After carefully assessing the situation, this last possibility was not what Schultze really thought. Later that day he noted in the KTB: 'I am of the opinion that we broke out from the North Sea unseen. My course 193° left me 120 nautical miles off the Irish west coast. Virtually no marine traffic sighted, only fishing boats on the Bailey Bank.' This situation changed swiftly, and on 28 August *U-48* was forced to make two alarm dives in order to avoid being spotted, the first on the approach of a British square-rigger, then a steamer. On each of the next four days it was necessary to dive at the approach of merchant ships.

On 1 September 1939 the sea was running at strength 2 to 3 with high swell. Visibility was only moderate under an overcast sky with occasional rain. That afternoon FdU advised by signal: 'Commencement hostilities against Poland.' They listened to Hitler's Reichstag speech. Schultze noted in the KTB: 'We have the feeling of being poorly off. The phrase "Atlantic forces" once sounded powerful, but what we have is not enough to pluck more than ten to twenty hairs from the fur of the British lion.' Schultze also said as much to his watchkeeping officers 'having regard to the lack of U-boat numbers *and* pocket battleships, of which I expected at least five or six'. In the KTB he wrote: 'We are at our waiting position. Two or three steamers pass by daily on a regular basis. Nice big tankers and freighters and a passenger liner amongst them.'

At 1230 hrs on 3 September 1939 the FdU signalled: 'State of war with Britain,' and at 1700 hrs the same day France also 'found herself at war with Germany'. At midday *U-48* entered naval chart square BE 64 (about 500 nautical miles west of Nantes). Wind was light from the north-west. Schultze urged the bridge watch to 'maintain 100 per cent effectiveness'. From now on every smudge of smoke sighted was to be reported immediately. Throughout 4 September *U-48* cruised at a few knots watching out for ships which the commander had to stop and search, and if need be sink. He felt the tension. Would his men match up? He felt certain they would.

To the KTB: 'I am patrolling north and south in my assigned sector and

The U-Boat War Begins: The First War Patrol of U-48

preparing to make war on commerce according to the Prize Rules.' The KTB also mentions: '4 September, sighted and stopped two tankers. The first was *Abadan*, 6,230 tons, in ballast from Le Havre to Mexico. Her papers in order, we allowed her to go. When stopping the second steamer a man of the gun crew was swept overboard by a rough sea. Fortunately his harness held him.'[1]

At 0815 on 5 September the bridge watch heard a dull noise to the south which sounded like a torpedo exploding. Shortly afterwards the radio operator announced the first reported sinking of the war by a U-boat: *U-47* (Prien) had stopped and sunk a steamer at 45°29'N 9°45'W. *U-48* continued on a westerly heading. The fresh south-westerly breeze drove a long swell before it. The sky was covered occasionally by swiftly passing cloud masses, visibility remained mainly good.

'Steamer 10° starboard ahead!' the watch called out.

'Man and load deck gun!' Schultze responded.

The gun captain appeared on deck with the gunners. The first 88mm shells were passed up to the bridge and sent down to the gun through a chute. *U-48* manoeuvred quickly into a favourable position. The commander sent by signal lamp: 'Stop. Send a boat with captain and manifest.'

They were all blind on the steamer's bridge. The ship steamed forward with nonchalant indifference.

'Deck gun, one round across her bow!'

The 88 roared, a long muzzle flame flashed from the barrel and the shell splashed into the sea 50 metres ahead of the steamer, which now stopped. While the gun crew reloaded, a boat was lowered and rowed across to the U-boat. The ship's master came aboard and handed Schultze his ship's papers for examination. These left no doubt: a Swede with a cargo for Oslo. 'In order,' Schultze declared, 'we must let him go. Gun crew unload and stand down.' The shells on deck returned to the interior of the boat the same way they had come together with the empty shell casing. The Swedish captain was rowed back to his ship, and once aboard he dipped the Swedish flag in salute and proceeded with his voyage.

Late on the afternoon of 5 September mast-tops were sighted on the horizon. The commander was summoned to the bridge and shown the top of a superstructure. Schultze dived the boat at once to avoid being seen and reported. Trimmed at periscope depth *U-48* headed at low revolutions towards her prey, the commander making occasional sweeps through the periscope.

'The ship has no nationality markings,' Schultze said as he crouched at the attack periscope, seated in the saddle, circling the column with touches on the foot pedal. The crew were at battle stations. Apart from the commander's commentary they were 'blind' and had to follow his orders precisely. When *U-48* was sufficiently close to the merchant vessel he ordered: 'Clear to surface! Bridge watch to tower. Gun crew ready to engage!' After a brief pause he continued, 'Radio room report at once if he transmits. Chief engineer – surface!'

In the tower Schultze peered over the battle-helmsman's shoulder at the boat's course. 'Boat is through!' Chief Engineer Zürn reported. Schultze unsealed the tower hatch and threw it open. Fresh air streamed into the boat. At the forward coaming of the tower he saw the bows of the steamer heading directly for *U-48*.

'Bridge watch, come up!' The lookouts came to the tower.

'Gun crew, man bow gun!'

All went smoothly in the frequently practised routine of everyday U-boat life. Shells were brought up to the bridge and sent down the chute to the deck gun. The first was soon in the chamber. The gun captain measured the range to the ship. 'Bow gun ready!' Signal flags ordering the steamer to stop fluttered from the extended sky periscope. 'Fire a round, just in case this captain is also blind,' Schultze ordered.

Sea state was strength 3, and when the first two shells splashed into the sea ahead of the steamer, she put her rudder hard over and hoisted the Red Ensign. Seconds later the *U-48* radio operator noted the distress call from the British ship: 'SOS from *Royal Sceptre*, chased and shelled by German submarine, position 46°23'N 14°59'W.'

'Steamer is transmitting and giving his position,' Oberfunkmaat Wilhelm Kruse, the radio petty officer, advised. By doing so the steamer had put herself beyond the protection of international law. Her intention in transmitting was to call up enemy warships to her aid, a hostile act.

'Fire at will at the steamer! Try to silence the radio room!'

Shells straddled the freighter in rapid succession. The gun crew slaved at the weapon, finally obtaining the first hits on *Royal Sceptre*.

'Radio room silenced!' the *U-48* radioman reported.

Schultze saw the steamer's lifeboats being lowered and ordered ceasefire in order to give the crew the change to abandon the burning ship. A few minutes later the radio operator of the stricken vessel began to send again: 'From *Royal Sceptre*: chased and shelled by German submarine. Leaving ship position 46°23'N 14°59'W.'

There's nothing else for it but a torpedo!' Schultze said when he was

The U-Boat War Begins: The First War Patrol of U-48

given the fresh report. 'Torpedo room, prepare single shot, tube 1!'

'Tube 1 ready for surface torpedo,' came the report from the bow room.

'Tube 1, fire!'

The torpedo was expelled by a compressed-air cartridge and once free of the boat ran independently, straight and true over the few hundred metres to the target. The warhead of 350 kilos of TNT hit amidships. The control room petty officer noted the time: 1338 hrs. *Royal Sceptre*, 4,853 gross tons, sank very quickly. Within a few minutes she was gone. For the first time the radio operators heard through the hydrophones the eerie breaking sounds of a sinking ship. They would hear it over fifty times more aboard this U-boat.

The *Royal Sceptre* radio operator had remained on the ship to the end, calling for help for the crew in the boats, and he shared her grave. 'Caps off, men!' Herbert Schultze exclaimed emotionally, 'Now you know who our enemy is. His name is defiance, if it's for the flag. He will not spare us, because he is prepared to sacrifice himself in situations of the greatest danger.'[2]

A few minutes after the ship sank, a lifeboat containing women and children was seen, and a second with crewmen heading towards France, over 400 nautical miles away. A short while later a lookout reported a second ship emerging from a squall. This was the British steamer *Browning*. When she had hauled up sufficiently close to read a flag signal flying from the periscope, Schultze hoisted: 'Turn south – 13 nautical miles. Pick up crew of steamer *Royal Sceptre*.' The *Browning*'s master could make no sense of the signal and gave the order to abandon ship even though he had not been fired upon.

'We have to round up the lifeboats and escort them back to the steamer so that she can pick up the women and children of *Royal Sceptre*', Schultze explained.

'But do we really want to let that fat tub escape, Herr Kaleunt?' the watchkeeping officer asked.

'We are pursuing commerce warfare in accordance with the Prize Rules. Just imagine the fuss Tommy will make if we do not adhere to them strictly. The British have each one of our submarines under a microscope and will use the most minor error to make propaganda claims of atrocities which stink to high heaven. Therefore we must run a "get-you-home" service for these people.'

U-48 headed at full speed for the *Browning* lifeboats which were being rowed at a furious speed. As the submarine approached them, the master waved with both arms while the crew raised their arms in a gesture of surrender. Schultze stopped the boat where the lifeboats could easily drift up to it. 'Listen, captain,' Schultze raged at the man, who was now standing up in the nearest boat, 'over there we have just left the crew of a ship we sank. You now row back to your ship, get aboard her, head for the lifeboats and save the shipwrecked people.'

The captain found this incomprehensible and stood mesmerised for almost a minute staring at Schultze, then gazed at the men on the conning tower. Here was some foul Nazi trick, but what it must be he had as yet been unable to fathom. 'For God's sake,' Schultze roared, 'worry about the people of the *Royal Sceptre* I have just sunk over there.' The medium-sized German commander, tending a little towards corpulence, indicated the direction to head by pointing towards it. The captain's problem was that he knew the Hun well from the last set-to, but this one was not running true to form. The lifeboats returned to the *Browning*, and after being heaved inboard the steamer headed for where the *Royal Sceptre* had been sunk. They found the boats and rescued the survivors.

'Radio room to bridge,' the radio petty officer reported, 'warning broadcast by two British coastal stations reads: 'To everybody – attention! Danger of U-boats.' and then repeated: 'Danger of U-boats at 46°23'N 14°59'W.'

'That will set their destroyers on the hunt for us,' Schultze promised, 'we shall make off for the north west at maximum speed.' At full ahead *U-48* disappeared out of sight of the British. When the *Browning*'s mastheads and smoke could no longer be seen, the commander went below to his compartment, hung his binoculars on their hook and threw his cap onto his cot. Then he let down the folding table, removed the KTB from its pigeonhole and entered the ship's name and details of the first sinking of the voyage. In conclusion he observed: 'I ensured the safety of the crew of the ship I sank according to the Prize Regulations. There were women and children in the boats. The ship's boats were not a place of sufficient safety for them.' This was the spirit of the U-boat mariner with which Dönitz had inspired his men. Nevertheless, on the very first hours of the war there occurred an incident which provided the enemy with a plentiful helping of atrocity propaganda.

* * *

After a five-hour consultation with Naval Control in the Royal Liver Building, Captain James Cook returned to the Donaldson liner *Athenia*,

The U-Boat War Begins: The First War Patrol of U-48

13,581 gross tons, and sailed from Liverpool for Montreal at about 1630 hrs on Saturday 2 September 1939. The liner carried 1,102 passengers and 315 crew. Although it was not necessary for an innocent passenger liner to do so, at the outbreak of war next day Captain Cook set a zigzag course, and had previously rigged his ship not to show any light by night. His mean course was westerly at 15 knots.

U-30, commanded by Oberleutnant-zur-See Fritz Julius Lemp, had recently arrived in marine square AM1631. At 1630 hrs on 3 September 1939 west of Rockall his lookouts reported a large steamer on a westerly course well north of the usual shipping routes. The distance was so great that Lemp did not expect to be close to the ship until nightfall. Lemp plotted her course and ascertained that she was zigzagging. At 1930 hrs when dusk fell and the ship had not set navigation lights, Lemp concluded that because she was a liner zigzagging and proceeding by night blacked out, she must be a 'troop transport or armed merchant cruiser'. He ordered tubes I and II flooded, and fired the two torpedoes at 1938 hrs.

The torpedo from tube I struck *Athenia* at the level of No.6 hold and caused flooding to the engine and boiler rooms as a result of which the liner stopped and assumed a 6° list to port. The torpedo in tube II jammed with rudder damage and it took several minutes to expel it. It then ran a circular course threatening to return to hit *U-30*, and Lemp was forced to take the boat deep to avoid the danger.

Upon returning to the surface, radio operator Funkmaat Georg Högel gave Lemp a note of a distress message being sent without pause by the stricken liner: '*Athenia* torpedoed, 56°44'N 14°05'W.' From *Lloyd's Register*, Lemp identified his victim as a passenger steamer. 'But why was she sailing blacked out?' he asked himself aloud. He decided to leave the scene immediately, swearing his crew to silence. He did not report the sinking to Wilhelmshaven, and thus Dönitz knew nothing of it.

Of the 1,417 persons aboard *Athenia* when she sailed, 128 lost their lives, the majority to accidents during the rescue operation. The liner did not sink until 1040 hrs on the morning of 4 September. The U-boat war had its first sensation. As was to be expected, the sinking was condemned by the British as a brutal assault on an innocent passenger ship contrary to maritime law. The Propaganda Ministry of the German Reich decided on the absurd explanation that since no German U-boat was responsible, it must have been done by the British in order to blacken the name of Germany with a dreadful atrocity at the very outbreak of war.

The enquiries which Dönitz had addressed to all U-boats were answered in the negative except by Lemp, who had recognised his error, ordered the strictest secrecy and did not reply. Not until 29 September when *U-30* entered Wilhelmshaven at the conclusion of her first war patrol and Dönitz came to the lock personally to greet the returning crew, did the veil over the *Athenia* incident finally drop.

On the quayside, Lemp saluted the FdU and stated: 'I report to the Herr Kommodore the return of *U-30* from patrol!'

'Heil Lemp! Heil the crew! How did it go?' Lemp's face fell: now he had to confess. Still saluting as he spoke, he said: 'I have to inform the Herr Kommodore that I sank the *Athenia*.'

'You did what, Lemp?'

'I sank the *Athenia*, Herr Kommodore. I believed the ship to be a troop transport or auxiliary warship. Only later did I have doubts when I read the SOS messages and appeals for other ships to come quickly.'

'A fine mess you have landed us in, Lemp,' Dönitz told him, 'I shall have to court-martial you for this.'

'I am aware of it, Herr Kommodore!'

'Very well then, Lemp. Until you are told differently, you must keep this matter strictly secret. And make sure your crew does too.'

'Jawohl, Herr Kommodore.'

The investigation into the case was conducted secretly. If Lemp were guilty he could be reduced to the rank of Ordinary Seaman, but the FdU became convinced that Lemp had acted correctly in the given circumstances. The only charge he had to face, and for which he received only a disciplinary punishment, was for his failure not to have been more painstaking in his examination of the liner before he fired his torpedoes at her.[*] Because of the possible political consequences of the incident, Hitler ordered the sinking of the *Athenia* to be kept secret. As a result, OKM had the offending page of the *U-30* KTB, copies of which went to various departments for assessment, removed and destroyed. It was the only known act of this nature by the U-boat arm in the Second World War.[‡]

---

[*] The meaning behind this statement is as follows. The German Naval Staff were convinced by a photograph of the sinking liner which they obtained from one of the rescue ships that *Athenia* was an auxiliary warship or could be mistaken for such. This photograph appeared in the *Völkischer Beobachter* edition of 23 October 1939 and showed a large naval-type radio installation about the liner's masts fore and aft, far larger than would be required by an innocent passenger liner. If Lemp had seen this installation he would have been justified in sinking *Athenia* without warning under international law. He was not justified in sinking her without warning on the basis of the zigzagging and running without lights at night only. See: Cay Rademacher, *Drei Tage im September, Die letzte Fahrt der* Athenia *1939*, Hamburg: Mareverlag, 2009, p 293. Tr.

The U-Boat War Begins: The First War Patrol of U-48

The first impression which the British Admiralty had derived from the *Athenia* incident was that Germany had begun unrestricted submarine warfare. That this was not the case was shown by the conduct of Prien, Schultze, Liebe, Rollmann and the other successful commanders of the time.

Further Successes for *U-48*

During the first week of the war, the *U-48* radio operators noted down several signals reporting sinkings. Kapitänleutnant Liebe sank the *Manaar*, 7,242 gross tons: *U-47* (Prien) was also successful, next came *U-34* (Rollmann). *U-33* (Dresky) was another of the first boats to enter the list, and on 7 September Prien struck again.

On the morning of 8 September 1939, *U-48* sighted a steamer. This was the British *Winkleigh*, 5,055 gross tons, owned by the Tatem Steam Navigation Co., London, loaded with an important cargo for the British war effort. When *U-48* hoisted a flag message the ship stopped at once and lowered a boat bringing over the captain with the ship's papers. One glance at these was enough to convince Schultze she carried contraband.

'Have your crew leave the ship, captain. I will signal requesting help to have you picked up,' Schultze assured him while passing down four loaves. The captain, broken-hearted, replied bitterly: 'White man kills white man!' Then as his boat pulled away from the submarine, he raised his right arm and shouted 'Heil Hitler!' From the bridge of *U-48* Schultze watched the lifeboats being set down with the crew. The radio frequencies were monitored to ensure that the doomed ship did not transmit news of her plight. At 0830 hrs on 8 September 1939 a torpedo was fired from 600 metres and hit the *Winkleigh* amidships, sending up a great column of fire. The ship sank on an even keel within a few minutes. Schultze had the position of the casualty broadcast over the distress frequency and could be certain that help would soon arrive to save the crew. Warships would turn up, if not a steamer whose captain had overcome his fear of the grey wolves to attend the site of the sinking 500 nautical miles west of Brest. At midday on the 8th, *U-29* (Kaplt Otto Schuhart) reported sinking the motor tanker *Regent Tiger*, 10,176 gross tons. *U-48* dived three times that afternoon when flying boats were seen, but remained undetected.

---

‡ In February 1940, 120 *Athenia* survivors and relatives of the deceased in the United States filed unsuccessful liability claims against Cunard, agent for the Donaldson Line. The defendants were only able to provide a passenger list and the naval architects' blueprints. The ship's papers and log book had been destroyed and thus the true status of the *Athenia* is not known. Rademacher, *Drei Tage im September*, pp 295–6. Tr.

U-48

After two quiet days, on the morning of 11 September the lookouts spotted the mast-tops of the steamer *Firby*, 4,869 gross tons, port of registry Hartlepool, owned by the Popper Shipping Co. Ltd. The deck gun was used to stop the ship. Her captain came over to the U-boat with the ship's papers. From these Schultze saw that the freighter was British and carrying contraband. After the crew had abandoned *Firby*, a single torpedo was fired from tube IV. The compressed air from the propulsive cartridge billowed back into the bow room. After a run of forty-five seconds, the victim was hit amidships and sank on an even keel ten minutes later. Schultze brought *U-48* over to the lifeboats and passed down bread, and dressings for two slightly wounded seamen before ordering the radio petty officer to send a message *en clair*, the text of which read: 'CQ CQ CQ for Mr Churchill, have sunk British freighter *Firby* at position 59.40 degrees N, 13.50 degrees W, rescue crew if you please.' This signal was read out in the House of Commons, for it almost seemed as though U-boat commanders such as Schultze were making every effort to communicate the news that Dönitz's U-boat arm was pursuing commerce warfare in exemplary compliance with the Prize Regulations. All further sinkings during September 1939 showed this to be the case.

On 12 September *U-48* turned for home. No more steamers were sighted, and on 16 September the boat traversed the Kattegat at top speed, reaching the pilot vessel *Süderau* at ten minutes before midnight to take aboard the pilot. The last leg of the voyage began at 0100 hrs on 17 September, *U-48* making fast at the Tirpitz Mole, Kiel, at 0550 hrs. Thus the first war patrol of *U-48* came to a successful conclusion. She had sunk three merchant ships of 14,777 gross tons. Twelve other boats were all due to return to port at about the same time for lack of fuel. To prevent the creation of a U-boat vacuum, allowing the enemy a chance to get his ships through unhindered, *U-28*, *U-31*, *U-32*, *U-35* and *U-53* remained in their operational areas while *U-26*, *U-27*, *U-29*, *U-33*, *U-34* and *U-39* sailed for home. Before the return to Wilhelmshaven described earlier, *U-30* (Lemp) put into Reykjavik to land two seriously-wounded crewmen and left at noon the same day.

These first war patrols had shown that commerce warfare in accordance with the Prize Regulations was being pursued even though it was a dangerous business for U-boats. Incidents in the U-boat war now created a great stir on both sides of the fence.

The Sinking of the Aircraft Carrier *Courageous*
While the patrol was ending for *U-48*, *U-29* (Schuhart) with three successes

The U-Boat War Begins: The First War Patrol of U-48

to date, still had torpedoes aboard and Schuhart was hoping to increase his tally before heading for home. At midday on 17 September at 50°N 14°W his lookouts sighted on the horizon a large transport, first by her superstructure and then her flat upper deck. Her course was favourable for *U-29*.

'Fast steamer with aircraft on the upper deck, Herr Kaleunt!' reported IWO Georg Lassen, in charge of the bridge watch. 'A very fat tub indeed, IWO,' Schuhart replied, 'and he is nicely placed for us. We shall go to periscope depth and prepare to attack.'

The dive went smoothly. *U-29* disappeared from the surface and shortly afterwards the hydrophone operator, Funkobergefreiter Schröter reported: 'Propeller noises, Herr Kaleunt! Including several destroyers.' Schuhart rushed to the hydrophone room and lent over Schröter's shoulder, listening through the parallel headset. He confirmed that the screw noises were from destroyers, recognising their sharp characteristic screeching. 'This big steamer must be a very important ship to have a pack of destroyers to escort her. We shall now have a closer look!' With this observation the commander hurried back to the control room, settled himself on the saddle of the periscope column and ordered the 'asparagus' extended. The periscope motor hummed. The tip being still covered by the wave crests, Schuhart asked for a half-metre higher. The chief engineer carried out this order precisely, and now the commander could make out, still very far off, the superstructure of a great ship and three columns of smoke which he guessed were trailing from the funnels of destroyers still unseen beyond the horizon.

Looking upwards he saw a shadow. 'Down periscope!' After raising the sky-periscope in its place he announced laconically, 'We have the full salad, aircraft circling the whole convoy.' He swept the skies. 'Four aircraft,' he told the crew at battle stations. 'Attack, Herr Kaleunt!' the coxswain advised. He was near Schuhart, bent over his charts and marking the positions of the first sighting.

'OK, the boat will attack the big transport.' *U-29* stalked the convoy ever closer. Now and again the large ship zigzagged, but once it had done so twice, Schuhart knew the mean course and could estimate where the convoy would cross his path. Two hours later, after a careful peep through the periscope, he saw what she was.

'Commander to everybody – the ship is not a freighter but an aircraft carrier!' A murmur ran through the submarine. Suddenly silence was restored at the commander's next order. 'Torpedo room, tubes I and II ready for a fan or two!'

U-48

'Tubes I and II ready!'

Seated in the saddle of the attack periscope, Schuhart swivelled around the column by use of the foot pedal. He identified the sweeper destroyer running a fast zigzag course ahead of the carrier. The purpose of this destroyer was to intercept and attack a U-boat on the bow of the great warship. A touch on the rudder brought *U-29* out of the swept quadrant. The aircraft carrier began to tower ever higher above the surface of the sea and already filled three-quarters of the optic.

'Torpedo room – *Achtung*!' The next order would be the one to fire. The torpedo mate waited on tenterhooks. 'Tubes I and II fire!' The compressed-air cartridge hissed: the torpedo mate's hands covered the push buttons should the electrical ignition process fail. 'Torpedoes running!'

The control room petty officer opened the vents of the equaliser tanks to admit seawater, compensating for the lost weight of the two discharged torpedoes and retaining the boat at trim.

'Port 20!' Schuhart ordered the battle helmsman. The latter repeated the order and *U-29* bore away on the new course to bring her away from the destroyers keeping pace alongside the carrier.

'Time's up!' shouted the coxswain, taking his eyes from his stopwatch. The seconds ticked by, then the first torpedo hit the carrier amidships, followed five seconds later by the second, 20 metres astern of the first. A geyser of fire and water erupted upwards.

'Aircraft carrier is hit – he is stopping – flames are pouring out of the holes caused by the torpedoes – white flames – we hit his aviation fuel tanks.' Schuhart reported his observations calmly one after another. Seconds after his closing words there resounded a fearsome breaking and grinding, and amidst a series of eruptions and explosions the aircraft carrier began to capsize. She was the Royal Navy's first casualty of the war: HMS *Courageous*, 22,489 tons displacement with a ship's company of 900. Of these, Captain Makeig-Jones and 514 of his men lost their lives.

Courageous and her strong force of escorts had been engaged on an anti-submarine patrol. Captain Roskill, author of the official British history of the Second World War at sea, criticised the decision '. . . that such a valuable ship should have been used for such a purpose. Probably this was attributable to pressure from on high, above all from the First Lord, Winston Churchill, to "take up the offensive against the German U-boats" rather than devote all energies to the defensive strategy for convoys and the escort of Fleet units'.[3] That this was the case is evident from Churchill's book: 'I was constantly at pains to discourage this defensive obsession by whatever kind of counter-attack possible. I could never be satisfied with this policy of "convoys and blockade".'[4]

That this kind of strategy against U-boats was not without its problems was demonstrated by the loss of the *Courageous*. A few days earlier, Kapitänleutnant Glattes in *U-39* had attacked the aircraft carrier HMS *Ark Royal*. Three torpedoes with magnetic ignition had been fired at her, but all three detonated prematurely. The columns of water betrayed the boat which was then attacked and sunk by the escorting destroyers *Faulknor, Foxhound* and *Firedrake*. The crew escaped in time and was taken prisoner. In this case it had only been a stroke of luck that preserved *Ark Royal*. The failure of the torpedoes saved the ship and not the large destroyer escort accompanying her.

This incident was probably the first significant failure of German torpedoes, a calamity which was to become more drastic as time went on, frustrating great chances of success so that finally one could say: 'The German torpedo disaster saved Britain from a far more serious defeat at sea than it eventually suffered in the Norwegian campaign at the time of Operation *Weserübung*.' The tragedy experienced by a series of U-boats whose commanders had aimed and fired at enemy capital ships and had had no success because the torpedoes failed will be outlined in later chapters. It was also a tragedy for the whole U-boat arm.

CHAPTER 3

The Second War Patrol of *U48*: Five Days – Five Sinkings

U-48 set out on her second war patrol only seventeen days after the termination of the first. The crew had enjoyed a short leave: on 4 October 1939 'Vaddi' Schultze was back on the conning tower, issuing his orders from beneath a large fur cap. Men of the 'departures committee' took their places on the quayside to shout their goodbyes

As when he left for the first patrol, Herbert Schultze did not look back: there was no point in it even if he had wanted to: it was one in the morning and pitch dark. By midday he had completed the passage of the Kiel Canal: at eight that night *U-48* was heading through the German Bight: on 6 October the boat battled through rough conditions in the central North Sea. The wind whistled bitterly cold from the north-east, then veered to come from the north-west. Huge rollers swept the foredeck and crashed against the tower, flinging regular cascades of spray over the lookouts. Before noon on 7 October the boat made a trial alarm dive to test the mettle of the crew, who could soon expect to be tussling with aircraft and destroyers as well as the elements. Schultze' officers were IWO Oberleutnant-zur-See Teddy Suhren, IIWO Oberleutnant-zur-See Otto Ites and chief engineer Oberleutnant-zur-See (Ing) Erich Zürn, a veteran group who welded the crew into a fighting machine.

Schultze, being a teetotaller, attempted to convince his men of the evils of alcohol at every opportunity. His three officers had served aboard *U-48*, built for Atlantic operations, since commissioning on 22 April 1939. 'Vaddi' was from Kiel and had found his sea legs at an early age. He had joined the Reichsmarine in 1930, and was already 'old' from the point of view of the young crew, already a 'father' at thirty years of age in 1939. The father image with centre-parted hair was present more in his grave expression than his behaviour aboard the boat. Herbert Schultze was very fond of the number seven to the extent that he would only steer a course divisible by seven. This may have been more legend than reality. However, the fact that the boat's mascot, a black cat 'with its back up' and hissing defiance, painted on the conning tower during the second patrol – many crewmen including Oberleutnant-zur-See Suhren wore it on their caps – hinted at Schultze's inclination towards superstition.

The boat sliced a course through the October chop towards the operational area. *U-48* was attached to Group Hartmann, put together by Dönitz and led by Korvettenkäpitan Hartmann aboard *U-37*. There was a special background to the assembling of this Group, for on 1 October 1939 Dönitz had explained in his KTB:

> Our situation is notable for the small number of U-boats available. In view of the congregation of enemy merchant ships into convoys I consider it inadvisable to scatter our boats singly over a very wide area. It must be our aim for U-boat groups to intercept convoys and destroy them with concentrations of the few U-boats available. To find convoys on the high seas is difficult. The basic approach must be to search in those areas through which shipping has its natural routes of passage. This is found south-west of England and around Gibraltar. The first has the advantage of being closer to home, but enemy reconnaissance of the coastal fringes is heavy and operates from many bases. Moreover at this time of year we have to reckon with unfavourable weather in this area. Gibraltar has the disadvantage of being a long haul, but since this cuts across the trade routes we can expect successes on the way, and there is a greater bunching of maritime traffic around the approaches to Gibraltar. The climate is considerably more favourable that in the North. We have few reports about the levels of reconnaissance, which can only be flown from Gibraltar itself or Casablanca, but our information is that it is maintained principally over the Straits. Therefore I have decided to concentrate the boats on the Gibraltar traffic.
>
> Implementation: The more determined and unexpected the appearance of U-boats there, the greater and more certain the result will be. The boats will be ready for operations at an assortment of dates. Accordingly they will depart on different days and take up initially an operational area south-west of Ireland, the most lucrative area for sinkings to date. When all boats are more or less in position there the FdU will order them to advance south, but depending on the situation.
>
> Korvettenkäpitan Hartmann has taken command of the Atlantic Group aboard *U-37* and when necessary will take over operations against convoys. If it appears to him that the prospects off Gibraltar

U-48

are not promising, he is authorised to order a new formation more remote from enemy bases along the west coast of the Iberian Peninsula which will concentrate only on north-south traffic.[1]

Thus the FdU set out the course which *U-48* and other boats would steer on the second wave of patrols. Six U-boats were non-operational because of yard lay-ups, special missions and damage. By 15 October 1939 only three were on hand for anti-convoy duty. One of these was *U-48*. Nevertheless, this second wave of U-boat attacks would produce great successes. What had become obvious after the first wave was that the available fleet of U-boats was insufficient to maintain a continuous assault on enemy shipping. As soon as the boats, on waiting stations since before war was declared, had fired off all their torpedoes, the oceans were void of U-boat activity.

At midnight on 8 October 1939, *U-48* stood west of the Shetlands, eight hours later north-west of Orkney and by 2000 hrs north-west of the Hebrides. From this point on, enemy air and naval patrols were to be expected. The lookouts were visited frequently by Schultze to ensure they remained on their toes. North-west of Ireland on 10 October, *U-48* found the seas deserted, on the 11th no smudge of smoke was ever seen. 'Is our course too close to the coast?' Schultze asked himself in his KTB entry. He pressed on further south: next day at 0700 hrs when the lookouts sighted a ship seven miles off the starboard bow and proceeding at 15 knots with navigation lights on he took up the chase. While this was under way a second steamer was seen, more favourably placed and moving more slowly.

'Diving stations. Alarm dive!'

Trimmed at periscope depth, Schultze allowed the second steamer to approach close so that he could order her to stop as he surfaced.

At 0734 hrs Zürn received the order to surface. The boat came up slightly bow heavy. The bridge watch and behind them the gun crew followed the commander up the ladder. Schultze had the ship signalled to stop, which she did immediately, lowering a boat for the master to come to the U-boat. He climbed aboard and up to the conning tower to present the ship's papers for the German commander's inspection.

This was the steamer *Lido*, 2,000 gross tons, bound for Dublin with timber. Since everything checked out Schultze released her, warning the captain that should he use his radio he would be sunk at once. The Irish captain assured him that he had no such intention: he intended to discharge his cargo, not spy for Britain.

The Second War Patrol of U-48: Fve Days – Five Sinkings

Schultze, disgruntled, watched the steamer disappear towards the Emerald Isle.

'We shall never win the war like this. Although the *Lido* is probably on the level, many others will shi . . .' At this point the devout Schultze fell silent, noticing that his IIWO, Oberleutnant-zur-See Ites, was waiting with interest for the remainder of the sentence.

'No doubt you would enjoy hearing your commander profane, Ites?' he asked with a frown.

'Well, almost . . .' Ites replied.

'Almost maybe, but in practice never!'

At 1610 hrs on 12 October the lookouts reported a large tanker on the port quarter. This was the *Emile Miguet*, 14,115 gross tons, which Schultze fired on and forced to stop. Upon being advised by his radio room that the tanker was sending an SOS with her position and repeating it without a break, Schultze opened fire at once. The tanker's crew took to the lifeboats and their ship was torpedoed from close range to ensure she settled quicker. During this operation the bridge watch sighted another steamer.

'This tanker is not going anywhere, so we shall investigate the new sighting,' Schultze explained and headed *U-48* for the new objective which was running without lights and with luck might easily have escaped notice. At 2024 hrs IWO Suhren ordered a single torpedo fired which exploded 100 metres ahead of the submarine's bow. This alerted the steamer to the presence of *U-48*.

'Steamer is transmitting distress message. Ship's name is *Heronspool*.'

'Begin pursuit!'

Once *U-48* had closed the range at full speed and turned towards the steamer for a second torpedo, the British ship opened fire from a gun on her stern. The second torpedo was loosed at 2045 hrs without result. Five minutes later when Suhren had the target in his sights once more a third torpedo was released at 2115 hrs.

'Time is up!' called the coxswain, stopwatch in hand. Nothing. In a rage Schultze slapped the bridge coaming with his open palm. 'This is a damn' fine mess. It borders on sabotage. Those jerks at the Torpedo Research Institute should be locked up for this!'

'Watch out, steamer is firing again!' shouted the bosun's mate as he saw a flash from the steamer's stern. Two shells plumed up in the sea as they exploded well away from the U-boat. With better training the steamer's gun crew could have damaged the U-boat and saved their ship.

'Bear away and make fresh approach.'

23

U-48

U-48 slipped out of the line of fire and under full cover of darkness crept up afresh on this tough nut. Teddy Suhren braced himself behind the UZO sight. The UZO were heavy binoculars which fitted on a rotating bracket set in a ring marked with the degrees of the circle. Used for surface attacks, the UZO installation was linked to the mechanical analogue computer below. The pedestal was located on the forward part of the bridge.

Suhren had the steamer in the optic.

'Ready!'

The fourth torpedo left the tube at 2305 hrs and streaked towards the target. Nothing.

'Steamer is shooting again!'

'God, he's stubborn!' Schultze cried in anguish, 'and we're going to waste all our torpedoes on this tub.' *U-48* ran another evasive semi-circle before firing the fifth torpedo at 2350 hrs. Nothing. Schultze bit his lip. In this situation he needed to express his feelings in a string of vile curses, but even now he exercised restraint.

'Men, the situation is hopeless, but no longer serious! We shall try our luck with the stern torpedo tube. Tube five ready?' The tube was reported clear to fire, and two minutes after the fifth torpedo, the sixth was loosed. This caused further uproar on the bridge when it detonated a bare 150 metres astern of the *U-48*.

'If it is the intention of the torpedo jerks to kill us, then they will surely do so,' Schultze remarked gloomily. 'How goes the reloading?'

'We are reloading tube II, tubes III and IV are to follow, Herr Kapitän. Tubes II and III will be ready together at 0100,' the torpedo petty officer reported to the bridge.'

The boat had put some distance between itself and its opponent while running a parallel course. It was 0101 hrs precisely when the 'mixer'[*] advised that tubes II and III were ready to fire.

'We shall attack again. Battle stations!'

'The new approach to the enemy ship commenced. The seventh torpedo was fired at 0116 hrs. It hit the steamer's forecastle and exploded.

'Steamer is stopping! Crew taking to the boats, Herr Kaleunt!' Suhren reported from the UZO.

'This time we've won our laurels,' the bosun's mate remarked.

'Yes, but he cost us seven torpedoes which we needed for later,' Schultze reminded him.

---

[*] U-boat slang for torpedoman.

The Second War Patrol of U-48: Fve Days – Five Sinkings

'Smudge of smoke in sight, starboard beam!' It was 0120 hrs.

'We'll leave the *Heronspool* to her fate, she's already much lower in the water and will certainly sink. Head for the new sighting.' *U-48* bore away on a fresh heading at full ahead both diesels for the new steamer, but this must have been a ghost, for no trace of her could be seen.

'Right, let's get back to the *Heronspool* just in case she tries to give us the slip.' When *U-48* sighted the abandoned steamer only her superstructure above bridge level was still visible. Schultze ordered not to bother transmitting the ship's position, as destroyers would certainly be arriving here soon.

The boat turned away. The next steamer was sighted at 0700 hrs. By then all tubes had been reloaded. At 0702 hrs Schultze took the boat down to periscope depth. The steamer wandered along, only two small rudder corrections were needed and *U-48* was in the right position to attack.

'We shall stop the steamer. Gun crew to readiness, bridge watch to the tower. Surface!'

Passing behind the battle helmsman Schultze glanced at the compass reading, nodded to the leading seaman at his post and waited for the chief engineer to report.

'Boat is through!' Zürn announced.

Schultze threw open the outer hatch and went up first for a quick look round before calling up the lookouts.

'Man the gun, bring up ammunition. Ready the weapon to fire a warning round across the steamer's bow!'

'Steamer is transmitting, Herr Kaleunt!'

'Destroy the radio installation!' Schultze shouted to the gunlayer at the 88mm. The first two shells howled into the nearby ship. The transmissions ceased abruptly. It was the French steamer *Louisiane*, 6,903 gross tons. She stopped.

'Hoist flag signal "Get into the boats".'

Once the lifeboats were clear of the steamer, *U-48* opened fire at 0835 hrs and shelled the *Louisiane* for ten minutes, aiming below her waterline. Once she began to settle the shooting was stopped: another ten minutes and the French freighter had gone under. Here follows the sinking of this vessel from the perspective of the ship's master:

The Sinking of the SS *Louisiane*

The French steamer *Louisiane*, master Captain Charles Bandon, had orders to proceed to a US port in the Gulf of Mexico as part of the hastily assembled Convoy OB 17. She was to load fighter aircraft to resist the German bomber offensive when it came. The freighter was a fine modern ship operated by the Compagnie Générale Transatlantique. Together with four similar ships sailing from Britain, she weighed anchor at Spithead on the morning of 11 October 1939 and joined a convoy escorted by several sloops and a corvette. The long haul head was south-westerly for the far side of the Atlantic. The warship escort was detached surprisingly soon leaving the merchantment to continue the voyage alone. It was not long aboard *Louisiane* before the three other freighters were lost to sight, all being bound for different ports and their captains at liberty to choose the course which suited them best. No German U-boats were sighted or reported on 11 and 12 October. Everything looked favourable for the crossing. A ship came by. Captain Bandon noted in the log that she was the *Heronspool*.

As darkness fell on the evening of 12 October, and the sky was already black astern, Captain Bandon saw flames lighting the western horizon. The closer he came the more imposing were the flames, and soon amidst the flickering tongues of red and yellow and the spouting oil he could make out the shape of a burning tanker.

'That will be the *Emile Miguet*,' Bandon observed to his wireless operator, whose door was open. 'Do you know anybody aboard her?' Jean Lebrun nodded, staring in horror at the flames. Somewhere in the vicinity there must be a German U-boat. The captain read his mind.

'I'm turning south now to get clear of this U-boat. If we keep on this heading the flames will illuminate us into a very visible target.'[2]

As his ship turned, through binoculars Bandon saw several lifeboats being rowed eastwards. Once he had completed a broad semi-circular evasive course and there had been no sign of the U-boat, Bandon breathed a sigh of relief. 'It looks like we've outwitted them,' he concluded, and brought his ship back to her original course to continue her voyage.

At first light, while drinking a cup of black coffee brought him by the cook, Captain Bandon was taken aback to see the sea foam to port 20° ahead and from the deeps appear on the surface a German U-boat exactly as portrayed on the charts. He heard the drone of her diesels and watched with horror as U-boat men poured out of the conning tower and manned the deck gun. The relay of shells had already begun and the muzzle plug was unscrewed from the barrel. Then the weapon was traversed to point at the French freighter.

'Send an SOS, Jean!'

The Second War Patrol of U-48: Fve Days – Five Sinkings

The young telegraphist rapped out on the morse key, 'SOS German submarine SOS'.

Ten seconds after this message the U-boat opened fire with the evident intention of silencing the wireless installation. The first shell hit the ship's bridge. The First Officer and Captain's ADC were killed, the helmsman and an apprentice at the wheel fell to the deck wounded.

'More shells followed,' Captain Bandon remembered later, 'and then the U-boat commander must have been satisfied that he had destroyed the radio room, for the firing ceased.' Bandon ordered everybody into the boats, including the radio operator, who had wanted to keep transmitting once he recovered from his shock. The *Louisiane* crew abandoned their ship, and only after all lifeboats were in the water and away did the Germans resume the shelling. The French freighter was riddled, many shells hitting below the waterline to speed her sinking. She disappeared below the waves at 0814 hrs at position 50°14'N 15°02'W.

'We shall head for the lifeboats,' Herbert Schultze ordered.

When *U-48* reached a point to intercept the lifeboats, the submarine stopped engines. 'Do you require water or provisions?' Schultze asked. Captain Bandon replied in English, 'Thank you, we have all we need!' As the lifeboats drifted past the submarine, Bandon saw the fighting cat painted on the conning tower. Then *U-48* submerged.

The lifeboats were rowed eastwards. All crossed their fingers and hoped that the radio message they had managed to get off had been heard. At midday the superstructure of two British destroyers appeared above the horizon. The *Ilex* and *Imogen* reached the lifeboats at 1300 hrs, took the survivors aboard and sunk the boats with machine-gun fire. Both destroyers then headed for England, rescuing on the way the crew of *Lochavon*, 9,205 gross tons, sunk by *U-45* (Gelhaar), and a short while later another detour was made to pick up the crew of *Bretagne*, a French steamer of 10,108 gross tons which had been in the same convoy as *Lochavon* and also sunk by *U-45*. This was a fast convoy. A third ship bound for Europe from Kingston, Jamaica, avoided torpedoes.

Aboard the two destroyers the passengers made a desolate sight. As the presence of German U-boats had to be reckoned with in this region, the crews remained at battle stations. Continual course changes occurred and occasionally one heard the detonation of depth charges dropped blindly as a deterrent. Suddenly hectic activity broke out. They parted at great speed then turned inwards towards a central focus which *Ilex* crossed first, dropping a depth-charge pattern. Then after the fountains thrown up by these charges subsided, *Imogen* followed suit.

U-48

'They have a German U-boat in an ASDIC pincer,' Captain Bandon told his men. Suddenly the sharp elongated bow of a U-boat emerged from the foaming and tossing seas, protruded a few metres above the surface, fell forward, the tower became visible and then the submarine lay as if dead on the waters. Men jumped from the tower into the sea. The destroyers fired a few rounds and then ceased fire. The U-boat, damaged in the pressure hull below the waterline, sank quickly.

Giant bubbles rose to the surface above the sunken boat and burst. In the sudden silence the shouted orders of the destroyer commanders could be heard. The two warships closed in on the tight group of U-boat men in the water, dropped nets over the ships' sides and fished them out, aiding the injured to clamber aboard. Thus ended the career of Kapitänleutnant Rudolf Dau in *U-42*. He had lost his cap but was easily recognisable by his red hair. When two British sailors attempted to search him, Dau drew a thick wallet from a side pocket of his leather jacket and tossed it into the sea, where it sank at once. The IWO of *U-42* watched these goings-on with a grin. Then he reached into his own side pocket – and brought out a comb, restoring a sharp parting to his wet hair. With the shipwrecked crews, Allied and enemy, that they had saved the two warships headed at high speed for England.

A few hours later the steamer *Karamea*, torpedoed by *U-45*, reached an Irish port and safety. From this disaster of independents, everything useful was gleaned which might improve the convoy system and provide ships with the most effective protection.

Fast Shooting

At 0917 hrs on 13 October 1939 an RN destroyer hove into sight and at once fired two or three salvoes at *U-48*. They fell close, but the submarine had dived urgently and gained enough depth to escape damage from the shelling. Schultze took the boat to 120 metres. The men remained at battle stations, the off-watch returned to their cots. The hydrophone operator listened to the rapidly approaching screws. The destroyer dropped a pattern of depth charges close to the boat but no damage ensued. Some kind of sonar was heard but no Asdic. *U-48* moved away from the destroyer at minimum revolutions, creeping speed. Standing in the control room near the chart table, Herbert Schultze conned the boat discreetly out of the danger zone. Hours went by. The fug in the boat grew ever thicker. Schultze ordered the use of potash cartridges to aid breathing. At last the destroyer screw noises became ever fainter.

At 1550 hrs the boat came up and 'hung from the periscope head at 16

The Second War Patrol of U-48: Fve Days – Five Sinkings

metres' as the chief engineer put it. A quick sweep of the horizon resulted in the sighting of a tanker at long distance. Schultze allowed this vessel to come up, and then surfaced, demanding by flag signals that she stop. The tanker's captain obeyed forthwith and did not transmit a radio message, coming aboard *U-48* with the loading manifest. This was the Norwegian tanker *Europe* with aviation fuel for Amsterdam. Her master's papers were in order and at 1700 hrs Schultze released the ship.

Between 1900 and 2040 hrs the upper deck torpedoes were transferred below. The manoeuvre went like clockwork, the commander observing in the KTB: 'Fast and determined, irreproachable execution of the task at night in grid square BE 3573.' The test dive at 0907 hrs on 14 October to ascertain the trim weights and oil consumption was completed in record time. Schultze insisted that every action had to be 100 per cent perfect and that no opportunity should be lost to reduce the time it took to submerge the boat. In an emergency seconds could be decisive in determining whether the boat and her crew sank or survived. Any crewman who made a boob which lost time could expect a 'rocket'.

At 1005 hrs a steamer was sighted zigzagging. Running surfaced to guarantee he would intercept her, Schultze worked his way forward at the limit of vision, diving at 1102 hrs and heading for the steamer. The order to surface and prepare for a surface attack followed at 1213 hrs. The deck gun obliged the British collier *Sneaton*, 3,677 gross tons, to stop.

'Steamer transmitting SOS and giving his position!' The *U-48* radio operator kept up a running commentary. 'Now their operator is saying that the crew is taking to the boats.'

'One torpedo!'

This time the torpedo ran straight and true to hit the stationary collier amidships. She sank quickly and as usual Schultze took *U-48* to the lifeboats to ensure they had everything necessary.

'Captain to captain!' he shouted when the boats were within earshot, 'Can we help you?'

'Thank you, we have everything,' replied the ship's bearded master, standing.

'A safe journey home!' Schultze called back. He noticed the incredulous looks they gave him. A few minutes later the lookouts sighted another steamer. *U-48* went to periscope depth. After a long survey of the vessel Schultze said in disappointment, 'She is Belgian. This time we must deny ourselves. We shall remain submerged. She will definitely have seen the *Sneaton* survivors.' *U-48* ran a parallel course with the Belgian ship,

Schultze watching through the periscope until the *Sneaton*'s lifeboats were seen. All had raised a sail to catch the favourable wind.

At 1517 hrs *U-48* surfaced. 'Give the boat a good airing, supercharge the port diesel,' Schultze ordered, instructions necessary to keep the submarine ready for action. No further sightings were made that day. At 0100 hrs next morning, 15 October 1939, Schultze signalled the FdU: '. . . After sinking four steamers and stopping two others I must consider my location compromised. Therefore I shall proceed tonight to southern boundary of my operational area and send signals Nr. 2331/15/50 and 2347/14/51 from there. After doing so I shall return to my northern boundary and hope to encounter further victims.'

That this was an inspired decision proved itself at 0840 hrs on 15 October when a steamer was sighted. *U-48* headed towards it at top speed surfaced, diving at 1012 hrs to approach close. When he raised the periscope at 1220 hrs for a peep he laughed and called to his IIWO standing nearby, 'Have a look, Ites,' and offered him the periscope saddle. Ites sat down and peered into the optic. 'Looks like a wreck, Herr Kaleunt.'

'It *is* a wreck, IIWO, and that of the tanker we sank three days ago.'

'The *Emile Miguet*? But surely she was much bigger?'

'What you see there is the forecastle, about 130 metres in length. The stern section broke off and sank. We must surface and sink the remainder.'

U-48 surfaced at 1230 hrs. The gun crew fired a hail of shells into the wreck. As the fifteenth hit a gigantic tongue of flame stabbed up. 'Those were the gases which built up in the tanker's holds,' the commander explained to the lookouts. The remains of the ship now burned with a dense black smoke visible for miles. It was bound to attract the attention of British warships and so Schultze left the wreck to her fate and set off for his operational area.

At midnight on 16 October *U-48* was south west of Ireland in square BE 3578. At 0650 hrs a vessel was sighted showing lights. By means of a flag signal hoisted on the periscope mast Schultze ordered her to stop and send over her master with the ship's papers. The *Lerdam*, 8,800 gross tons, was bound for Rotterdam. Schultze was not entirely happy with the documents and sent a boarding party to check the alleged cargo of cotton. It corresponded with the manifest and so Schultze let her go. At parting Schultze requested fresh meat and fifty eggs from the Dutch captain which were provided at once, all payment being categorically refused. Schultze would not let himself be outdone and – much to the regret of his own crew – presented a bottle of cognac to the Dutch crew. Then he hoisted the signal

The Second War Patrol of U-48: Fve Days – Five Sinkings

'Safe journey' and watched the *Lerdam* steam away to eventually arrive safely at her port of destination.

At midday on 16 October, moderate seas with north easterly breeze, scattered cloud and good visibility prevailed in square BE 3564. Any ship entering the lookouts' range of vision was bound to be seen. By midnight *U-48* had sailed south to BE 6578 without seeing any vessel: at 0908 hrs *U-46* reported: 'Enemy convoy in square 6831.' This was the adjacent quadrant to the south for which Schultze quickly charted a course, heading for the convoy at maximum speed. The boat pounded southwards all day until at 1930 hrs *U-37* reported: 'Convoy has dispersed'.

That the commander wished to release a few strong words was evident to the crew from his facial expression. Boatswain Brandes hid a grin when he saw Schultze's grief. They had sped here all day at top speed, burning tons of fuel for nothing

'Go to 77°.'

'77° it is, sir!' the helmsman confirmed. The course was divisible by 7. This occurred so often that the crew suspected the commander was superstitious, although nobody dared tax him about it. *U-48* ran on at high speed in the hope of finding some of the steamers from the dispersed convoy, and the commander's luck was in, for at 2014 hrs in square BE 9153 two steamers were sighted, both navigating unlit. Immediately he received the report the commander leapt up from his bed, sprinted down the narrow passageway and swung himself through the bulkhead hatch into the control room.

'Coming up!' he roared and climbed the ladder.

'Port 10° ahead, Herr Kaleunt!' Schultze raised his binoculars. The first steamer was very near and could be seen clearly. 'Surfaced attack!' The UZO binoculars were brought up and placed on their column. Suhren as Torpedo Officer stood behind the apparatus and aimed it at the first steamer. At 2030 hrs he gave the order to fire. In the bow room the torpedo mate waited, hands covering the manual release knobs for the eventuality of electrical failure. A cloud of vapour from the compressed air cartridge stabbed back into the bow room. 'Torpedo is running!' the mate called out. The control room petty officer flooded the forward tanks to equalise the sudden loss of the torpedo weight. Where the torpedo finished up nobody knew, for no explosion was heard. The next torpedo was due to hit three minutes later. This struck the steamer below the mast aft. The ship, estimated at 5,000 to 6,000 gross tons, came to a stop, her crew took to the boats and *U-48* turned away to pursue the second ship.

At 2100 hrs a destroyer was seen approaching from ahead on a parallel course about 400 metres off the beam and heading for the first casualty. As a precaution Schultze reduced speed to slow ahead so as to cut back the diesel noise, but the destroyer's commander had eyes only for the sinking steamer, and to save its crew.

'Fire torpedo at destroyer from stern tube!'

This one should have hit, for the warship was on a straight course. What happened to this torpedo remained a mystery, and the destroyer gave no sign of realisation that she had come under fire.

'Very well then, we shall pursue the second steamer.'

U-48 soon came across her quarry. Once in her sights *U-48* ventured even closer to be sure of obtaining a hit. Schultze wrote in the KTB:

> 2310 hrs, square BE 9231, first torpedo at the second steamer. Range 150 metres very close. No explosion heard. Possibly the torpedo had not yet risen to the set running depth and passed below target's keel. The steamer discovered us and transmitted an SOS, reporting position and 'German U-boat'. She is the British *Sagaing*, 7,986 gross tons. At 2320 hrs second torpedo failed. If possible I am hoping to sink this ship with the deck gun at dawn. Therefore I am presently keeping contact with her on the assumption that early tomorrow or during the day the convoy will reassemble. Sent radio message as per radio log.

U-48 kept pace with the steamer at 13 knots at the limit of visual range. At 0345 hrs, the BdU sent signal 0223/18/41: 'To *U-48* – begin voyage home.' Schultze was not ready to let *Sagaing* off the hook, however, and at 0400 hrs he informed his KTB: 'We shall pursue *Sagaing*!' *Sagaing* was keeping a good lookout of her own, and at 0655 hrs transmitted her position and reported 'I am being tracked by a U-boat'.

Another steamer had wandered into the range of vision of *U-48*, and then others at about 0715 hrs, all steering to the east. *U-48* signalled: 'Enemy convoy in sight' and sent regular position reports to allow other boats to home in on her signals. At 0732 hrs a destroyer arrived, forcing *U-48* to make an alarm dive. Schultze continued the story in the KTB: 'We dived and went to 120 metres (deepest point 132 metres). The destroyer depth charged us. We counted off 31 explosions. I assumed that acting on my radio signal *U-37* and *U-46* will have found the convoy by daybreak and attack. I therefore stayed a little longer submerged since it appeared necessary to give the crew some rest. At 1645 hrs we resurfaced and transmitted a signal to the FdU confirming that the boat is returning home.'

The Second War Patrol of U-48: Fve Days – Five Sinkings

On 17 October 1939, 150 nautical miles north west of Cape Finisterre, *U-46* (Sohler) established contact with Convoy HG3 and called up *U-37* and *U-48* to join him. *U-37* was the first to find a target and sank the *Yorkshire*, 10,183 gross tons. Nine minutes later the bridge watch aboard *U-48*, approaching at high speed, heard a second torpedo explosion. This time it was from *U-46* sinking the *City of Mandalay*, 7,028 gross tons. *U-48* continued towards the convoy at high speed. 'We are almost there,' Schultze commented upon sighting the first column an hour later. All ships of the convoy were now heading north to get clear of the U-boats.

At 1900 hrs *U-48* went to periscope depth, and eighteen minutes later Schultze fired a fan of two torpedoes at a 6,000-tonner, but both missed. He immediately tried a third from the stern tube, but this also failed. Now hunted by a corvette, *U-48* was forced to pull away, but once the corvette regained the convoy *U-48* returned to the fray.

'We shall attack!'

U-48, surfaced, ran at full ahead towards two favourably-placed steamers, of 6,000 tons and 5,000 tons respectively, which 'Vaddi' Schultze had selected. Teddy Suhren stood at the UZO. The last two torpedoes were ready in the tubes. Just as this fan of two torpedoes were released, the entire column of the convoy altered course. This saved the two ships targeted, but after the running time had elapsed both torpedoes hit the British *Clan Chisholm*, 7,256 gross tons by *Lloyd's Register*, which sent a distress message and sank ten minutes later at 45°10'N 15°05'W.

All three Hartmann-Group boats had scored against the convoy, and were now hunted by British and French destroyers. The U-boats left the scene safely, but next morning upon surfacing they were bombed by Sunderland flying boats and forced back under. Short signal to BdU from *U-48*: 'From convoy sank *Clan Chisholm* 7,256 gross tons, no torpedoes left.' Minutes later the BdU replied: 'Bravo *U-48*. Come on home.' When the commander announced this to the crew, relieved jubilation swept through the boat. *U-48* turned about and began her return to Germany while *U-37*, sent into the lion's den of Gibraltar, sank three independent ships in a furious four-hour foray, and the Greek *Trasyvoulus*, 3,693 gross tons, on the way home.

At 1215 hrs on 19 October, *U-48* sighted a steamer, diving at 1240 hrs to get within range to bombard the merchantman with the deck gun. At 1332 hrs after surfacing and recognising this ship as the *Rockepool*, 4,892 gross tons, Schultze opened fire with the deck 88mm since he had no torpedoes. The British freighter had two guns on the poop and returned fire with these, forcing Schultze to dive, since a single hit on the pressure hull would rob

U-48

the submarine of her capability to submerge. With such a long and dangerous voyage still ahead of her, *U-48* would have had no hope of getting home under these circumstances.

Rockepool had sent an SOS with her position, and Schultze thought it worthwhile to shoot again from a different angle, resuming fire at 1412 hrs: however now a destroyer appeared from nowhere and headed straight for him. *U-48* dived, ending the encounter with the *Rockepool*.

Upon resurfacing at 1542 hrs the telegraphist morsed to the FdU: 'Return of *U-48* continuing.' Beyond the north-west coast of Ireland the boat passed the western Hebrides and at 1600 hrs on 21 October stood north-west of these islands. At 0945 hrs next morning west of the Shetlands an aircraft came up from astern and cut across the boat's path diagonally about two miles ahead. *U-48* was seen and reported, for at 1015 hrs two destroyers appeared. They were initially about six miles apart but sailed inwards towards each other. Schultze decided to pass between them, flooding down to bridge level and succeeding in his escape.

On 23 October 1939, *U-48* entered the northern North Sea to be greeted by heavy rain during the evening. The entrance to the Skagerrak was passed at 0800 hrs next morning, and the Kattegat at 1600 hrs. At midnight in the Little Belt a small 250-ton U-boat was passed running northwards, but it failed to answer recognition signals. At 0945 hrs on 25 October, *U-48* moored at the Tirpitz Mole, Kiel, entering the yards next day for an overhaul which lasted until 20 November.

The crew divided into three watches for leave. On the 26th Schultze reported his return from patrol to Dönitz, having sunk five enemy merchant ships of 37,153 gross tons. He also reported the devastating failure of the torpedo issue, which had frustrated an even higher tally of sinkings. Dönitz, recently promoted to Konteradmiral and made BdU (Commander-in-Chief, U-boat arm), promised immediate remedial measures. After this second patrol by *U-48* he wrote in his report: 'A very successful voyage, particularly so since it lasted only three weeks. *U-48* fired all her torpedoes and reported five failures. It is superfluous here to go further into the causes and effects. I am keeping the Torpedo Inspectorate continually informed and they have been made aware expressly of the urgency of the matter. The BdU is in the closest contact with them.' This addressed once more the question of the torpedo misery, which would develop within a brief time into a total fiasco.

Special Mission: Scapa Flow

Once *U-48* had returned to Kiel, only three boats remained on hand for anti-

The Second War Patrol of U-48: Fve Days – Five Sinkings

convoy work. This was due to losses and special missions, and boats refitting after returning from patrol. Although the second wave of U-boat attacks had been very successful, it was now evident that the number of U-boats available for operations was insufficient to inflict those intolerable losses on merchant tonnage which would encourage the enemy to sue for peace. As soon as the last of the second wave of boats in the Atlantic fired the last torpedo, a U-boat void existed.

Before *U-48* sailed on her third patrol there occurred that great feat of U-boat history when a German U-boat penetrated the heavily defended British naval base at Scapa Flow. On 9 October 1939, *U-47* under Kapitänleutnant Günther Prien sailed on this mission. Dönitz's plan for a U-boat to enter Scapa Flow and if possible sink an enemy capital ship there had been carefully worked out and offered to Prien, who was at liberty to accept or decline it. Prien accepted. The idea was to pass through a narrow gap between two grounded wrecks in the Holm Sound shallows and look for a target in the bay of Scapa Flow.

On the evening of 12 October 1939, *U-47* reached the Orkneys where Prien informed his officers of the mission. Early on the 13th the boat rested on the bottom in 90 metres and at 0445 hrs the crew was told that this patrol to Scapa Flow would take them into the lions' den itself. When darkness fell on 13 October, *U-47* surfaced and headed for the naval base at slow ahead. Flickering polar light threatened the operation at the last moment, illuminating the boat for all to see, but IWO Oberleutnant-zur-See Engelbert Endrass considered it the best shooting light for the boat. His opinion convinced the hesitant Prien. Off the Rose Ness light the lookouts sighted a small steamer. Prien flooded down as a precaution, and this proved a wise measure when a fishing boat appeared a short time later heading directly for *U-47*. Prien took his boat down, for if she were seen in these waters the operation would be over and the Royal Navy would set up a great hue and cry in pursuit of the intruder.

At 2307 hrs *U-47* grounded violently in 30 metres. The fishing boat, or possibly naval trawler, left the scene as quickly as she had arrived and at 2331 hrs Prien brought *U-47* back to the surface. Having identified Holm Sound, Prien headed for it. The strong current drew the boat towards it. At the last moment the block-ship was seen. Coxswain Spahr noticed the error and corrected the course. A few seconds later and *U-47* would have entered Skerry Sound instead of Kirk Sound. Once inside Kirk Sound channel, Prien ordered surface running on the electric motors only.

The rising tide swept the boat in the direction of the wrecks. At the

U-48

narrowest point between Mainland and Lamb Holm, *U-47* drifted directly towards the last obstacles. The battle-helmsman was forced to correct the course constantly as Prien manoeuvred his boat very precisely to pass between the two wrecks. At the last moment he saw the hawser connecting them and dived the boat to avoid it. *U-47* was now in Scapa Flow, and free to reconnoitre the main anchorage of the Home Fleet.

Bosun Dzillas pointed out a shadow to the watchkeeper, Oberleutnant-zur-See Endrass, who was stationed behind the UZO on the bridge. All tubes were ready for firing. Shortly afterwards a second large warship was seen astern of the first. *U-47* believed she had two capital ships before her tubes. Prien ordered two fans of two torpedoes each to be fired. The first fan ran successfully, but one torpedo of the second fan stuck in the tube, the electrical ignition having failed.

U-47 made a turn. All awaited the expected torpedo explosions. Not until long after the running time was up did they hear a hit. They thought this was on the shadow which Prien had identified as HMS *Repulse*, but actually hit the anchor chain of HMS *Royal Oak*. Nobody aboard the ship appeared to notice the attack. They heard the noise, but passed it off as a delayed-action bomb dropped by the Luftwaffe nearby. The second fan had no result, and neither did a torpedo fired from the stern tube during the turn.

Prien put some distance between himself and the battleships at which he had fired. All tubes were empty save for the failed torpedo which had jammed in one. The crew worked at a feverish tempo to reload. According to Korvettenkäpitan Wessels, *U-47*'s chief engineer, the process took only twenty minutes, an incredibly short record time.

Prien had the courage and tenacity not to give in and returned to the fray even though he was aware that 'destroyers might have been alerted by the first explosion and could be on his trail'. Three torpedoes had been reloaded and the discharge cartridges refilled with compressed air. Prien intended to fire all three torpedoes at the anchored ship. Endrass stood at the UZO. He had the old battleship in his sights, and it filled the optic completely when the order came to fire. All three torpedoes ran. *U-47* turned away with rudder hard over and started for home. Immediately after the call 'Time is up!' the first torpedo hit just forward of the ship's bridge, the second abaft the bridge and it seemed that the third also struck.

The night came alive. The battleship *Royal Oak*, 29,150 tons displacement, broke apart as a magazine exploded, capsized and sank. Three hundred and seventy-five of the ship's company survived, twenty-four officers and 809 ratings went down with the ship. *U-47* made off at full

The Second War Patrol of U-48: Fve Days – Five Sinkings

speed and negotiated the Narrows successfully, reaching the open sea at 0215 hrs. Captain Roskill's opinion of this *coup de main* by *U-47* reads:

> Meanwhile in Scapa Flow Bay it was now accepted that in all probability a German submarine had got through the barrier defences. The hunt for this vessel, carried out with all available forces, was unsuccessful. We know now that this operation had been very carefully planned by Admiral Dönitz. Kaptlt Prien deserves the highest recognition for the courage and determination with which he executed the Admiral's planning.

Dönitz was promoted immediately to Konteradmiral on the strength of this success and made C-in-C U-boats (BdU). The promotion was announced by Grossadmiral Raeder aboard *U-47* on her return. On 18 October Günther Prien received the Knight's Cross from Hitler's own hand at the Reich Chancellery in Berlin.

Hitler's Visit to the FdU: The First Torpedo Failures
Before Prien's exploit, on 28 September 1939 Hitler had visited the FdU's HQ at Wilhelmshaven. After inspecting the honour guard, Dönitz made his report to Hitler in the presence of Raeder and Generaloberst Keitel. The address was entitled: 'Operations of the U-boat arm to date and the future intentions of the FdU with regard to U-boat policy.' Dönitz summarised the situation as follows:

> 1. The pressure exerted on the enemy by the German U-boat arm is, as before, very great and not less than in the Great War
> 2. Britain lacks the advanced technology to overcome the U-boat peril.
> 3. Although the British defences have made some advances, these are met by great strides in U-boat technology, in particular:
> (a) the boats make less noise;
> (b) the torpedoes make no splash when expelled, which formerly betrayed the boat's position; and
> (c) the track of the torpedo cannot be seen and its effect is greater than previously.
> 4. The U-boat arm has made fairly great advances in telegraphy, which has enabled operations to be planned for distant theatres. The concentration of ships into convoys can therefore be matched by concentrating U-boats into packs.

U-48

5. After considering all questions relating to the U-boat War, the FdU is convinced that in its U-boats Germany has the means to hit Britain decisively where she is weakest.

6. The U-boat War can only be pursued successfully if there are sufficient boats available. The figure is at least 300. The requirement from armaments planning is therefore to build a significantly greater number of U-boats than had originally been envisaged.

7. Given enough boats I believe in a decisive success by the U-boat arm!

An attentive Hitler followed this precise summary, which also brought to his attention the fact that the September results proved the point Dönitz was making that substantially more tonnage could have been sunk if enough submarines had been available. In conclusion, from now on U-boats had to be built as a priority. There followed an hour-long reunion attended by the Führer and all U-boat officers at the naval hostel in Wilhelmshaven. This was the first and last visit by Hitler to his U-boat men and to the command centre of the U-boat arm.

From the opening days of the U-boat War it had come as a bitter surprise to many commanders that the lethal weapon which the improved torpedo was claimed to be was often 'blunt'. A series of U-boat commanders reported in short signals that torpedo failures had robbed them of deserved successes. In his KTB entry at 1517 hrs on 2 October 1939, the FdU noted: 'Numerous premature explosions of torpedoes reported.' This was the first warning sign in the war that a serious problem existed with the torpedo issue. The same day he signalled: 'To all boats: everybody attack blacked-out vessels between 44° and 62°N, and from 7°W to 3°E.' Unfortunately for his purpose he was unable to conjure up torpedoes which could be guaranteed to work. At Scapa Flow, Günther Prien had had to fire seven torpedoes at a moored battleship to obtain two certain hits (plus one which exploded against the anchor chain earlier). Any other commander would have returned home without success.

After his KTB entry of 2 October, Dönitz examined all torpedo reports from his commanders. Since 6 September there had been reports of torpedoes exploding prematurely well short of the target. On 14 September when *U-39* attacked the aircraft carrier *Ark Royal* from a range of only 800 metres, Kapitänleutnant Glattes had fired two G7a magnetic-ignition torpedoes which simply could not avoid exploding as soon as they passed below the keel because the intensification of the magnetic field close to the iron ship provoked the detonation. However, the two torpedoes fired at *Ark*

The Second War Patrol of U-48: Fve Days – Five Sinkings

Royal never made it to the keel since they exploded 100 metres short of the target. *U-39* was seen and depth-charged by the destroyer *Foxhound*. She was sunk but her crew saved.

On 31 October *U-25* fired four torpedoes at short range at a stationary steamer north west of Cape Finisterre. All four failed. On 7 November *U-46* (Sohler) returned from patrol having sunk one tanker, but he had fired seven failures at a convoy, and two at a cruiser stopped at a 90° shooting angle. Both torpedoes fired exploded prematurely. The cruiser was alerted and left at high speed. Sohler was lucky that the cruiser had had no destroyer escort or probably his boat would have suffered the same fate as did *U-39*.

On 30 October *U-56* (Zahn) penetrated the destroyer escort surrounding the battleship HMS *Nelson* and fired a fan of three which ran straight and true for the British flagship from 800 metres. Besides the ship's company there were VIPs aboard the battleship in the shape of the Commander-in-Chief Home Fleet Sir Charles Forbes, the First Sea Lord, Admiral of the Fleet Sir Dudley Pound and the First Lord of the Admiralty, Winston Churchill. Above the screw noises of the escorts the *U-56* hydrophone operator heard the hard metallic impact of a torpedo against the side armour of *Nelson*. The torpedo failed to explode. The second also struck and failed to explode. That evening Zahn signalled the BdU: '1000 hrs, *Rodney*, *Nelson* and *Hood* with ten destroyers in square 3492, course 240°. Fired three torpedoes, failures.'

With that it was clear to Dönitz that he was not only short of sufficient submarines, but that he had a grave problem with the torpedoes. Most of the boats which had been lost at the Front for uncertain reasons could have been sunk as a result of torpedo failures when ships and escorts identified the place from where an attack had originated and subsequently attacked the submarine.

Admiral Dönitz demanded that the TVA (Torpedo Research Institute) Eckernförde launch an immediate investigation into the causes of the defects. He was rebuffed to a certain extent by the head of TVA, Konteradmiral Wehr, who insisted that the problem was due to chance failures. From earlier torpedo development problems of which he was aware, Wehr's explanation was eventually proved to be a deliberate lie. As early as June 1937 Wehr, then in the rank of Kapitän-zur-See as head of TVA Eckernförde, had recognised that the G7a and G7e torpedoes ran at a significantly greater depth than set. An attempt was made to correct the fault by the installation of a depth-adjustment device (*Tiefenfeder*), and the first test firings with it showed a marked improvement. Oberingenieur

Mohr (who built the Neger human torpedo which became operational in 1944) was in charge of test firing and considered the results inadequate, but Wehr ignored him and on 16 July 1937 ordered the Torpedo Inspectorate to install the *Tiefenfeder* generally, declaring at the same time that the device would guarantee 'a tolerance not exceeding 0.5 metres' across the board.

Because of bureaucratic slackness the 'improved' torpedoes were not delivered until 1939. Alarming reports had been received from Spain following German naval operations there during the civil war. Naval Command was appalled and ordered the Torpedo Testing Commission (TEK) set up in 1937 to run tests on German torpedoes under the closest scrutiny. This was carried out in August 1938 by the torpedo boat *Albatros* and highlighted the catastrophic situation. The head of the TVA chose to ignore these results and on 20 March 1939 stated that the tests had been carried out 'with unsuitable torpedoes used on unsuitable targets' and concluded against his better knowledge, 'The trust of front-line commanders in their weapons has been compromised without justification. The torpedo is in all respects ready for operational use.' All further memoranda received following testing and exercises which complained if defects of various kinds were suppressed by Konteradmiral Wehr and not forwarded to his superiors.

On 8 October 1939, a few days after the first official memorandum on torpedo failures in Dönitz's KTB, the head of the Torpedo Inspectorate Vizeadmiral Götting convened a special conference at Dönitz's urging to be held at TVA Schiessplatz Nord. As a result of this conference, torpedoes with magnetic pistols were withdrawn from service. U-boats were only to use torpedoes which exploded on impact. This placed special importance on the depth-keeping of contact torpedoes. Although Konteradmiral Wehr was present at this conference, he made no comment implying that the depth-keeping was defective. On the way to Vizeadmiral Götting's car, Kapitän-zur-See Rudolf Junker, Götting's Chief of Staff, asked Konteradmiral Wehr, 'Is the depth-keeping reliable?' to which Wehr replied, 'What would be unreliable about it?'

That not only something, but something decisive, was not reliable was reported by Korvettenkäpitan Kattentidt, a TVA officer in charge of a firing trials section. He went over the head of Konteradmiral Wehr to the TEK head, Kapitän-zur-See Albert Scherf, directly and informed him on 20 October of concerns regarding the depth-keeping. Scherf alerted Vizeadmiral Götting, who summoned Wehr to see him the same day. All the

The Second War Patrol of U-48: Fve Days – Five Sinkings

files were gone over, and in the evening Vizeadmiral Götting informed Dönitz: 'Our most recent information reveals that there are problems with torpedo depth-keeping. All torpedoes should be set to run two metres shallower than the draught of the target.' This meant that U-boat could not use torpedoes against destroyers because they would have to be set to run so shallow as to be visible and thus betray the submarine firing them.

Dönitz reported the matter to his superiors immediately and demanded flawless torpedoes. Grossadmiral Raeder dismissed the admirals responsible, but more evidence was needed before a case could be made out for a court-martial. Claims that Dönitz was prepared to let it go at that are incorrect.

On 20 January 1940 Dönitz received official confirmation of the report made orally about torpedo depth-keeping, and in his KTB next day he wrote: 'This is an ominous failure and I decided yesterday to order U-boats to set contact-pistol torpedoes to run at no more than four metres.' At the next conference, attended by Dönitz, the heads of the Torpedo Inspectorate, the TVA and TEK, these changes in the operating depth were confirmed. It was admitted that the cause of premature detonation had still not been identified. 'Which means,' Dönitz confided to his KTB, 'that the usefulness of the torpedoes is highly limited. The contact torpedoes are liable to run too deep, and the magnetic type to explode prematurely.'

On 5 November 1939 a new 'irreproachable' pistol detonator, the 'Pi A+B' was delivered to *U-28* and *U-49* for testing. They sailed on 8 and 9 November respectively, *U-49* being the first to report back: 'G7a detonated prematurely: G7e failed to explode.' The BdU considered this 'a bitter disappointment'. Other boats sent in similar reports one after the other. Dönitz wrote: 'The confidence of commanders and crews in the torpedo has suffered a major blow. The loss to us of tonnage not sunk by reason of known torpedo failures can be estimated at a total of 300,000 tons at least.' This did not cover the entire spectrum of the torpedo calamity. By the Norwegian campaign these 'wooden swords' would save the Royal Navy from a crushing defeat.

Not only the devastating torpedo situation caused the BdU concern: the question of U-boat construction had not been addressed with the necessary energy, contrary to his expectations, and the time was approaching when he would have less U-boats at his disposal than before the outbreak of war if the losses and transfers of boats to the training flotillas grew any larger. The much-vaunted Z-Plan was to have provided the German U-boat arm with more than 190 U-boats by the end of 1944. Hitler had not hinted at the

U-48

possibility of war against Britain until 1939, and thus the U-boat was not even remotely ready for operational development. Only fifty-seven U-boats were on hand when the struggle against Britain at sea took shape as economic warfare in which the U-boats would play a decisive role. Once war began, the construction of U-boats should have been pursued immediately and as the top priority. The extent to which wishful thinking and reality ran their separate courses in this respect will be shown in the following text.

The new U-boat building programme set up within the framework of the Mobilisation-Armament Plan, which Hitler discussed with Raeder during their first wartime conference on 7 September 1939, provided boat numbers which would not even be sufficient to cover the forecasted U-boat losses. Moreover, the increased recruitment of personnel to the U-boat arm required ever more boats to be diverted from the Front for training purposes. The increase in boats (ignoring the likely losses) was to be seven in 1939, forty-six in 1940, and then ten boats per month from 1941 onwards. When it is remembered that the 1918 Scheer Building Programme foresaw the construction of thirty(!) boats monthly, it is clear that this 'little programme', as it was called, had not the slightest prospect of putting the U-boat arm into a position to win the economic war against Britain. Dönitz and Naval Operations Command (SKL) were convinced that this programme had to be increased at all costs. The bulk of the effort in the commerce war against Britain, as the naval planners saw it, would rest almost exclusively on the U-boat arm during the first year of war. Raeder left the 7 September conference for his HQ with this knowledge, and after explaining it to Dönitz, the latter raised with him again the matter of the 300 U-boats he needed and which had to be provided as soon as possible if the commerce war were to be decided in Germany's favour. Thus forearmed, Raeder now argued that the military means to reinforce the economic war against Britain must be focussed on U-boat construction.

> The economic war against Britain is primarily in the hands of the Kriegsmarine. Deliberately abstaining from high-risk encounters (as the U-boat war requires), Britain and France are limiting their long-term activities to propaganda and economic warfare. Nervous at suffering casualties, their measures have the one and only aim of severing all Germany's trade links. A ruthless control of merchandise and merchant shipping, linked to the most heavy-handed political and economic pressure, hinders the neutrals in their merchant occasions and compels them to support Britain's economic war against

The Second War Patrol of U-48: Fve Days – Five Sinkings

Germany. The methods they are using force German policymakers to erect a determined front to prevent this and strike back, using the *same* methods of brutal economic warfare.

Without doubt it must be recognised that the Kriegsmarine is being affected most strongly by the questions of economic warfare in its war against Britain. It is being called upon primarily to handle the demands of economic warfare in the military sector. The strategic objective of offensive naval policy – paralysing the enemy war economy by cutting off his trade routes, together with the defensive task of protecting our own trade routes – indicates unequivocally the total extent of economic warfare. That is the sense in which the war at sea must be seen as a component of the overall economic war. It is reiterated that the military weapon to carry through the economic war at the present time is the few U-boats we have.'[3]

Resulting from this, at 1700 hrs on 10 October 1939 Raeder put before Hitler his new U-boat construction plan and suggested that in order to force it through some of the boats could be built in the Soviet Union, where they were willing to help. Hitler refused this categorically. The expanded U-boat building programme would develop thus:

Physical stock 10 October 1939: 59 boats
Increase to year end 1939: 5 boats
Physical stock, end 1939: 64 boats
Increase to year end 1940: 54 boats
Physical stock, end 1940: 118 boats
Increase to year end 1941: 250 boats
Physical stock, end 1941: 368 boats
Increase to year end 1942: 349 boats
Physical stock, end 1942: 717 boats

These boats would consist of fifty small and 667 medium size U-boats. Based on initial results and the experience of the Great War, losses would run at 7 per cent. The question of equipping training flotillas with boats was not addressed in this 'milkmaid account'.

One thing was evident to Dönitz: an increase in two boats monthly in 1939, and 4.5 boats monthly in 1940, and twenty-one boats monthly in 1941 would result in no overall increase in U-boat numbers in the opening years of the war. It was also clear to him that losses would rise once the Royal Navy became fully committed in the U-boat war.

By the end of 1939, twenty-eight U-boats had failed to return from patrol.

U-48

During this period precisely twenty-eight new boats had entered service, a net increase of nil, but there were twelve operational U-boats less that at the outbreak of war because these had been transferred to the Baltic to train new U-boat crews in the school flotillas.

On 1 November 1939, Grossadmiral Raeder wrote a memorandum summarising the negotiations:

> The U-boat War has now received all possible intensification against merchant shipping. Even passenger liners sailing blacked out and those in convoy can now be sunk without warning. All we lack is a declaration of siege against Britain whereby even neutral shipping can be torpedoed without warning after previous notification to the neutral States. After conferring with the Luftwaffe C-in-C, merchant ships in convoy are being attacked without warning by aircraft. This is permitted under international law.

At point (3) of his memorandum Raeder wrote:

> The U-boat building programme thus far has not been declared a priority by the Führer because the repair of Army equipment and supply of munitions remain in the foreground for the time being. With the current apportionment of steel, metals and labour, the major U-boat building programme cannot proceed. A reconsideration is promised for December. It will require persistent pressure to carry through the major U-boat programme. Signed Raeder.

The intensification of the war against merchant shipping mentioned in this OKM report leads to questions about the U-boat War regarding the Prize Regulations which appeared on the agenda at every session of the Naval Staff.

The Intensification of the U-boat War
On 16 October 1939 in the presence of General Jodl, Raeder addressed Hitler on all matters in the memorandum Raeder had given him shortly before. Under point 'a' of the memorandum he had asked permission to torpedo without warning any merchant ship definitely recognised as enemy. In his opinion passenger liners could be torpedoed if in convoy. Raeder reminded Hitler that he had already issued orders to sink passenger liners without first calling upon them to stop *if* they were sailing blacked-out by night. He also proposed that Italy, the USSR, Spain and also Japan should be forced to sign a declaration that their ships would not carry any contraband in future or be treated as were all other neutrals.

Under point 'c', Raeder reported that the Soviets had placed at his disposal a well-situated naval base to the west of their ice-free northern port of Murmansk. He was thinking of stationing a depot ship there for U-boats to put in for repair.

The most important question arising from the intensification of the U-boat War was the operation of German U-boats in the war on commerce under the Prize Regulations. What was allowed in such operations had been set out in the 1936 London Protocol from which Germany had accepted verbatim the points in Article 74 and enshrined them as the German Prize Rules of 1938. Naval Operations Command and Raeder as its head (he styled himself 'Chef der SKL') had decided to observe the Prize Regulations for as long as the enemy allowed the possibility. Raeder had expressed this unequivocally in his 'Battle Instructions for the U-boats of 3 September 1939'.

Just as had been recognised very quickly in the Great War that this manner of running the U-boat War paid no dividends, in what was to become the Second World War it was noticed equally quickly that the enemy was not prepared to honour the Prize Regulations himself, but use them for his aim of destroying the U-boats. Britain's 'Confidential Orders' of 1938 and the 'Defence of Merchant Shipping Handbook' issued the same year contained instructions which formally contradicted the idea of observing the Prize Regulations. British merchant ships were to open fire immediately on any U-boat sighted, reporting its position and their own by radio so that anti-submarine forces could be called up. British merchant ships were already being armed with one or more deck guns 'for defence'. On 1 October 1939 all British merchant ships, or foreign merchant ships flying the Red Ensign, were being ordered by radio to ram any German U-boat seen. These British measures deprived their merchant shipping of the protection of the Prize Regulations, for the action posed unfair danger to any U-boat commander intending to proceed surfaced in accordance with the Prize Regulations or who stopped his submarine to receive a ship's master bringing his papers for inspection.

This flagrant abrogation of the Prize Regulations was the reason why SKL gradually abandoned them, for it would have been both reckless to observe their provisions and a criminal abuse of U-boat crews to expose them to such danger. All merchant ships which accepted the British instructions were automatically considered to be naval auxiliaries and accordingly lost the protection of the Protocol. The same applied to any merchant vessel in convoy with a warship escort. For these reasons, SKL and the BdU matched every British step in these matters of international maritime law with a counter-measure and extended the latitude in the rules of engagement for the U-boat arm.

'This whole development led the Germans to introduce rules of engagement for their U-boats which corresponded more closely to their nature and reduced to an acceptable level without any breach of international law the risk in deploying them.'[4]

Hitler's personal restriction on U-boats that passenger liners and all French ships should not only not be sunk but not even be stopped had been relaxed extensively by 23 September 1939 after it was seen that Britain and France would not be prepared to entertain peace negotiations following a successful conclusion to the Polish campaign.

CHAPTER 4

The Third War Patrol of *U48*: Cruiser in Sight!

During the morning of 20 November 1939 *U-48* finished re-equipping at Kiel and cast off from Tirpitz Mole on her third war patrol at 2230 hrs. *U-47* had sailed on 16 November followed by *U-35*. *U-31* also left on 21 November.

Exiting the Kiel Canal at 0500 hrs on the 21st, *U-48* met her 2.Minesweeping Flotilla escort beyond the Brunsbüttel Lock at 1600 hrs for the run through the declared minefields. After detaching the minesweepers at midnight, the boat headed for Fair Isle. Immediately beyond the German Bight, the BdU signalled at 1750 hrs on 22nd: 'Nr 1659/22/56 attack formation *U-47*, *U-35*, *U-31* and *U-48*.'

U-48 and *U-31* had sailed through the North Sea to the operational area almost in company. *U-48* covered 236 and 164 nautical miles respectively on 22 and 23 November. At 0515 hrs Schultze evaded a destroyer which appeared not to have seen the boat: at 1230 hrs he dived the boat because of two aircraft which could not be identified.

The freshening wind drove long rolling seas towards the boat from the west-north-west: *U-48* rose over the crests and plunged into the valley between each. Whoever did not have his sea legs after this would never have them. Great banks of cloud moved swiftly across the sky. The barometer read 995 millibars. The bridge watch dressed up in 'seal ware' – thick oilskins and a sou'wester – and harnessed themselves to the rail running around the bridge coaming to prevent being swept overboard by the sea.

Just after five next morning a destroyer was seen changing course towards *U-48*: when Schultze was about to order an alarm dive it made another course change and disappeared into the mist. At 2015 hrs in grid square AN-M 1461 east of the Orkneys the lookouts reported a vessel to starboard showing lights. Schultze recognised her as a tanker and kept her under observation while formulating his decision.

'We shall have this one. I estimate a tanker of 6,000 tons.'

U-48

The first torpedo was fired at 2332 hrs from 1,000 metres. No explosion ensued.

'We shall pursue the tanker and position ourselves for a second torpedo.'

Sailing at the limit of visual range, Schultze was about to close in for the attack when he saw a destroyer approaching. An hour passed while he allowed the warship to pass on. The second torpedo left the tube at 0030 hrs on 26 November from 1,500 metres. One hundred and eighteen seconds after firing and thus at a range of 1,770 metres the plume of the torpedo explosion rose up at the tanker's bow. She was the Swedish *Gustav E Reuter*, 6,336 gross tons, and came to a stop, sent an immediate SOS and followed it with: 'I have struck a mine.'

After this success *U-48* returned to her original position by way of the Northern Passage. The lighthouses of Fair Isle and Sumburgh Head showed from time to time, enabling an accurate fix of position. Schultze dived the boat at 0807 hrs on 26 November to reload torpedo tubes, safer and less awkward work submerged. He considered it impossible to reload on the surface in Sea State 7 to 8 and storms of Force 9 on the Beaufort Scale. He surfaced briefly at 1430 hrs for an hour or so but judged the weather too rough and went back down to 40 metres. The hydrophones detected no propeller noises. The sea was clear of shipping.

While recharging batteries late that evening a radio message was brought to Schultze: '2035 hrs FT 1710/26/93: *U-48* reconnoitre east of Shetlands-Lerwick Bight.'

On 27 November, with the boat submerged to avoid the tempestuous seas, depth charging was heard at 0420 hrs, but no shipboard sonar or Asdic: the seas were empty on resurfacing at 0942 hrs. The boat made an alarm dive for a single aircraft at 1250 hrs, resurfacing twenty minutes later. A destroyer was avoided by diving deep at 1345 hrs: at 1705 hrs *U-48* came up and made for Lerwick Bay. At eight the commander confirmed his position by the Sumburgh light, the boat was south east of the Shetlands, wind Force 5 from the west-north-west, sea state moderate, cloudy with moderate visibility, though occasionally very dark during squally showers. *U-48* reached Lerwick Bay at midnight and steered for the anchorage. No ships, patrol boats nor obstructions were seen. Half an hour later in signal 1834/27/48, *U-48* reported her intention to return to her prescribed area of operations.

At 0150 hrs when a blacked-out warship was reported by the IWO, Suhren, the commander came to the bridge for a look through binoculars.

'A cruiser. About 10,000 tons.'

The Third War Patrol of U-48: Cruiser in Sight!

The cruiser was off the port beam and running in the opposite direction: she disappeared rapidly into a squall. Schultze reversed his course but once he saw how the storm-force winds swept the sea over the boat and even swamped the tower he realised that the conditions put a pursuit out of the question. In a Force 8 to 9 with hail it would be fruitless to search for and then attempt to make contact with this cruiser. He explained in his KTB:

> I assume that the cruiser was attempting to obtain a lee close to the coast from the hurricane-force winds. I decided to return to Lerwick Bay. Accordingly I dived the boat at 0157 hrs and cruised submerged. We entered the Bay again and penetrated the inner harbour. We sighted nothing except two small fishing vessels seeking shelter and left again at 1400 hrs.

At 1410 hrs *U-35* morsed: 'AA 1325/61 returning into our patrol sector.' *U-48* surfaced at 1550 to crash through the icy storm. The vicious wind took the lookouts' breath away. Schultze came to the bridge frequently to look round and judge whether it was more favourable to submerge. In the control room he chatted with his chief engineer, Oberleutnant (Ing) Zürn, a Swabian from Stuttgart. Zürn had a birthday on 23 July, Schultze one day later, but Zürn was from the 1927 cadet intake and belonged amongst the 'ice-grey' veterans.

'How is it with the fixtures and fittings?' Schultze enquired.

'We should request a major overhaul when we put in. Not all is well.'

'I shall make a strong case to the Great Lion.'

'Which will mean Christmas leave.'

'Fine, Zürn, but for the time being we shall keep this to ourselves. I am worried that the men may be encouraged to drink.'

'Young men are bound to want to let off steam, Herr Kaleunt.'

'True. We old men are beyond good and evil in that respect, aren't we?'

'I do not quite see it like that. I should be happy to spend a few weeks with my family and down a few glasses.'

'Well OK, but I will not allow a party aboard.'

The commander returned to his curtained-off compartment to rest, for even though he stood no watches, he had always to be ready if he were summoned to the bridge. At 2305 hrs a blacked-out steamer was sighted under escort by a destroyer. The commander was informed and came up for a look.

'Must be a very valuable ship to have a destroyer escorting her. We shall sink her!' He ordered the boat to come about and then headed at full speed

U-48

for a position off the bow of the enemy merchantman. Once he had made enough progress he dived the boat to periscope depth to creep up submerged. The moon was very bright and the boat could not have remained on the surface without being spotted.

The Battle with a Q-ship

U-48 achieved a favourable shooting position and Schultze fired the first torpedo at 2332 hrs. The range was extreme and the torpedo passed ahead of the target. This showed the commander that the ship was moving at very slow speed. *U-48* had to change her position. This was possible even underwater, for according to the latest estimate the freighter and escort were making only five knots. The low speed surprised him. Proceeding at slow ahead had several interpretations, one of which was that the destroyer was escorting a valuable ship which had suffered damage. The other idea Schultze preferred not to consider.

U-48 fired a second torpedo at 2355 hrs. This exploded after a short run of 23 seconds. The range to the target was 1200 metres, therefore the torpedo had detonated prematurely. The destroyer turned towards *U-48* at high speed, Schultze electing to make an alarm dive. On his first sweep with the periscope subsequently, he saw that the destroyer had returned to its ward without dropping any depth charges, and neither did she use Asdic or sonar to locate the U-boat.

This convinced Schultze to put the steamer in the other category. It must be a Q-ship.* The slow speed and the course, straight as a ruler with no zigzags, pointed to it. After surfacing, he had the telegraphist tap out a warning to all U-boats in the area. *U-48* made herself scarce, but at 0205 hrs next morning, two hours after transmitting the warning, another destroyer appeared escorting a blacked-out steamer. This 'couple' was also going nowhere fast and sailing straight and true. Schultze and the bridge watch concluded that this was another Q-ship.

At 0700 hrs a steamer appeared with four or five destroyers as escort. Schultze watched this slow-moving armada from various angles in an attempt to establish its purpose. He suspected it might be a hunter-killer group. At 0713 hrs one of the destroyers detached from the squadron. Schultze could not reach the freedom of the dark horizon against seas coming from the north-west, and so he decided to submerge. The hunter-killer group now attacked. The first depth-charge patterns were dropped at

---

* An apparently innocent merchant ship equipped as a decoy with hidden armament and a trained naval crew to ambush surfaced U-boats.

The Third War Patrol of U-48: Cruiser in Sight!

0745 hrs by when *U-48* was already at a considerable depth and relatively safe. Each series consisted of four to five depth charges dropped at specific distances from each other and exploding at a range of depths. The next attack followed at 0900 hrs and the third at 1115 hrs.

Schultze took *U-48* even deeper and made timely changes in his course in his attempts to escape the destroyers. At 1230 hrs when depth charges exploded perilously close to the boat, he considered that his latest course change had saved her from a direct hit and certain destruction. What he could not prevent, however, was the increasing level of damage to the boat and the growing danger which that brought with it.

The hydrophone operator reported other depth charges exploding at a great distance. This led Schultze to assume that another boat was also under attack. The hunt against *U-48* lasted seven hours. Her survival was due to the clear-headed captaincy of Schultze, who seemed guided by the hand of Fate to make his decisions at precisely the right moment each time.

'This depth charge hunt,' he wrote later in his KTB, 'was definitely a reprisal for *U-47* sinking their cruiser.'‡

Upon resurfacing, the commander had the port diesel supercharged, and switched on the fans to thoroughly air the boat. At 0148 hrs on 30 November the BdU ordered: 'FT Nr 2252/29/95 *U-48* and *U-47* proceed to Atlantic.'

To the Attack Again!

In a westerly Force 8 gale and high seas which constantly swept the bridge, causing the lookouts to snap on their restraining harnesses, Schultze gave the order at 1012 hrs to continue submerged, thus cutting his rate of progress by half. Depth-charging was heard astern at 1203 hrs, and not until 1655 hrs did *U-48* resurface. The distance covered in the day was 142 nautical miles. At 0520 hrs on 1 December 1939 Fair Isle was sighted to port. *U-48* dived to avoid a fishing boat at 0946 hrs. 155 nautical miles were sailed on this day, and 146 the next. On 2 December the BdU asked *U-47* and *U-48* to report fuel levels so that he could calculate how far south they would be able to operate.

Next day both boats were struggling through rough seas with a high swell and gale-force winds. No shipping was seen. *U-48* pounded and pitched and rolled. The telegraphist sent a short signal in the Weather Code reporting the conditions. Only 116 nautical miles were covered that day. Prien signalled: 'To BdU. Because of weather situation no offensive activity possible.'

---

‡ i.e. the battleship *Royal Oak*. Tr

U-48

Schultze told his telegraphist to repeat the same message. The BdU replied: 'To *U-47*, *U-48*: if the storm continues, both boats divert to Finisterre.' Both boats continued at slow revolutions. At midday Schultze surfaced briefly to recharge the batteries. Once the boat was fully aired, he submerged again at 1730 hrs.

On the surface at 0530 hrs on 5 December it was found that the weather had improved. Despite the cloud, visibility was good but a very heavy swell persisted. That day 188 nautical miles were covered, but not a smudge of smoke was seen. Next day at 0325 hrs two westbound destroyers were seen and avoided. These were the only vessels sighted until the morning of the 8th even though 132 nautical miles were logged on the 7th.

Thick fog had forced the boat to submerge early on 8 December for fear of being surprised by enemy warships. After the hydrophone operator reported 'screw noise' at 0900 hrs, from periscope depth Schultze saw two steamers running zigzags. After surfacing he saw the escorts and turned away quickly: he assumed he had been seen but thought there was a still a good chance of sinking one of the merchant ships. At 1120 hrs at periscope depth again *U-48* described a broad curve to the most favourable shooting position, and fired at 1155 hrs from submerged.

'Torpedo running!'

It hit the British steamer *Brandon*, 6,668 gross tons, and the ship sank within ten minutes. The location was square BF 1532. As soon as the torpedo struck, the second steamer turned away and left the scene so fast that she could not be overhauled. Through the periscope Schultze watched the escorts head for the site of the sinking. Although one of these turned towards the submarine there was no pursuit. Upon surfacing at 1332 hrs there was also no sign on the second steamer. Minutes later the disappointment turned to glee as a convoy hove in sight to starboard. The boat headed for it, and upon reaching an advantageous position for a submerged attack at 1448 hrs Schultze decided to dive the boat. Just as he closed the tower hatch he glimpsed an aircraft. At 15 metres depth there were four explosions in the immediate vicinity. The bombs shook the boat severely causing minor equipment failure and light bulbs to burst. The situation was restored to normal within a few minutes. Though *U-48* went deeper she was detected by the active sonar of destroyers. Schultze ordered more depth. At 1510 hrs two depth charges exploded immediately above the boat and would have sunk her had she not gone deeper.

'Go to X plus 30!' (i.e. maximum depth plus 30 metres).

At 1535 hrs three depth charges shook the boat. The trim gauge burst,

The Third War Patrol of U-48: Cruiser in Sight!

and fuses on the torpedo director and electric motors burnt out. Schultze put the boat on the sea bed at X plus 50 metres and switched off all auxiliary machinery to thwart the enemy sonar. Erich Zürn the chief engineer was in his element. He put all his men to repair the damage in the control room and at the switching tables. One after another most, but not all, of the 'damage clear' reports came in. The hydroplane operators worked surely and promptly. The damage had to be fully repaired if the boat was to survive.

The destroyers continued their hunt for the U-boat. Towards 1800 hrs they gained an Asdic contact, and sent down ten depth charges, but too shallow, though causing the wash basin and toilet bowl aboard to crack and more light bulbs to fail, together with the revolutions counter in the tower. If the boat remained in this position on the sea bed, Schultze felt certain that she would be destroyed in perhaps the next attack. He could either surface and be shot to pieces or attempt to get away from the grave where *U-48* had come to rest.

'Chief engineer, come up ten metres.' The boat lifted off the bottom and moved off gently at X + 40 metres. The screw noises of the enemy destroyers, preparing for a new attack run, became softer, and at 1845 hrs, Schultze ordered the boat to rise to periscope depth. From there he counted a wide circle of twenty enemy ships. No effort was to be spared by this large force to bring the 'hunt' to a successful conclusion with a 'kill'.

'Surface, but no noise,' Schultze hissed. On the surface the diesels started up. He was horrified at the noise, he was sure this would cause the boat to be discovered. The enemy warships did not seem to have noticed.

'See the two ships at 10° to starboard? We shall run between them, the gap is widest there.' The boat was flooded down, and headed for the gap. A defect in the water coolant plant put the diesels out of commission for several minutes, and the boat eventually hummed through the gap on the E-motors, 'putting the enemy's nose out of joint', as Schultze boasted in the KTB. The effort to escape the circle of death was successful, and by 2000 hrs the commander had to hand a list of the substantial damage – 'all command elements, the gyro and magnetic compasses out of service, electric lamps and switches out, some outboard vents loose, ventilation piping damaged'.

'All technical people to the task, Zürn, we must have the boat operational again as soon as possible.' Everybody understood the importance of this work and that perhaps his own contribution to the repairs would save the boat. That evening during their labours the BdU noted in his KTB: 'The presence of *U-47* and *U-48* at the approaches to the English Channel and

U-48

south of Ireland resulted in the first sinkings of steamers there . . . *U-38* fired twelve torpedoes – many failures – they had the new pistols, what is wrong now?' The question needed to be resolved: the future would show that the Torpedo Inspectorate had not come to grips with the problem.

By midnight much of the damage aboard *U-48* had been repaired and two hours later the boat was operational once more: at 0630 hrs on this 9 December the lookouts sighted a blacked-out tanker with an unidentified type of aircraft escort. Although the boat was not fully battleworthy, Schultze decided to attack because the target, a tanker, represented 'prime game'. The first torpedo fired at 0644 hrs produced no result, Schultze expected it to miss since at the moment of firing it, the boat's head had moved off the line of aim and altered the angle crucially. At 0646 hrs the stern tube torpedo was fired, this also missed. The failure was put down to the poor visibility and damage to the UZO. The third torpedo released at 0710 hrs struck the tanker amidships. She sagged noticeably. The casualty was the *San Alberto*, 7,397 gross tons, which now began to transmit SOS, then the very recently introduced code for an enemy submarine, 'SSS'. No position was given. Her crew took to the boats. Once he saw that the tanker was doomed to sink, Schultze continued his patrol, remarking in the KTB, 'This success is our revenge for the evil depth charging.'

U-48 dived twice on 10 December, enabling repair work to be carried out on the valve of the engine room bilge pump. This lasted from 1250 to 1532 hrs. The distance run this day was 54 nautical miles. On 11 December *U-47* signalled that she had turned for home. *U-48* reported similarly. There had been several failures of electrical torpedoes (ETOs) and with regard to the continuing calamity Dönitz expressed himself: 'One thing can now be established: the measures which the Torpedo Inspectorate had promised would remedy the cause of the failures have *not* achieved this aim.' And on 14 November, in order to highlight the connection, he made the point in his KTB: 'The influence of the torpedo failures on U-boat operations has substantially reduced the effectiveness of the U-boat war. The long lay-ups in the yards come additional to that. Cause: the various weaknesses of the boats which are only now becoming apparent at the Front. The major weak point is the exhaust valves. Because of the shallow submergence practised hitherto [in peacetime the maximum permitted depth was 50 metres] none of the weaknesses we are seeing now had appeared.' On 15 December the BdU had a conference with the senior yard managers on shortening the lay-ups to three or four weeks.

To return to *U-48*. On 12 December the bridge watch sighted another

The Third War Patrol of U-48: Cruiser in Sight!

submarine. Schultze submerged until its identity had been established as German. Recognition signals were exchanged. It was Prien in *U-47*. The boats closed to loudhailer distance. Schultze and Prien traded experiences, then parted with mutual good wishes for a safe return. At 1820 hrs the BdU signalled: '1728/12/95 to *U-48*, extend operations to area west of Channel.' Schultze had already decided on this independently, and so now he had the approval of the BdU.

At 0755 on 13 December a steamer was sighted zigzagging. Schultze took the boat to periscope depth and manoeuvred to attack. The torpedo fired at 0838 hrs was a failure for causes unknown. After eight minutes it was heard to explode which indicated that it blew up at the end of its run miles away. Hearing this explosion the steamer made off at triple full ahead. When *U-48* surfaced at 0920 hrs the telegraphist copied a convoy report from the repeat signals broadcast. Schultze headed for the alleged convoy at midday, but despite long searches in quadrant 4125 nothing was found either on the 13th nor the 14th. Finally a lone steamer was discovered at midday on 15 December, and having identified her as Greek from periscope depth, Schultze surfaced and brought her to a stop with a round across the bows from the deck gun. This was the *Germaine*, 5,217 gross tons, with a cargo of wheat for Cork. When in reply to Schultze's questions the ship's master admitted that he had orders to enter the Bristol Channel, that decided the matter. Schultze told him to return to his ship and put the crew in the lifeboats since he would now sink the *Germaine*. As soon as the crew was safely away, the steamer was torpedoed and sunk at 1740 hrs. Previously the steamer had been allowed to send an SOS after her master promised not to give his position nor mention a U-boat. The message was answered very quickly by the Norwegian steamer *Venland*, which headed for the lifeboats of the Greek ship. Next morning the *U-48* telegraphist brought Schultze a signal confirming that the *Venland* had picked up the *Germaine* crew.

At 1812 hrs on 17 December Schultze signalled: 'To BdU, request route for home.' The answer arrived swiftly, and since he had enough fuel left to do so, Schultze headed for Germany at full speed, travelling 277 nautical miles on 18 December. It was the commander's declared intention to arrive home early to obtain Christmas leave for his crew. Next day the boat passed through the central North Sea and crossed the German Bight. The BdU noted in his KTB that evening: 'After *U-48* passed through the Fair Isle passage into the North Sea on 19 December, there was no single U-boat left in the Atlantic. A total void of U-boats exists. Not until January-February can we expect up to fifteen boats there.'

U-48

On 20 December *U-48* signalled: 'To BdU: Passed Norderney running in.' At 1005 hrs *U-48* left the Brunsbüttel lock for the Kiel Canal, and after a day's run of 174 nautical miles made fast at the Tirpitz Mole at 1730 hrs. Four pennants representing 25,618 gross tons of enemy shipping sunk fluttered from the sky-periscope. The BdU commented: 'Another successful voyage by *U-48*. Her commander brought her out safe from the most grievous depth-charging and returned the boat home despite serious damage.'

After Schultze had made his report to the Great Lion on 21 December, the boat was cleared out, including all remaining provisions and the unused torpedoes. Kapitänleutnant Herbert Schultze prepared an Experience Report for Dönitz which is copied below in its entirety:

Experiences and Considerations After Three War Patrols

General:
Efficiency: The efficiency of boat and crew correspond completely to our peacetime impressions and expectations. Overall it is probably more than we thought could be expected as regards personnel and equipment.
Personnel: Morale and enthusiasm stem directly from the officers and the boat's success, and are thus decisive for crew efficiency. Maintaining a precise routine of sleep, reveille, meal-times, boat cleaning, torpedo care, the most punctual watch changes, observance of military etiquette and the imposition of the strictest discipline are extraordinarily important for upholding and preserving crew morale as well as efficiency.

The composure and determination of the officers, or their nervousness and indecisiveness, radiate undiminished over everybody and have the corresponding positive or negative effect of efficiency, and by implication success. The alarm bells are to be regarded as sharp, incisive commands. Cursing and swearing, horrified shouts such as 'There's a destroyer!' 'Aircraft!' and suchlike are to be avoided and given as calm, clear and unmistakable reports – and only as loud as need be to ensure it is relayed forward. Sightings should always be introduced: 'I see at so-and-so distance/point of the compass . . .' This will endow the reports with conviction and expert exact identification.

Partial crew changes after long voyages are initially distressing

Herbert Schultze, commander on eight war patrols.

A British ship sinking after being torpedoed.

A tanker aflame along its entire length.

The hydroplanes position on *U-65*.  The hydroplanes position on *U-65*.

Relaying orders by telephone.

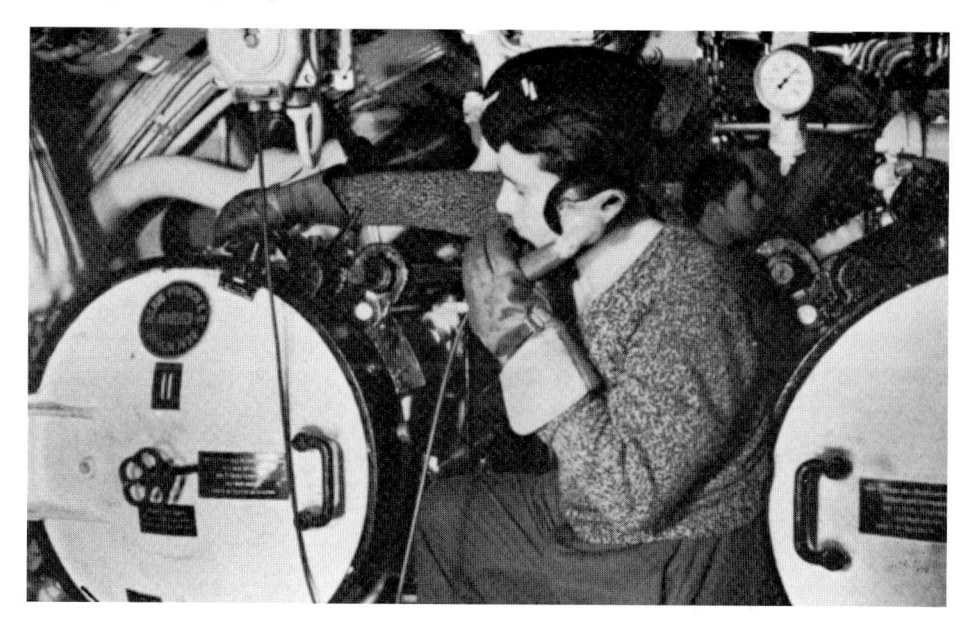

U-48 ahead, *U-65* close to the fishing smacks.

U-48 putting into Lorient, 25 September 1940.

U-48 leaving the St Nazaire locks.

U-48 putting to sea.

U-94 arriving at St Nazaire.

Grossadmiral Dönitz, BdU (commander-in-chief U-boats).

The legendary racing driver Hans Stuck visiting *U-48* at St Nazaire.

Racing driver Hans Stuck on the *U-48* gun platform.

A warm farewell.

U-47 under Günther Prien leaving for her last patrol, astern is *U-99* which also failed to return.

U-48 taking torpedoes aboard at Kiel.

A torpedo being lowered into the interior of the boat.

The torpedo, held by a crane. being fed through a cradle into the interior.

Commissioning of *U-123* at Bremen, 30 May 1940.

U-123, Kapitänleutnant Moehle, during the boat's commissioning ceremony.

The boat at Lorient.

U-124 and *U-95* shortly before sailing, 24 February 1941.

U-95 at Lorient, 24 February 1941.

U-46 leaving St Nazaire, May 1941.

Grossadmiral Raeder congratulating Kapitänleutnant Schuhart on his sinking of the aircraft carrier HMS *Courageous*, (right) Dönitz.

Hans-Rudolf Rösing, second commander of *U-48*.

Erich Zürn, *U-48* chief engineer on eight war patrols.

U-65 engine room, Brest, August 1940.

U-65 diesel motor room.

U-100 running into Lorient, 1 September 1940.

Seven sinkings pennants on the extended periscope.

Konteradmiral Dönitz awarding decorations to *U-38* crewmen.

The Third War Patrol of U-48: Cruiser in Sight!

for comradely circles but later unimportant because of quick reacclimatisation. These changes do not prejudice the efficiency of the boat unduly if the change is limited to a few (two to four men). Changing the coxswain or boatswain, however, should only be done with the commander's agreement because these men fulfil extraordinarily important roles and have a special personal collaboration with the commander. The commander can only part with such successful veterans with a heavy heart and unwillingly

Medical conditions such as headache, toothache or stomach-ache, small injuries, pimples, crabs – even the difficult case of stomach ulcers – can be treated and relieved with the means aboard.

Spiritual influence was significant in the last voyage. Fear of depth-charging is inevitable when the boat is severely shaken, but the thought 'It will end soon' and 'prayer' are just as helpful as the stolid idea 'I die a noble death' and 'It's all sh . . .' – though naturally not until it seems that all hope of escape is lost.

Materials:
The Boat: The pressure hull is first class, as has been proved by the deep dives we made. The Germania Werft machinery is reliable with only minor problems to date. The torpedo tubes have proved good and reliable. The subject of torpedoes is addressed separately since they are decisive for tactics and the prospects for success.

The attack periscope is only adequate to a very limited extent as regards light strength and sharpness at the edges, but manipulation is very good. After various improvements the misting-up of the mirror occurs less frequently. In my opinion the upper part of the periscope head can be doubled in diameter for better light and sharpness at the edges without making it more visible, given cautious use. The distance-run calculator and the position dead-reckoner are unreliable and frequently defective. Both are a very great navigational aid, although not so far absolutely essential. The echo-sounder has been outstanding and allowed me to navigate without problems from the west coast of Ireland to the German Bight without needing to take navigational sights or used the radio-D/F.

The use of fishery charts for the North Sea has much to recommend it because of more accurate information on depths. The magnetic compass must be compared to the O-gyro every four hours in order to have a clear picture at all times about deviation during activities such as torpedo testing, electrical charging. (Keeping a running list for this purpose is advisable!)

Gunnery Installations: The use of the deck gun is too greatly limited by the lack of freeboard. It can be used in conditions up to Sea State 3 to 4 taking into account the disadvantage of sailing with one engine half-ahead alternating with one engine slow ahead

The MG C/30 is unreliable on this mount and because of where it is sited on deck practically useless. Whether it would be much better to have it on the tower must be seen. I accept this will eventually be the case. The MG C/34 I consider very useful and I can see many uses for it, e.g. when stopping illuminated ships at night to extinguish searchlight.

Upper-deck torpedo storage is very useful. Transferring below can be done in favourable conditions, even floating condition B, running before the swell with one or both E-motors at slow ahead to deprive the swell of energy. This transfer can only be done at night, of course, when there is no chance of being surprised. Ballast tank 5 flooded for stern, ballast tank 1 for bow transfer.

The torpedoes have provided plenty of cause for complaint to date. Misses have been put down to failures to some degree, while errors in torpedo handling and setting errors have been blamed for failures which would otherwise have hit. In any case disquiet and a lack of confidence in the most important weapon of the U-boat arm has been the result. One major demand cannot be shelved! Premature detonation, and the torpedo exploding at the far end of the run, must cease and be impossible. They represent a deadly danger to the boat and by day prevent the attack being repeated.

Reason: Each such explosion notifies every enemy merchant ship and warship of a failed U-boat attack (The word gets round quickly!) It is followed by 'SOS SOS chased/torpedoed by submarine, position' etc, and very soon one has the whole foxhunt on one's heels, no prospect of repeating the attack, which after the first or second unnoticed miss without explosion might still have been successful – but now even the independent steamer will divert or zigzag, increase speed, drop depth charges, or open fire!

An ETO was flooded in the tube, cause not known exactly, it should not happen! A leak through the bow door is possible but not proved.

The Third War Patrol of U-48: Cruiser in Sight!

Requirement: We must have torpedoes which can be set to run at all angles. It is not right to rule out the possibility of fire-control systems merely because the number of these torpedoes is limited. The safety distance of detonator pistols must be known for certain. A 'fan' with seven seconds interval between torpedoes is not a true fan.

Tactical Experience:
(1). Tactics to date: A lone U-boat patrolling an individually assigned large sea area was successful at the beginning of the war when the enemy had not organised his convoy system fully. Some steamers continue to sail as independents, feeling safe with two deck guns.
(2). Directed attack on convoy: Is good, but will have only limited success until more U-boats become available. Convoys apparently scatter at the first torpedo hit and the few U-boats which manage to arrive find themselves watching the ships of the erstwhile convoy heading off in all directions. Ships attempting to escape from U-boat concentrations are easily able to do so if the boat can be forced to dive by a few escorts.

Activity in the Various Sea Areas: I consider an extended stay in shallow coastal waters such as the St George's and Bristol Channels, and the English Channel, risky because of the threat by the outstanding British defence organisation (U-boat reported sighted by aircraft or naval vessel, or after ship torpedoed, results in immediate counter-measures by strong anti-submarine groups). After an aerial attack (four bombs) I was forced to dive, and twenty minutes later the convoy destroyer escorts were there – in very good order – we without weaponry to respond – depth charges very accurate. Not possible to listen because we settled on the bottom, everything switched off, despite that, one precise attack after another. Only my dive X+55 [maximum safe depth 200 metres + 55 metres] and the outstanding discipline in the boat enabled us to survive the heavy depth-charge barrage with tolerable damage.

In these relatively narrow seas mentioned above, there is no prospect of collaboration by U-boats against a reported convoy because the approach to and the attack on the convoy will again meet strong naval defences near the coast and only rarely be possible, and moreover time is lacking for the approach.

U-48

An attack on convoys in shallows of less than 50 metres will only be successful submerged shortly before dusk, otherwise only surfaced at night because the defences are called up immediately.

A means must be found to combat from great depth destroyers and patrol vessels attacking with depth charges. I am thinking of released mines, light acoustic gyroscopic torpedoes, gas bombs, mock periscope mines and similar. Active sonar itself must come soon, enabling us to fire blind from 20–25 metres down.

Attack Experiences: The awareness of being really unseen comes gradually at first. At night one is completely unseen and this knowledge must be used to form a conviction that:
(1) The enemy under attack and on the defensive is in the weaker position because he cannot maintain alertness as aboard the attacking U-boat by reason of weariness at dull and unrewarding activity of long duration.
(2) Our night binoculars are probably streets ahead of those of the enemy, and thus the gigantic shadow we see clearly and hugely does not mean by any stretch of the imagination that he sees us on the same scale!
(3) The small U-boat in sharp outline could only be discovered on rare occasions by the target ship in attack and torpedo exercises in the Mecklenburg Bight even though the most alert and responsible eyes were keeping lookout through the best optics available.
(4) That one only accepts combat with merchant ships if one is convinced that the opponent is shooting worse than oneself, that he has more fear than oneself and therefore initially always shoots worse than the U-boat, provided the U-boat gunnery officer has not forgotten procedure and in the heat of the moment sets the wrong elevation or mis-uses the slide rule. Such a gun battle is exciting and raises the fighting spirit of the crew uncommonly well, and therefore should be done once, provided the horizon and sky are not left unwatched. That is always the danger for us: concentrating too fixedly on the opponent and limited attention and observation of the other dimensions!
Bridge Watch: Therefore keep lookouts organised – watchfulness – do not allow tiredness to creep in. Strict division of 90° sectors must be controlled. In parallel with the sighting report to the commander about ships, the size and kind of ship, and approximate course and bearing to be reported. The watchkeeping officer on the bridge must

The Third War Patrol of U-48: Cruiser in Sight!

have authority to turn the boat towards or away from the sighting according to his judgement of the situation. He is trained to think and act independently and only in rare cases will he be able to do any real damage while the commander is on his way to the bridge. During the day he is certainly free to give the alarm!

Continuous D/F and working out the compass deviation are of fundamental importance and the point must be hammered home that when a vessel is sighted, the first thing to do is D/F!

Dive deep and surfacing must be heard throughout the boat so that the forward torpedo tubes, outboard vents, bilges, etc are carefully watched. At 'go fast to great depth' pumping must be done with all means available instead of flooding because of the very significant reduction of volume of the boat. The deep dive can then occur dynamically at high speed! If possible trim with men, trim with water on reaching required depth! The manoeuvre 'All men to the bow!' etc should only be called for in the most urgent situations of danger because of the haste and excitement it causes. 'Ready with lifejackets and breathing apparatus' must also be practised frequently in wartime so that in emergencies this order does not appear an extraordinary measure and lead to greater alarm, and also ensures that everybody actually does have a breathing apparatus.

My Thoughts on Naval Policy: The fate of the *Admiral Graf Spee* gives us much food for thought. It concerns the commerce war in which our U-boat arm is involved. At the Falklands in 1914 the cruiser squadron was lost: at the Cocos Islands the *Emden*, in the Rufiji the *Königsberg*. All including the *Königsberg* were lost because they ventured dangerously near to the coast without having exhausted their military possibilities. If *Graf Spee* went into the River Plate and got involved in a battle there, the next step of putting into Montevideo almost certainly sealed her fate if she could not leave again at once. The story of this 'pocket battleship' and her cruise cannot be closed without thinking of her creator, Admiral Zenker! How far-sighted was the tactical and strategic concept of this warship type and how the legacy of this admiral might have continued if, building on the experience of the World War, a common 'pocket battleship'/U-boat tactics could have been devised, tried out and used successfully in this war. I am thinking of U-boats as scouting vessels and escorts, perhaps in the form of a protective circle or line for the 'pocket

U-48

battleship' alternating with attack tasks and in return keeping enemy anti-submarine vessels away from the U-boats! Or perhaps U-boats with a submersible U-ship of 4,000–6,000 tons carrying provisions, fuel, torpedoes, etc.

Despite the *Graf Spee* case, the effectiveness of the 'pocket battleship' as commerce raider is not questioned. The 'pocket battleship' is doubtless *the* commerce raider of today just as is the U-boat, and both, united in a common tactic, unbeatable! Similarly, co-operation with merchant raiders. Another thought is this: just as Q-ships can be built to combat our U-boats, we can do the same for their cruisers and destroyers. How is now clear: when one of our torpedo-carriers disguised as a merchant ship is stopped by a destroyer or cruiser, fire torpedoes and hinged flaps drop exposing guns!

The third help is the Luftwaffe. In my opinion all three – surface forces, U-boats and long range bombers – must be tightly yoked under a Commander-in-Chief Commerce Warfare [BdH] against Britain in planned co-operation to respond to convoys reports. The BdH will command the signals facility, collate reports from raiders, pocket battleships and our own anti-cruiser/destroyer Q-ships. Spies etc will provide opportunities for U-boat attacks. Their reconnaissance reports and contact-keeping signals will deliver the already weakened convoys to our bombers for operations near the unloading ports where it is always difficult for U-boats because of the anti-submarine defences.

Independent of the BdH the destruction of the unloading ports is a task for the operational Luftwaffe. Directed by a single hand, the ponderous convoy system will be shattered by the relatively few forces at our disposal, forcing Britain to abandon the system, the disadvantages and losses being so great that the favourable outcome of the war will be brought closer for this reason. Within the final 300 nautical miles which the convoy has to sail it must be attacked day and night by U-boats, and by day by aircraft, and on the last night have to negotiate a minefield. If they survive all that, they will have to unload in ports where the quays are in ruins with many mines and in constant threat from the air. This will allow British seamen no respite after the dangers of the crossing.

I do not believe that these are wild fantasies, for in the end the entire war-planning process is always a question of planned and

The Third War Patrol of U-48: Cruiser in Sight!

executed organisation of forces together with other fundamental requirements. Bringing the war to distant theatres by commerce raiders and U-cruisers in the South Atlantic, Indian and Pacific oceans seems equally possible. It would constitute a threat on all the seas and tie down strong (enemy) forces far removed from the real North Atlantic theatre, a weakening of the enemy's available anti-submarine forces there.

Besides these real tactical concepts it is probably inevitable that Norway and Sweden should be occupied at the earliest opportunity. The increasing mining of the North Sea makes the return of U-boats and surface ships to Germany ever more difficult, and the question of having bases closer to the operational areas will become ever more urgent![1]

CHAPTER 5

The Fourth War Patrol of *U48*: General Observations

The cleaning-out of the boat was completed by the evening of 21 December 1939. Next morning *U-48* entered Germania Werft for a general overhaul which lasted from 23 December 1939 to 20 January 1940. On the latter morning *U-48* sailed with her full crew for a trial voyage, which was completed satisfactorily, and after Chief Engineer Zürn had ironed out a few minor defects the boat returned to Tirpitz Mole for the scheduled remaining work. Re-equipping next day was a difficult task, for everything had to be stowed in the narrow tube in such a way that nothing was inaccessible. Once this was completed on the afternoon of 21 January, *U-48* took on board eight mines from the Mining Office (*Sperrzeugamt*).

In accordance with Operational Order Nr 22, *U-48* was to lay mines and then 'hunt at will'. She would continue and intensify the mining schedule given to the U-boat arm at the outbreak of war. Provisions and torpedoes were loaded from the *Memel* on the morning of 23 January. To conclude the fitting-out, on 24th the ice protector for the bow tubes was fitted at Deutsche Werke to prevent damage to the boat during the passage through the Kiel Canal. That afternoon the crew was given shore leave.

A Review of the Minelaying Programme
At the afternoon situation conference with the Führer on 22 November 1939, Grossadmiral Raeder had set out his planned minelaying operation along the English coasts. Besides the German destroyers, which had laid not less than 540 mines off the English east and west coasts, aircraft of the coastal air groups dropped seventy-seven mines in three nights in the Thames and Humber Estuaries and off Harwich. A number of ships had run foul of these mines and been sunk. In order to expand this activity Raeder proposed to declare a broad strip of the English coast a mined area, and on 1 December Hitler gave his agreement.

The Fourth War Patrol of U-48: General Observations

Building on this conference and Hitler's consent, the minefield *Schottland* was declared. Its purpose was to put a stop to shipping along the English east coast, enabling German U-boats to 'sink ships without warning under the fiction of hitting a mine'. 'The declaration of this minefield is a prelude aimed outwardly purely against the enemy's military operations and not against neutral shipping. An extension of the area to the south linking to the British declared minefield is intended soon after the first announcement.'[1]

In furtherance of this intention, on 1 December 1939 the following bulletin was broadcast over German radio and also in the Warnings to Shipping announcements:

> The Government of the German Reich hereby gives notice that within the framework of its operations against British naval forces and their bases along the English east coast, mines have been laid in an area bounded in the North by the degree of latitude of Kinnaird Head to 0°30'W, in the South by the degree of latitude from St Abbs Head to 1°30'W, in the East by the line connecting the points mentioned.

At first no mines were laid, and the BdU was given freedom to operate U-boats in that area from 2 December. In accordance with the plan, U-boats here were to remain 'invisible'. With reference to the mining operations at the Führer conference of 30 December 1939, Raeder reported that the mine barrier along the English east coast had been extended in December by destroyers and U-boats. Mining was currently in hand by U-boats along the English west coast. One of the U-boats which was to participate in the west coast mining in January 1940 was *U-48*.

After the ice-breaker *Wotan* cleared a path through the Kiel Canal between 2330 and 0830 hrs on 25 January, when even this ship experienced particular difficulty in forcing a way through the thick ice, *U-48* made fast at Brunsbüttel Lock. The morning was spent in shipboard work, the afternoon free. *U-48* could not put out because the ice escort was not expected until next morning, a fact of which Kapitänleutnant Schultze had been advised by telephone from Wilhelmshaven.

At 0800 hrs on 26 January 1940, *U-48* cast off from Brunsbüttel to follow a *Sperrbrecher** ice-breaker to the lightship *Elbe I* under tow by the tug *Löwe*. On the voyage to Heligoland the engine revolutions did not exceed 300/min from which the commander and chief engineer Erich Zürn

---

* A *Sperrbrecher* was a requisitioned merchant ship packed with barrels and cork to make her virtually unsinkable, and usually equipped with a very heavy flak armament. Tr.

U-48

suspected that the propellers had been damaged by ice. *U-48* entered Heligoland harbour and secured alongside *U-41* at 1720 hrs. On the morning of 27 January a diver examined the propellers and found that both were seriously damaged. Upon being notified of this, the BdU ordered Schultze to put back to Wilhelmshaven to repair, and *U-48* sailed at 1245 hrs. At 1500 hrs the Jade pilot came aboard from Lightship 'F' and at 1927 hrs the boat moored at entrance 3, Wilhelmshaven, proceeding at 2045 hrs to the U-boat base to make fast alongside *Donau*. On 28 January the boat removed to Westwerft for greasing, left the following day, tested trim and returned to the U-boat base. This is mentioned to show that everything did not always go smoothly, even leaving port had its difficulties, especially in ice conditions, and such minor delays could hold back a boat for days.

At 0800 hrs on 30 January 1940, *U-48* left entrance 3. There was thick ice in the Jade. As before, the run to Heligoland island was made with an ice-breaker escort. Ballast tank I astern was flooded to reduce the risk of ice damage by bringing up the bow and making the steel protector more effective. *U-48* passed Lightship 'F' on the port beam at 1608 hrs, and at 1800 hrs *U-48* made fast in the U-boat basin at Heligoland.

Next day the boat topped up fuel at the west mole and released the ice-breaker. At 1500 hrs *U-48* sailed on her fourth war patrol. A Force 6 easterly gale was blowing across the German Bight. Sea state was 5, rough, clouds scudded by overhead but visibility was good. Schultze, wearing a fur cap with a high crown, looked like a polar explorer. By the evening wind and sea conditions in the German Bight had worsened, and these conditions persisted on 1 February 1940, causing Schultze to submerge the boat at 0758 hrs. The engine room staff were given emergency drills, to which time had rarely been given previously: these were repeated in the early afternoon. Crossing the central North Sea passed uneventfully, and by the early morning of 2 February conditions had calmed. Naval trawlers were sighted at 0705 hrs and 0750 hrs on an easterly bearing and a third at 1115 hrs. An evasive course was steered to escape attention. Shortly afterwards Fair Isle was sighted and the boat dived to pass the Fair Isle passage by night. At 2000 hrs she was south of the Shetlands. Another near-gale was blowing from the south-east with heavy sea and overcast, but visibility was good. Schultze noted that the Sumburgh Head light was out. No patrol vessels were seen in the Northern Passage.

From her position north of the Shetlands on 3 February the boat pounded her way to north-west of the Hebrides by evening with slackening wind and calmer sea 'to reach position 1769 Mitte'. West of the Hebrides and north-

The Fourth War Patrol of U-48: General Observations

west Ireland on 4 February nothing was sighted; at 2045 hrs Schultze ordered a test dive to 55 metres and checked the trim. From 2125 hrs *U-48* continued on the surface towards the operational area. At 2233 hrs a vessel showing lights was seen, and the commander summoned to the tower.

'We shall go closer and give him the once over.'

The ship appeared to be Norwegian, and Schultze approached close to stop her by lamp signal at 0010 on 5 February. She was the Norwegian steamer *St Villa*, 900 gross tons, bound for Bergen. Being a neutral ship with neutral cargo he released her. To the enquiry 'British patrol boat?' Schultze responded by lamp 'Good voyage!' and they parted. Otherwise nothing was seen during 5 February. Towards 2000 hrs it began to rain: at midnight there came a strong swell accompanied by poor to moderate visibility, poor hunting weather. A steamer sighted at 1630 hrs was flagged to a stop. She was the Danish *Anna*, 1,200 gross tons, Genoa to Norway with animal fodder. As her course was right and nothing suspicious was detected she was released having been delayed only thirty minutes. Subsequently sea and horizon were empty for long hours: a fishing vessel was avoided at 1040 hrs on 7 February, and at 1230 hrs an armed steamer, possibly an auxiliary. Schultze estimated 7,000 to 8,000 gross tons, bearing 240°. She had a gun on the stern and through binoculars Schultze notice a rangefinder on the bridge. *U-48* submerged and once trimmed at periscope depth crept up on this opponent to reach the best shooting position. At 1305 hrs the torpedo fired from tube II at an estimated range of 700 metres missed for too great a lateral angle. The commander admitted candidly: 'I goofed by erroneously setting the indicator at 322 instead of 335 degrees, and therefore the aim was 10° off. Otherwise it was the classic B3 attack – bow, angle 90, speed 14 and should have hit amidships.'

Schultze surfaced, but the heavy swell and steamer's speed of 14 to 15 knots prevented *U-48* obtaining the correct shooting position again. He gave up the chase and continued on the set course. At 1600 hrs the boat was south of Ireland in square 1888 East running towards the intended mining area at the western end of the English Channel. In the early morning of 8 February action was required to avoid a number of naval trawlers, and *U-48* submerged at first light. The commander ordered preparations for the minelaying and allowed the crew members not required for this to rest.

He set the boat on the bottom at 36 metres, but such was the chafing and grinding on the sandy bottom in the current, with screws of patrol boats reported very close by the hydrophone operator, that at 1130 hrs he decided to proceed submerged at minimum revolutions over the next seven hours

U-48

before surfacing and heading for St Albans Head to lay his mines. In the English Channel the night was dark, sea fairly calm with low rain clouds, all preconditions for a quick unloading of the mines were met. Schultze reported as follows:

Completion of Minelaying Mission
I considered the completion of the minelaying mission to be a priority in order to continue the patrol without being unduly encumbered. For the following reasons I decided to press forward even at the extra expenditure of fuel taking into account:

1. The new moon on the night of 8 February.
2. The trim of the boat and its seakeeping in the conditions were so poor that I feared the ballast must be incorrectly stowed. A check showed that the compensatory ballast of around 900kgs for the bow door covers dismantled after the second patrol had not been removed after they were refitted.
3. Therefore I needed to have the five bunkers emptied quickly and the mines away in order to be at least ready to some extent in a seaway.
4. The weather was favourable for entering the Channel with westerly winds, and the new moon easily causes a change in the weather.
5. I had only eight torpedoes and reckoned on five cubic metres fuel for each, thus I had enough fuel to proceed in excess of cruising speed.

Carrying Out the Mission:
After I had to remain close to Start Point submerged all day, towards 1830 hours I headed at full speed for Portland in order to lay the mines from the surface. The night was black, the horizon could not be made out, even the peak of the bow could not be seen in the darkness. I ran the boat into the uncertain blackness by guesswork – if we had rammed anything we would only have been able to feel and hear, so uncommonly dark was it.

At 2315 hrs we had dead-reckoned to where we expected to see the Anvil Point light. It did not appear. What next? As dark as a pig's belly, hazy and now fog! So, check by echo-sounding. According to the Channel depth charts we were approximately right, but still in doubt. I assumed that the British had extinguished the light. Should I now stay a full day and risk a change in the weather because of the

The Fourth War Patrol of U-48: General Observations

new moon? The weather was presently favourable. I could not spend much time just looking, and a whole day submerged is the worst! The solution came to me lightning fast – I shall sail a three-mile square, sounding the sides and diagonals, and look for the match to the chart.

On the third leg the echo-sounder failed, and destroyers and patrol boats alarmed us occasionally, but finally we got the set working again thanks to the excellent work of my chief engineer. Finally I had the feeling that we were in the right place. The question was: would we find the sand bar? 'Course 270° – one minute gone, two minutes gone' reported the coxswain. The heads drop, long faces, cursing.

'Group flashes 265°, very weak ahead,' the officer of the watch called down.

'Then we are all right,' came the voice of the bosun's mate.

'Let's go. Prepare to lay mines.'

We found the sand bar by echo-sounding and a brightly-lit ship – Dutch flag – apparently at anchor about 200 metres off. We were moving at top speed on the electric motors, the diesels were too noisy. We sowed the mines according to the prescribed plan. I dropped two TMC mines intentionally in the British declared area because the pilotage instruction stated, 'Five nautical miles clear of the Shambles lightship'. The original British area had been cleared and ships coming from the east used a closer line of approach. Whether the Shambles lightship had changed position we had no means of knowing, however.

The radio beams are so precise that other operations are possible. Now we left at full speed in order to put this dangerous place behind us. And behold! A favourable wind arrived from the east, slowly strengthening until it shrieked at gale force. Then came the red sky of dawn and we spent the day in the cellar sleeping the sleep of the just.

The commander's report only hints at the great difficulty in placing mines in the correct position on the enemy's doorstep. It was a mission carried out with élan in tricky weather.

At 0300 hrs on 9 February the Anvil Point light was spotted after surfacing. Its candle-power had obviously been much reduced. Laying the TM mines had lasted from 0335 to 0415 hrs, and *U-48* dived at 0715 hrs to proceed submerged until 1600 hrs. Still in the English Channel, they found a heavy sea running with gale-force winds. Rainclouds hung low and the night was black as pitch. At 2005 hrs a ship showing lights came up from astern, a Dutch steamer. Four hours later in square 2486 Otto at the western entrance to the Channel the wind strength and sea had abated somewhat. It was raining.

Two Dutch steamers were seen but allowed to pass on at 0340 hrs on 10 February, six hours later an Italian freighter hove into sight: this was the *Ettore* which could not be attacked because of her flag. At 1105 hrs Schultze surfaced and at 1400 hrs manoeuvred to attack a ship just sighted. She was zigzagging. At 1610 hrs she was steering 85° and changed to 140°, and twenty minutes later she was steering 85° again. At 1640 hrs Schultze took the boat to periscope depth to sneak into the ideal attack position, and surfaced once there. The bridge watch hurried behind Schultze to the tower, the deck gun was manned and within seconds the men had a round in the breech. Signal flags ordered the ship to stop. She was Dutch. The clock showed 1703 hrs. From the distance four reports were heard which sounded like shells hitting home. First Mate Van Deyck of the *Burgerdijk*, 6,853 gross tons, came aboard *U-48* with the ship's papers. She had a full cargo of soya beans, cereals and general foodstuffs bound for Amsterdam. Though ostensibly innocent, Schultze decided he must sink her. The steamer had been zigzagging. Her first mate had admitted when questioned that his ship had instructions to enter the control port at the Downs, and it was suspected she had radioed to warn of the U-boat. This was an encrypted signal of groups with an encoded signature sent on the distress frequency at 1736 hrs. 'I consider it possible,' Schultze wrote, 'that the steamer *Burgerdijk* sent it, and include this suspicion in my reasons for sinking the ship.'

In order to divert attention from this warning signal and also assist the crew in the lifeboats, Schultze allowed the *Burgerdijk* telegraphist to send an SOS at 1805 hrs 'Collision sinking' with the ship's position. Then the crew took to the boats and pulled away from the doomed freighter. At 1840 hrs Schultze ordered Suhren, 'One torpedo for the *coup de grâce*'. He preferred not to shell the ship for help was certainly on the way already to save the crew in the boats. The torpedo sped the 600 metres to the stationary *Burgerdijk*, hit her amidships and broke her apart to sink at 49°45'N 6°30'W. A little later the radio room reported that Lands End had repeated the *Burgerdijk* signal and that the Dutch steamer *Edam* had responded. She was 110 miles from the sinking and promised to attend directly. Schultze was now confident that the Dutch crew would be saved.

After a major improvement in the weather by the morning of 11 February, Schultze decided at 1600 hrs that the swell was light enough to ship torpedoes inboard from the upper deck storage. This work began at 1900

The Fourth War Patrol of U-48: General Observations

hrs. First the seawater in ballast tank IV had to be expelled. The boat ran before the swell at low revolutions on the E-motors and when necessary was flooded forward or astern respectively as the work demanded. Schultze had rigged an improvised canvas cradle which not only made the job easier but prevented the sea entering the boat through the torpedo hatch. Nevertheless it was difficult and dangerous work, as Schultze complained in the KTB: 'The torpedo rig is still much too unwieldy and difficult, especially the big chute. It is time that the engineers took a really serious interest in the matter, for while transferring the torpedoes below the boat is helpless.' The job was completed by 2100 hrs, and all torpedoes were now either in the bow room or the tubes ready to sink a whole row of enemy vessels, provided any came in sight.

At 1800 hrs on 12 February *U-37* signalled: 'Suspicious steamer, going in.' Ten minutes previously the bosun of the watch had sighted a convoy and Schultze was hurrying towards it. The convoy consisted of fourteen ships bearing 260° escorted by four destroyers. A flying boat was circling overhead. When a destroyer turned towards *U-48* at 0805 hrs, Schultze dived at once and ran beneath the convoy, the safest place to be. While the ships rumbled past overhead, Schultze was left with the impression that after ridding herself of the mines and bringing down the torpedoes from the upper deck, the hydroplanes were not answering the controls satisfactorily. The boat had not been checked for trim following the torpedo transfer. As a result of the false trim the boat dropped 80 metres like a lift before the chief engineer managed to hold her and succeed in the difficult task of bringing the boat back to periscope depth.

When Schultze peered through the attack periscope, the lens was milky. It was impossible to see through it, and even wiping the mirror did little to improve the vision. The cause of this fresh calamity was the new control room hand from *U-45*. He had suddenly decided to turn on the periscope heating, a custom from his former boat. The previous *U-48* artificer, who had left the boat a sick man, had been strictly forbidden to indulge in this 'bad habit' following previous adverse experiences.

'After the frantic attempts to stabilise the boat, ' Schultze wrote, 'I was ready to attack despite the milky-glass periscope. Shooting angle receptor responded to my question "Shooting angle incorrect". When I repeated the enquiry it replied "Shooting angle correct". We had become involved in a big, obtuse situation. Nevertheless I fired the torpedo and it hissed past the target.'

At 1000 hrs *U-48* surfaced and reported the convoy by radio signal, then transmitted regular homing signals. At midday the boat stood south of Ireland. The weather was overcast with mist, moderate visibility, wind freshening.

The *Ark Royal* Affair

At 1201 hrs the BdU signalled: 'Congregate in the Channel. A bird in the hand is worth two in the bush.' A little later the message was repeated with a supplement hinting that especially valuable targets would soon present themselves. This order was to remain in force until expressly rescinded. What could be so important as to entice *U-48* and all other German units into the Channel?

A *B(X) Meldung* (an agent's report of special urgency) sent on 10 February 1940 contained information that the aircraft carrier *Ark Royal*, the battlecruiser *Renown* and the heavy cruiser *Exeter* had left Freetown and that at midnight on 11 February at specific co-ordinates 200 nautical miles north-west of Madeira *Ark Royal* would be steering 15° at 22 knots, the other two warships trailing her 180 nautical miles astern at 16 knots.

On 12 February a new *B(X)-Meldung* provided the exact position of the carrier, escorted by four destroyers, at 0900 hrs. Because *U-48* was west of the Channel, together with *U-26* and *U-37* with which she had closed ranks on 13 February, she received orders to await the *Ark Royal* in the new operational area in the Channel approaches, and when she turned up, sink her. The BdU then added an additional observation in his KTB:

> A short while after sending this order *U-48* reported a westbound convoy. Because the boat had contact with the enemy and may be close to success, I consider it incorrect to intervene in the *U-48* operation. At midday on 13 February a signal was received from the given co-ordinates from which it could be seen that the boat must have re-established contact with the convoy. She had run off so far to the west and was so far from the Channel approaches (340 nautical miles), and additionally would have to battle against an easterly gale, that it would take her at least two days to get back.
>
> The conduct of the *U-48* commander will have to be investigated after his return. When it was already doubtful if it was right to let him remain at the convoy after losing contact and having my order, he should under no circumstances have put the boat so far west that it was finally impossible for him top carry out my order.[2]

The Fourth War Patrol of U-48: General Observations

Back to *U-48*

Despite the order of the BdU, I have decided to maintain contact with the convoy by day and attack at night since this appears to me correct, and to home in by my signals all other boats – *U-37, U-26, U-28* and *U-29* – whose presence I assume in these waters. My attack periscope moreover is not serviceable for daytime attack. It can be *the* day of the convoy attack. Around fifteen to twenty steamers, four destroyers and one flying boat have been seen. The convoy is making nine knots, wind is easterly, and good for the approach. Everything extremely favourable to destroy the convoy. And I have the exact co-ordinates, am reporting my position regularly as to latitude and longitude since I have no G-quadrant chart aboard. Unfortunately I do not know which boats will actually attack or be able to. The *U-37* signal was in the G-square. Where is that? I had reported to Wilhelmshaven that because of the mining operation I had no G-chart, and what would be the situation if other boats sent homing signals and reported a convoy in a G-square. I was told that this should be converted immediately into the standard grid square and then the message re-sent. Why have G-charts at all? If it has to be decoded and recoded, double bubble for the U-boats. Signals should be shorter, not longer!

From his point of view, Schultze was right. A big convoy and five to six U-boats nearby could have resulted in a convoy battle with enormous success whereas the business with the aircraft carrier was only a report which could change at any moment should *Ark Royal* receive fresh orders.

The secret G-square system was meaningless if a boat did not have the chart and had to wait for the G-position to be converted into the standard marine-grid square chart position. All these matters had been criticised again and again and many opportunities for improvement discarded because the U-boat arm was too weak and the engineer's staff were not interested in reading forward or back in order to take a closer look at these numerous problems.

Herbert Schultze was aware what this 'refusal of an order' might mean for him, but he could not act in any other way because he was with the convoy. However, the boats he assumed would home in on his signals had been ordered to assemble for the aircraft carrier, and had obeyed the order. Schultze knew how difficult it was to keep proper contact with a convoy from dusk onwards and explained this to his watchkeeping officers, urging them to maintain maximum alertness. Following that he left the bridge for the moment, which he later recognised as a serious error, for a few seconds later an escort destroyer turned towards *U-48*, which responded by diving

U-48

deep. After the hydrophone operator reported that the enemy warship had wandered off astern, Schultze ordered 'Surface!' He headed the boat at full ahead on the previous bearing of the convoy – and could not find it. He had overshot when it turned and lost contact.

First he searched along the previous course. Seeing lights to the south he headed for them and found they were naval trawlers. More weak lights were seen to the west. He headed for these and – lo and behold! more patrol vessels and naval trawlers. The convoy was gone. Naturally this changed the situation decisively. Now there would be no successes and an extremely sour Great Lion to face when he got home.

Schultze wrote in his report:

As I understand it: destroyers by day ahead and to the sides of the convoy, at dawn and dusk a sweeper astern. Meanwhile the convoy made a hook turn, and when looking for it on the former course ran into a clever assembly of patrol boats and naval trawlers with lights, which one confused at first with steamer lights. Suddenly one is right in the middle of them. All this happened in mid-ocean at 49°50'N 11°25'W.

It is clear that these vessels form a U-boat hunter-killer group which spreads out across the convoy route and waits like the fire brigade for a U-boat alarm and attack report, responding at once. Moreover they pretend to be harmless fishing trawlers, and set a great array of navigation lamps: three coloured lights in the upper mast, between them two white lights visible from all angles. Just like on the Cockburn Bank.

Therefore one day's work and effort seemingly wasted. I still did not know if the other boats were homing in on my signals. The weather remained favourable for night attack although visibility was very poor. A freshening wind up to Force 6. The search along the presumed course during the night bore no success.

More would be said about all this ashore.

Ark Royal, *Renown* and *Exeter* ran into Channel ports on 15 February 1940 and eluded the U-boats waiting for them. At 0400 hrs on 13 February, *U-48* stood south west of Ireland drifting before rough seas from the east. At midday Schultze reported the weather together with his fuel and torpedo status. At 1524 hrs the BdU signalled: 'To *U-26*, *U-37*, *U-48*: new disposition of boats.'

The Fourth War Patrol of U-48: General Observations

The *Sultan Star* Sunk
U-48 patrolled the area ordered. Wind and sea were calmer. At 1405 hrs on 14 February the boat dived for seventeen minutes when menaced by a flying boat: at 1555 hrs a steamer was sighted. Three minutes after working out the steamer's course and speed, *U-48* returned to periscope depth. The steamer was steering zigzags on a mean course of 40° for St George's Channel. At 1639 hrs Schultze noted in his KTB: 'I think this is a P&O ship, black hull with brown/yellow superstructure. The steamer has an air escort. The hydrophone operator also reported a second screw noise which might be coming from a destroyer or some other escort vessel.'

While submerged Schultze fired a torpedo from tube I at a range of 1,200 metres. It struck after 88 seconds running time, throwing up a towering plume. A few minutes after coming to a stop the steamer began to settle. She was the *Sultan Star*, 12,306 gross tons, and sank at 1710 hrs. The sinking was confirmed by a radio report from London. Immediately afterwards a destroyer turned towards *U-48*, forcing her to dive; four depth charges shook the boat but no damage was caused save for a few smashed glasses. Four more depth charges came down every fifteen to thirty minutes. Schultze maintained a depth of 70 to 75 metres and whenever the hydrophone operator reported that the destroyer had begun a new run-in to attack, the commander would remove *U-48* swiftly from the danger zone. At 1845 hrs the hydrophone operator detected propellers, initially weak and later inaudible which he thought must have come from a submarine chaser of the *Kingfisher* class: the depth charges fell very close but were apparently less powerful than the usual sort.

Schultze surfaced at 1920 hrs. It was a bright, moonlit night. A number of vessels showing lights could be seen near where *Sultan Star* had gone down and were probably engaged in rescuing her survivors. At 2000 hrs a Sunderland flying boat was seen. Schultze commented in the KTB: 'Every time a convoy or independent valuable ship appears it is accompanied by one of these Sunderland seaplanes flying short- or long-range reconnaissance.' At 2015 hrs a blacked-out small vessel identified as a submarine chaser was sighted and avoided.

At midnight *U-48* left the scene for Ushant to see if there were any tankers about. When one was sighted at 0915 hrs on 15 February heading for the English Channel, Schultze got into an attack position on her bow but was forced to dive by a flying boat. After resurfacing at 1115 hrs he made up for lost time and by 1245 hrs was ready to attack at periscope depth. The

U-48

target was the Dutch motor tanker *Den Haag*, 8,971 gross tons. A torpedo was fired from tube II at 1359 hrs at a range of 1,400 metres. After 112 seconds running time the torpedo hit the tanker amidships, tearing open the hull. A huge column of fire erupted as Schultze watched through the periscope: quickly the tanker began to break up and sag amidships. Her fate was certain, no second torpedo was required. At 1423 hrs *U-48* surfaced and established her exact position from Funksonne shore beacons.

U-48 passed next day south of Ireland through chart squares Otto 1470 to 1383 and the morning following sighted a steamer at 0740 hrs. A heavy sea was running before a Force 8 gale and no attack was possible. The steamer was steering 320° to 340° degrees, which to Schultze seemed an odd course, and at 1400 hrs when he sighted her again bearing 80° there was no doubt in his mind that it was the same ship. The weather improved, the gale began to blow itself out and he availed himself of the chance to attack submerged. The swell was so high that the periscope was often buried for long periods forcing him to resurface so that the lookouts could find the steamer once more after she was lost to sight: finding her on the starboard quarter he dived again.‡

At 1830 hrs a torpedo from tube III missed because Schultze miscalculated the speed of the target. During the approach manoeuvre she had been steaming at 8 to 9 knots, but once the boat dived she cut her speed significantly. 'Now I decided to attack and sink her on the surface,' Schultze wrote in the KTB, and at 1840 hrs when he surfaced he measured her speed at 9 knots.

At 2000 hrs a second vessel hove into sight, a Dutchman on the opposite heading and showing lights, and then on the port bow a blacked-out patrol boat. *U-48* sailed a course to outfox the patrol boat and at 2036 hrs fired a torpedo from tube IV from an estimated 2,000 metres at the mysterious steamer. The torpedo hit astern, and as soon as it did so, 'the steamer burst into bright flames which coloured the sky blood-red. The cargo must have been benzene in barrels or powder. Size about 6,000 to 7,000 gross tons. The patrol boat stood by the burning ship. I turned for home.' This had been the *Wilja*, 3,396 gross tons, which sank at 49°17'N 8°15'W.

At 2310 hrs *U-48* signalled the BdU: 'Am returning home. One torpedo stern.' The westbound Dutchman maintained radio silence, probably fearing it would be interpreted as a hostile act to signal anything and thus attract for

---

‡ The targeted ship must have cut her engines, for otherwise the hydrophones operator would have obtained her bearing relative to the boat's head from the propeller noise. Tr.

The Fourth War Patrol of U-48: General Observations

himself the same fate as the steamer. A patrol boat or destroyer which Schultze had to avoid appeared to have no interest in the burning wreck as far as he could make out.

On 18 February *U-48* headed for Germany in conditions of moderate wind and sea with rain showers. By midnight she was west of Ireland on course for the Western Hebrides. On 20 February at 0844 hrs, while diving to escape the attentions of an aircraft, a bomb fell in the wake astern; the aircraft continued to circle and forced *U-48* to dive again at 0917 hrs when Schultze came up to see if it had gone. The aircraft was seen to leave at 0927 hrs after which *U-48* surfaced. At midday when the boat stood west of Fair Isle a destroyer and three patrol boats appeared requiring a wide change of course to avoid them. Towards midnight on 21 February Schultze determined that the passage north of Fair Isle was clear of vessels: visibility was very good and he could see the Sumburgh Head light. At 0200 hrs he avoided two blacked-out destroyers seen in company with three patrol boats exhibiting lights as a lure: he was attacked and bombed by an aircraft at 1040 hrs while diving but no damage was done.

At 1313 hrs the Great Lion sent a signal ordering the boat to return home by Route II. This was not possible the same night, and since visibility was poor Schultze submerged at 1407 hrs. After hearing depth-charging in patterns of three at a great distance, *U-48* surfaced at 1725 hrs to reach the central North Sea shortly after midnight on 22 February, and then dived at 0420 hrs because of thick fog. The crew was sent to rest as the boat cruised towards Route II. Once in the German Bight on Route II and surfaced two aircraft, probably German, were seen at 2335 hrs, and at 1010 hrs on 23 February *U-48* made fast alongside *U-52* at Heligoland, leaving for Wilhelmshaven next morning. A period was spent at anchor near the lightship 'Fritz' at 1430 hrs when thick fog came down. At 0745 hrs on 24 February *U-48* surfaced and fell in astern of an ice-breaker for the last leg to Wilhelmshaven, reaching entrance III to the north lock at 1145 hrs and making fast. Boat-cleaning began at 1230 hrs after which the crew was allowed ashore.

On 25 February the BdU came to welcome boat and crew home, and an hour later *U-48* set off for Kiel, mooring at Brunsbüttel Lock at 1815 hrs. Next morning she accepted the hawser of the tug *Monsun* and with the ice-breaker *Hessen* leading passed through the Kaiser Wilhelm Canal to Kiel and to tie up at Germania Werft at 1700 hrs. That day Schultze made his report to Dönitz. After the usual questions and answers the Great Lion turned the conversation to address Schultze's 'refusal of an order'. Subsequently

U-48

the BdU made the following observations on the voyage:

> The boat carried out the mining operation swiftly and well, and moreover sank 34,130 gross tons of enemy shipping [later admitted by the British as 31,526 gross tons]. It results in *U-48* having the highest figure of tonnage sunk, 110,000 gross tons, at the current time. This is an excellent achievement. It must be assessed all the higher because the patrol was a mining-and-torpedo operation. Nothing is known yet about the success of the mines laid, but this can certainly be expected, and will be added to the figures for sinkings thus far.
>
> As regards the decision of the commander to pursue the convoy, I have determined from his report that he committed an offence against military discipline by acting contrary to the order I gave him. In view of the impressions under which he laboured it later became clear to the commander that he had acted wrongly. I have therefore decided to take no further action.

Thus spake Karl Dönitz, the Great Lion honoured by U-boat men: he took his commanders' errors for what they were. In his own KTB Herbert Schultze composed this summary:

> Following reflection on the circumstances and after discussing the matter with the BdU I recognise:
>
> 1. It was a wrong decision to remain at the convoy and neglect to obey an order given by radio to proceed to the new attack location in the English Channel.
> 2. At the latest after having lost contact with the convoy I should have set out for the position ordered instead of attempting to resume contact that night by pursuing vague courses.
> 3. That I had no G-square charts on board was obviously known to the BdU, and my considerations and worries were uncalled-for and can only be explained in that a young commander is inclined in many situations to feel himself left to his own devices and accordingly misinterprets the assessment of Command and its measures and even sets them aside in the conviction that he has a better grasp of the situation itself.

That Karl Dönitz did not give him short shrift is clear from his award to him of the Knight's Cross of the Iron Cross for surpassing the 100,000 gross tons target for sinkings.

The Fourth War Patrol of U-48: General Observations

On 1 March 1940 the men of *U-48* paraded on the Tirpitz Mole at Kiel to witness the commander of the most successful U-boat in the Commerce War at that time, Kapitänleutnant Herbert Schultze, become after Günther Prien only the second U-boat man to receive the Knight's Cross. The 'Hurrahs!' of the assembled men echoed across the pier, and Herbert Schultze accompanied the Great Lion on his inspection of the honour guard. The boat had sunk sixteen ships of 109,074 gross tons at this stage, an outstanding effort in the trade war against Great Britain.

CHAPTER 6

Wooden Swords: The Fifth War Patrol of *U-48*: Preparations for *Hartmut*

Once all boats still at sea at the end of February 1940 had returned to Germany, the BdU had nothing available for Atlantic operations. Dönitz spared no effort in his aim of having eight boats ready for Atlantic operations by mid-March. Six small U-boats were to be equipped and readied for mining operations and for work at the northern end of the English Channel, but on 4 March 1940 Grossadmiral Raeder put an end to this planning with the following order: 'Departures further U-boats to be stopped at once. Boats already at sea not to operate along the Norwegian coast. Accelerate operational readiness of all naval forces, no special readiness.'[1]

On 5 March Dönitz received the first information about what lay behind codeword Operation *Weserübung*: Norway and Denmark were to be invaded in a lightning strike by Geman forces. For Norway, landings were planned at Narvik, Trondheim, Bergen, Egersund, Kristiansand and Oslo. Naval forces and troop transports were to bring up the occupation troops, while more would be flown to Stavanger, Kristiansand and Oslo. Admiral Dönitz learned that the B-Dienst wireless-monitoring service had confirmed definite British preparations to intervene militarily in Norway, which if successful would stop the essential German iron ore supply through Norwegian ports from mines in Sweden.

The BdU was ordered to protect German surface naval forces on the way out and provide further protection after they had entered and anchored in their destination ports. He wrote of this after the war:

> For this purpose it seemed appropriate to have the U-boats take up their positions, and as thickly as the limited number of U-boats allowed, immediately after German forces had entered the relevant

Wooden Swords: The Fifth War Patrol of U-48

fjord. The enemy's point of main effort had to be Narvik. Because of its remote location and commercial importance for the iron ore supplies to Germany I expected the main enemy attack to fall here.

Furthermore the U-boats were to oppose British landings. In the majority of cases, possible landing sites were so numerous that if we did so we would not be able to secure the fjord, and would also expose ourselves to the danger of either being at the wrong place with too strong a force, or at the right place with too weak a force. For this task it seemed more advisable to assemble U-boat groups initially on standby in the open sea near the endangered regions. These groups could then pursue an enemy force and isolate a landing site when the direction where the enemy intended to carry out landings had been identified.

One thing at least was certain: this time, if B-Dienst observations were correct, the enemy would be coming, and that was much preferable to having U-boats in the expanses of the Atlantic searching for him there. It also seemed certain that out of the operation the U-boat arm would reap a harvest of successes, being deployed as it was *en masse* before the Norwegian coast, the goal of strong enemy naval forces.

These groups in their advanced waiting positions at sea had yet a further task: to tempt those enemy naval forces which might attempt to disrupt the sea routes from Norway to Germany.

These three goals could be achieved equally well if the enemy were intercepted on the way to his target. Therefore it was important to place U-boats along the enemy's line of approach, and if possible close to his own bases. The fulfilment of all these tasks . . . required a large number of U-boats. We did not have sufficient available. I therefore ordered that U-boat training in the Baltic should be halted temporarily and the six small boats of the U-boat School be transferred to the Front.[2]

The BdU also made operational two U-boats undergoing trials. These boats abandoned their working-up programme and reported operational status after fitting-out. This meant that all operational U-boats were now involved in the Norwegian operation, and the BdU could be sure that *any* penetration of Norwegian waters by the Royal Navy was *bound to* end in disaster for them.

The plan worked out by Dönitz with the Operations Staff for the distribution of boats provided thirteen for the protection of German landings sites. Stavanger and Trondheim would receive two boats each: a total of five were for Bergen of which two each would be at each of the main entrances and the fifth had to block the harbour directly. For Narvik, the Norwegian port from where iron ore was shipped to Germany, an echelon of four U-boats was planned.

Additionally two U-boat packs as attack groups for the event of British landings, or their resistance to German landings, had to be prepared at sea to intervene. The first group, lying in wait in the north, north-east of the Shetlands, would consist of six medium-size boats, and the more southerly group of three would wait east of the Orkneys. A third group, four 'dugouts', would form a patrol line east and west of Pentland Firth, where heavy naval traffic was expected. Finally, two boats would lie off Stavanger, and three off Lindesnes, their purpose being to intervene to separate German seaborne traffic from enemy naval forces by determined torpedo attacks on the latter. In all, north to south under the Norwegian coast, and between Shetland/Orkneys and the port of Bergen, a total of twenty-six (later twenty-seven) U-boats were at readiness in nine groups. The seventh of these groups would also operate in the English Channel if necessary.

Dönitz provided each commander of these boats with a copy of the orders for Operation *Hartmut* under seal, the envelope being endorsed: 'These orders will be opened only at sea and on receipt of the codeword.' Together with his Staff officers Dönitz was convinced that this unique major operation committing all German operational U-boats to the attack had to result in a complete and devastating victory. He wrote:

> Even the training boats and those just released from trials had crews and commanders with Front experience and some of them had been very successful in the period since war began. Thus Prien in *U-47* and Schultze in *U-48* were amongst the commanders listed for the Norwegian coast. I was therefore very confident as regards the prospects of success for my U-boats.[3]

On 2 April 1940 SKL advised that X-Day for *Weserübung* would be 9 April. On 6 April all U-boats at sea received the order to open the sealed envelope containing the operational order *Hartmut*.

U-48 in the Norwegian Campaign

On 4 April 1940, forty-eight hours after Dönitz received the date for the operation, *U-48, U-9, U-14, U-56, U-60* and *U-61* left their bases and headed for their holding positions. *U-7, U-10, U-19, U-25, U-30, U-34, U-47* and

Wooden Swords: The Fifth War Patrol of U-48

U-49 had sailed the previous day, so that fourteen U-boats were congregated tightly in a limited sea area. On 5 April *U-1*, *U-2*, *U-4*, *U-5* and *U-6* put to sea, and on 6 April *U-50* and *U-64* escorted Ship 36, the raider *Orion*, out from Kiel while *en route* for their own patrol areas off Norway.

The course of *U-48* took her to the northern sector, off the Shetlands. Upon arrival she sailed a limited patrol. Once the *U-48* telegraphist passed him the order to open the envelope for *Hartmut*, Schultze knew that the waiting period was over. The orders placed him off Narvik in support of the Narvik Group. He headed there at full speed. Ten destroyers carrying invasion troops of 1.Gebirgs (Mountain)-Division under Generalmajor Dietl had already arrived. Off Narvik, *U-48* sighted a destroyer. IWO Suhren and Schultze disputed its nationality. The commander thought it was German, Suhren considered it enemy. Suhren wrote of this incident:

> I had served aboard a destroyer as midshipman and knew what German destroyers looked like. That thing there was as British as you could get! The commander said, 'Give him the recognition signal!' to which I replied, 'What for? We have to dive! And the quicker the better!'
>
> Schultze gave in reluctantly as I stood my ground: the destroyer had come close, showed us his broadside and was training all his guns on us. Then we dived – and down came the depth charges!
>
> Schultze raged: 'This is all your fault that we have German depth charges raining down on us!' I replied, 'They are not German, they are British, and they sound so loud because we are in this narrow fjord and the noise echoes off its steep rocky banks.'
>
> After the eighth depth charge I mentioned in passing, since I had a hunch, 'If he is British, he will now send down five more. Today is Friday 13 April, and the Tommy will drop thirteen depth charges, just you see, Herr Kaleunt!' 'Vaddi' Schultze looked at me as though this were some kind of bad joke, but look you, the destroyer dropped five more and then made off.'[4]

Immediately after resurfacing, the bridge watch sighted *U-46* (Sohler) just leaving the fjord. Schultze shouted over, 'Commander to Commander: you should run into the fjord with me!'

'But I have orders to leave for a new position.'

'Your orders have been cancelled. You should follow me. Wireless messages are no longer getting through.'

'OK, you lead, I shall turn and follow.'

U-48

U-48 led the way into the inner fjord, both boats making progress gingerly. They passed through the Narvik main fjord, being forced to dive repeatedly when British aircraft appeared. Meanwhile Schultze had established through radio transmissions with *U-46* that all ten German destroyers in Narvik Fjord had been sunk by the enemy and that numerous British destroyers held the inner fjord. The battleship HMS *Warspite* was also around somewhere. That was a target which Herbert Schultze could not let pass by. While sailing through the fjord waters they heard the sound of battle from various arms of the fjord and feared that this 13 April 1940 tolled the death knell for the German destroyer arm.

Torpedo Failure!

As *U-48* dived once more to avoid a destroyer, Schultze said: 'This time we must bag one of the big boys. Not like 11 April.' On that evening of 11 April, the boat had fired a fan of three at a group of large cruisers. No hits had ensued. All torpedoes exploded prematurely. The BdU concluded in his KTB report: 'This report of torpedo failure, together with the reports from *U-51* and *U-25*, gives rise to the strongest suspicion regarding the viability of the magnetic pistol. The question of torpedo failures threatens the success of the entire U-boat operation. Following the signals from *U-51* and *U-48*, the radio message sent by *U-25* also suggests the possibility of premature detonation.' *U-51* (Knorr) made two attacks on British destroyers entering Vestfjord on 10 April. If these two attacks had met with success, they would have created circumstances at least reducing to some extent the disaster of the German losses in destroyers. As the British destroyers were leaving, *U-51* and *U-25* (Schütze) both made an individual attack without result because of torpedo failure.

The attack by *U-48* on 11 April had been directed against the heavy cruisers *Devonshire*, *Berwick* and *York*, which had been deployed against German naval forces along the Norwegian coast between Trondheim and Vestfjord. *U-48* attacked twice: both times Schultze fired with all forward tubes and all torpedoes failed. Shortly afterwards an attack by *U-37* (Hartmann) also failed against the cruisers *Glasgow* and *Sheffield*. While *U-48* was penetrating Narvik Fjord, *U-38* (Liebe) was also attacking British heavy units. His torpedoes fired at the cruiser *Southampton* failed: *U-65* (von Stockhausen) had the same experience of torpedo failure after firing at the Polish passenger ship *Batory* carrying British troops. On 14 April the battleship *Valiant* survived a torpedo attack from *U-38*. Off Vaags Fjord, following torpedo failure *U-49* (von Gossler) was detected by the destroyers

Wooden Swords: The Fifth War Patrol of U-48

Fearless and *Brazen* and sunk with depth charges. From the flotsam a number of secret documents were salvaged including a chart with the positions of the German U-boats. As if that were not enough, on the night of 16 April *U-47* (Prien) fired two fans of four torpedoes each at a troopship and cruiser at anchor, all eight torpedoes failed.

Was *U-48* any luckier than the others after entering Narvik Fjord?

On 14 April *U-48*, which in company with *U-52* (Salman) had received instructions from the BdU Operations Division to reconnoitre, proceeded as ordered. The intention of the BdU was to obtain a picture of the prevailing chaotic situation in Norway and give the boats the opportunity to seek out enemy units and not wait until these happened to stray into their designated patrol areas. That day, Schultze sighted the battleship *Warspite* in Vestfjord. Schultze approached as close as he dared. Watching from the periscope saddle, the colossus filed the optic. He ordered a fan of three torpedoes fired. All failed. In the afternoon, Schultze reported to the Great Lion by signal that the second attempt to get to Narvik port had failed after he was driven off by enemy destroyers in a heavy depth-charge attack.

On 15 April, the BdU received a string of reports, each more depressing than the previous one.

'*U-48*: torpedoes fired at destroyers failed.'

'*U-65*: two torpedoes at troopship in Vaags Fjord failed.'

'*U-47*: four torpedoes at anchored troopship failed.'

'*U-47*: One G7a failed, three Etos failed to detonate, Vaags Fjord.'

Dönitz confided to his KTB:

> These signals are depressing. The hope for an improvement in the situation and better results from the changeover to contact pistols has come to naught. I placed my most competent commanders at the hottest spots. From their reports and my knowledge of the personal attributes of the men, it is beyond doubt that they approached the mission with verve, and tried and did everything possible.

In response to an enquiry to the Torpedo Inspectorate given the highest priority, it was confirmed that *U-65* and *U-48* had been issued contact pistols with four-bladed propellers. The report read: 'These pistols have the risk of remaining inactive. They were issued to the boats without adequate testing.' This was a reply which in wartime in every country in the world would have resulted in an immediate court-martial. Frantic meetings on the subject of torpedoes abounded. Ever more references and instructions were issued to boats at sea. Again and again U-boat commanders attacked and suffered the same disappointment, and were then subjected to the heaviest depth-charge attacks because the intended victim remained afloat and unharmed and went on the offensive itself.

On 19 April 1940, *U-3*, *U-5*, *U-6* and *U-48* ran into their bases one after another. When Herbert Schultze was making his report to Dönitz his feelings got the better of him. He accused those responsible for the debacle of sabotage and demanded their immediate arrest and court martial. He would testify personally as to how often and for how long he had been making reports about torpedo failures. It took some time for Dönitz to pacify him and prevent him losing his head completely. He gave Schultze his solemn assurance that he would personally see that this was done. Prien arrived in *U-47* on 26 April and was also furious, describing his attacks and the torpedo failures in minute detail. When he had finished and Dönitz assured him that he would be successful on the next operation, Prien replied: 'Jawohl, Herr Admiral! But only if we get torpedoes which work, and do not have to fight with wooden swords!'

The list of boats which had attacked large British warships and troop transports was very long. If only half the torpedoes fired had exploded at the target, it would have inflicted a devastating defeat on Britain. The only German U-boat to succeed was *U-9* (Lüth) which sank a transport on 20 April. Commanders such as Kretschmer, Prien, Schultze and others had been in dead-certain shooting positions but were denied by torpedo failures. Neither the magnetic pistol not the depth-setting devices worked as designed.

'The torpedo crisis is a national tragedy,' Grossadmiral Raeder declared. The question now confronting Dönitz was whether he could continue to send to sea U-boats equipped with dud torpedoes. Every unsuccessful attack through torpedo failure brought the U-boat involved into danger of being sunk itself. In a conversation with Korvettenkapitän Godt, Chief of the Operational Staff, the latter stated to Dönitz that it would be irresponsible to send U-boats to sea armed with such torpedoes. 'I felt however,' Dönitz wrote, 'that at this stage I could not bring the U-boats to a standstill without damaging the arm to an inestimable extent.'[5]

In the weeks following the debacle, Dönitz visited one flotilla after another and also the Baltic training centres where he spoke to commanders and crews and gave heart to the demoralised men. At the same time the matter was at last before the Reich War Court. The new Torpedo-Inspector, Konteradmiral Oskar Kummetz, had previously sought to have the question clarified, but even he, after a short period in office, was forced to admit that the torpedoes with which the U-boat arm would engage the greatest sea power in Europe had not been properly tested in practice.

By 20 April 1940 Grossadmiral Raeder set up a special commission to investigate the causes of torpedo failure. When the first results of the commission's deliberations were delivered in mid-May, Dönitz described the torpedo failures as criminal. Raeder reported:

> 1. Following the experience with G7a and G7e torpedoes during the Norwegian operation I ordered an investigation into the causes of the defects and to what extent blame is to be apportioned.
> 2. The investigation revealed that defects in the torpedoes, and deficiencies in their preparation before issue were decisive, i.e.:
>
> (a) Depth keeping and running at depth of the G7a and G7e torpedoes were not satisfactory in these weapons to be used at the Front.
> (b) The explosive pistols were not fully serviceable technically (magnetic) or did not comply with requirements (contact).
> (c) At the Kriegsmarine Werft Torpedo Establishment and the testing works of the Kriegsmarine Torpedo Research Institute, deficiencies were identified in the preparation of torpedoes prior to issue. This matter is being investigated separately.
>
> As a result of these findings, the Kriegsmarine Commander-in-Chief has ordered preliminary proceedings leading to court-martial to be instituted against those members of the Torpedo Research Institute responsible.

In the words of the U-boat commanders who had experienced the total failure of the torpedoes under the Norwegian coast, this was the understatement of the year. In other words, the torpedoes did not just have defects, they were totally useless. They had no weaknesses – they were a disaster.

Admiral Wehr, head of the TVA, and two of his senior staff were convicted and sentenced on 23 July 1940 at the conclusion of enquiries by the Reich War Court investigatory commission. The Torpedo Research Institute was made the scapegoat even though the situation was known at the highest level at the latest by the time the trial results were published in August 1938 that U-boat torpedoes under manufacture were largely duds. The fact that Günther Prien had had to fire seven torpedoes at Scapa Flow to sink one battleship could still be kept secret, but so many failures experienced by all these commanders off Norway could no longer be suppressed. What is not sufficiently appreciated about this calamity is that British faces at the highest level paled when the truth was discovered. Their capital ships and cruisers and troop transports had not been saved by their own escorts but by German U-boats being equipped with 'wooden swords'.

Rowe H Saunders, the British naval historian, informed the author that Britain would have been ready for peace if the German U-boat arm in *Weserübung* had sunk all the British major warships fired at from close range. 'This alone would have motivated Britain to accept the peace feelers Hitler put out in his Reichstag speech of 19 July 1940 and brought a swift end to the war.' The extent to which this torpedo calamity was deliberate sabotage to damage the German Reich by 'enemies within' was not investigated by the Reich War Court on the premise that 'what ought not to be, cannot be'.

Shortly after the Norwegian campaign Herbert Schultze fell seriously ill and had to surrender his command to his successor, Kapitänleutnant Hans-Rudolf Rösing. Rösing had joined the Reichsmarine in 1924 and was thirty-five years of age when he took over *U-48*. He was considered an outstanding expert. He had been involved in the expansion of the U-boat arm from the outset and as the commander of several boats in the initial phase was known as a level-headed but bold naval officer. He came from a family with a naval tradition and was the son-in-law of Konteradmiral Looff, who had commanded the cruiser *Königsberg*, which in the Great War had finally been sunk in the Rufiji River in East Africa after a long resistance. The proven watchkeeping officers Suhren and Ites, and the chief engineer Zürn, remained aboard. Rösing would sail this very successful boat on her next two patrols and also achieve great success. In the following chapters I can give an account of these two voyages from the KTB which Rösing placed at my disposal.

CHAPTER 7

The Battle of the Atlantic: *U-48* under New Command – Sixth War Patrol

The OKW instruction to the BdU on 1 June 1940 was basically: 'The strongest possible U-boat presence in the Atlantic.' These words began that dramatic encounter with its highs and lows which naval historians now know as 'The Battle of the Atlantic'. No German U-boat had been in the Atlantic Ocean for the previous three months, as all available boats had been concentrated around Norway since March. There they had experienced the torpedo calamity, the failure of most torpedoes, that puzzling misfortune which cost the U-boat arm great success and brought the German troops in Norway so close to the edge of the abyss that consideration was even given to having them intern themselves in Sweden.

The BdU Operations Division with its HQ at Sengwarden near Wilhelmshaven had no definite intelligence about the enemy situation in the Atlantic at the beginning of June 1940. In this critical situation, Dönitz sent Kapitänleutnant Oehrn, his first staff officer, Operations Division, into the Atlantic as commander of *U-37* on 15 May. His shore position was taken over by Korvettenkapitän Werner Hartmann. When *U-37* reached the area north-west of Cape Finisterre, Oehrn soon reported that he had sighted and attacked enemy shipping. Of five torpedoes fired with magnetic pistols, two detonated prematurely and two others did not explode at all. This was a crushing report, for Admiral Dönitz proof-positive that the magnetic pistol was not sufficiently reliable for the Front. He banned its use at once and ordered that only torpedoes with the contact pistol were to be used.

When *U-37* returned to Wilhelmshaven on 9 June 1940 after a patrol lasting only twenty-six days, the boat had sunk ten ships of 41,207 gross tons, amongst them the French *Brazza*, 10,387 gross tons, while the *Dunster Grange,* 9,494 gross tons, had been seriously damaged by shelling. Oehrn had thus proved that the fighting abilities of the German U-boats had not suffered providing they had the right torpedoes. The BdU stated: 'The next boats went out convinced they could do the same as *U-37*. This got them over the Norwegian fiasco psychologically.'[1]

The Battle of the Atlantic began. Here Dönitz hoped to prove the fighting abilities of his 'wolf-packs' – as the U-boat groups were now called by the British – against convoys and in the hunt for independent ships. Another commander had left on patrol on 26 May 1940, Hans-Rudolf Rösing in *U-48*. He was numbered amongst the handful of commanders who hoped for success against convoys with an almost legendary boat. As previously stated, he had taken over the boat from Herbert Schultze, who had been forced to step down temporarily at the beginning of May for health reasons. When taking his leave of boat and crew Schultze said, 'Remember that you all have a reputation to protect, and I shall return to keel-haul you should you fall off at all under my successor.' *U-48* already had five patrols behind her, and could boast a tally of sixteen ships sunk of 109,074 gross tons, and her commander had been awarded the Knight's Cross.

The same officers were retained. On 26 May *U-48* cast off on her sixth war patrol. The fifth had been the unlucky Norwegian operation. The off-watch men of 7.U-Flotilla saw the boat off. *U-48* negotiated the Holtenau Lock and the Kiel Canal. *Sperrbrecher 9* provided the submarine with her escort from Brunsbüttel to the lightship *Elbe I* and was then released.

On the second day out a small hatch began to leak. Rösing set the boat on the seabed at 28 metres for an improvised repair with lead wire. On 29 May the telegraphists sent the agreed short signal to the BdU that the boat had passed 49°N. During the next test dive the chief engineer noticed that the faulty hatch was admitting water again at 25 metres. Rösing took the boat deeper to establish the safe diving depth. At 50 metres there was a ton and a half of water in the boat. Obviously the patrol could not continue in such circumstances: in the first depth-charge attack the boat might be forced deep and beyond the point of recovery. 'We shall put into Bergen, Suhren,' he told the IWO, then signalled the BdU: 'Am at square AF 7871. Small screwed access hatch heavy leak at 50 metres. Cannot repair with shipboard tools. Request repair Bergen.'[2]

The reply came quickly: 'Go at speed to Trondheim. Repair. Replenish. Mine and submarine danger in the Trondheim approaches. Enter through Frohavet.'[3] On the run-in to Trondheim, *U-48* had to dive three times for aircraft before entering the fjord through Frohavet west of Husöy. The hatch was replaced and in a test dive was also found to leak, though not as much as the previous one and only at greater depths.

The Battle of the Atlantic: U-48 under New Command

Successful Patrol

U-48 left Trondheim for the open sea on 3 June 1940 through the Frohavet, escorted by an He 115 floatplane of KFlgr.506 which then returned to its base. The lookouts sighted the first steamer on 5 June. She appeared suddenly from the evening mist. Taking advantage of the poor visibility, *U-48* got ahead of her bow before diving and making the approach at periscope depth.

'We shall fire a torpedo from the stern tube,' Rösing announced from the attack periscope. The eel* was made ready and a few minutes later the commander gave the order to fire. The control-room petty officer flooded the after tanks to restore the trim, the stopwatch ticked off the seconds.

'Time is up!' reported the IIWO. The tension was great as the time passed. They accepted that the torpedo must have missed.

'Probably ran under the freighter,' the 'mixer' reported from the stern room.

'What depth did you set it for?'

'Four metres as ordered, Herr Kapitän!'

'We will let him get away a bit.' Rösing had a few peeps through the periscope. Once the distance suited him he surfaced the boat. The bridge watch stood ready, and as soon as the chief engineer reported that the upper hatch was clear, Rösing opened it and went to the bridge. No aircraft.

'Bridge watch come up!'

At full ahead on both diesels *U-48* pursued the ponderous freighter. Rösing had the 88mm gun readied and the shells heaved into the tower for forwarding down the chute to the foredeck. Then came the order to fire. The first rounds splashed close to the freighter, the explosions throwing up huge geysers of water. The small ship lost way immediately, and came to a stop as the fourth and fifth rounds hit. Through binoculars Rösing saw the ship's boats being lowered.

'Cease fire! Let the crew into the boats first!'

Once the boats were sufficiently far from the burning steamer *U-48* resumed fire. It took seventy-seven rounds to sink the freighter.

'Head for the lifeboat port side ahead.' *U-48* slid alongside the small craft. One of the seamen had tied a shirt to an oar and was waving it. A man seated forward in the ship's boat appeared to be the captain. 'What ship?' Rösing asked him.

'The ship's name is *Stancor*,' came the reply. Then he requested some

---

* U-boat slang for a torpedo. Ed

water, which they had forgotten to bring. Rösing had a container filled with fresh water and passed down. Then the U-boat left the lifeboats. *Stancor* was a British freighter of 798 gross tons. She went down at 58°48'N 8°45'W.

Next day a heavily-laden steamer was sighted on course for the North Channel. She had a large-calibre gun at the stern.

'We shall attack.'

The diesels thundered louder as the submarine built up speed and was quickly in position to fire. The first torpedo left tube IV at 0007 hrs, but passed below the target. At 0203 hrs the boat was again well placed to attack. The attack computer confirmed the geometry.

'Tube 1 – *los!*' As the torpedo left the tube, *U-48* reared up and was restored to the horizontal by flooding the trim tanks. 'Torpedo running!' the 'mixer' reported. As a precaution he had also hit the manual-release switch in case the electrics failed. 'Time is up!' A second later a huge column of water and fire rose high at the ship's centre from the torpedo hit.

'Hit amidships' the captain advised the crew unnecessarily. The dull thud of the hit, the explosion bursting the ship's interior both left no room for doubt.

'Ship is sinking very quickly!' Twenty seconds after the torpedo hit the British steamer *Frances Massey*, 4,212 gross tons, had gone. *U-48* left the scene at half ahead through a calm sea. A second steamer was sighted half an hour later moving at a fast speed

'Full ahead both!'

The screech of the diesels rose to a dull rumbling as *U-48* headed at 16 knots to her favourable attack position. The range was 3,000 metres when Rösing ordered a torpedo fired. The commander saw the flash of the detonation.

'Hit forward 30,' he told the crew. Then came the thunder of the hit. The steamer was quickly in flames.

'SOS from *Eros*, sinking at 55°33'N 8°26'W. She says, torpedoed by submarine, we are sinking!' After thumbing through *Lloyd's Register*, the radio operator added, '*Eros* is British steamer, 5,888 gross tons.'

After hearing the sound of heavy aircraft engines the horizon to starboard was scoured. The IWO gave the alarm.

'Diving stations, clear the tower!'

The lookouts slipped through the tower hatch and down into the control room, Rösing being the last to leave the bridge when the flying boat was already very near. 'Hatch shut!' he reported as he secured it with a turn of

The Battle of the Atlantic: U-48 under New Command

the locking wheel. The chief engineer flooded the tanks and the boat headed down at a steep incline, being levelled off at 40 metres. All waited for the bombs to come down, but it remained quiet. Apparently the flying boat had not seen them, or was only interested in rescuing the crew of the *Eros*. At periscope depth fifteen minutes later the commander searched the sky first then had a 360° sweep with the attack periscope. There was no sign of the torpedoed steamer.

'Bridge watch ready in the tower!' he ordered, then opened the upper hatch. A draught of fresh sea air surged through the boat as the lookouts climbed the ladder.

'We shall head for the *Eros*. I want to make sure she went down.'

The boat ran towards the spot where the ship had been torpedoed. If she had not already sunk, which was unlikely since the hydrophone room had not reported sinking noises, she should still be visible.

Aircraft from astern!' the port astern lookout shouted, 'following the wake!'

'Alarm, dive fast!' In the frequently practised routine, the men on the tower tumbled into the interior of the boat, and for the second time that night Rösing sealed the hatch with a fast turn of the wheel as *U-48* submerged. A bomb fell in the wake but exploded well astern. Nevertheless the commander had the rudder put hard over to bring the boat to 90° off her previous heading. That this was the correct reaction was proved when a second bomb fell directly on the spot where the boat would have been had her course not changed. Twice more than night and on the morning of 7 June 1940, *U-48* was forced to submerge fast. Rösing then decided to stay down for a few hours.

The *Eros*, whose sinking all had taken for granted, did not sink. Destroyers had been quick to the rescue and took her in tow to the nearest British port. On the late afternoon of 7 June in calm airs, the sea as smooth as glass, Rösing decided to bring down the upper deck torpedoes. He reported by radio to the BdU: 'Off North Channel sank two steamers, torpedoed a third. Wind 0, sea 0, hazy, square AM 4941.' Two days later on 9 June a neutral Swedish freighter was sighted and allowed to proceed. The following night *U-48* came across a brightly-lit, very fast steamer. It took until the early hours until she was in a favourable shooting position. A single torpedo was fired at 0110 hrs from 600 metres range. It hit amidships 39 seconds later and unleashed a hellish cascade of further explosions which tore the ship apart within a minute. This had been the *Violanda N Goulandis*, 3,598 gross tons, a Greek freighter which sank at 44°04'N 12°30'W. *U-48* left the scene at full speed.

U-48

At 0843 hrs *U-43* (Ambrosius) made a sighting report. He had sighted a convoy and was transmitting homing signals for other U-boats. As *U-48* headed for this convoy, *U-29* (Schuhart) reported another. A request was sent for a homing signal to the second. The BdU intervened: '*U-29, U-43, U-46, U-48, U-101* operate against targets reported by this group. Command tactical leadership by *U-48* commander. If does not arrive and attack necessary, by contact boat.' Rösing issued no instructions to the four other boats made subordinate to him by this order. Correctly judging the situation he told himself that *U-46* and *U-101* had each been heading for one of the two convoys without knowing which, and he himself did not know the individual positions of the other four boats. All this made a co-operation co-ordinated and led by himself impossible. *U-48* was unable to reach either convoy. On 11 and 12 June *U-46* (Endrass) and *U-101* (Frauenheim) sank a total of four ships while *U-46* also torpedoed the tanker *Athelprince*.

Early on 14 June the *U-48* lookouts sighted a heavy cruiser of the *London* class heading south-east at high speed and closing quickly. *U-48* dived. When Rösing had the cruiser's upperworks in the optic, the target made an 85° turn away at high speed, thus denying *U-48* her opportunity. The cruiser was so fast that no U-boat, not even surfaced at high speed, could hope to catch her. Immediately afterwards four small bombs were dropped very close to the boat: Rösing saw them splash into the water through the periscope. Apparently an aircraft had seen the submarine in the very transparent waters. *U-48* dived at once to 30 metres and ran off one mile before returning to periscope depth. With his initial sweep with the sky-periscope he saw a biplane with floats, obviously the cruiser's shipboard aircraft. This machine would have reported the U-boat, as a result of which the cruiser turned away. This occurrence showed Rösing how useful it was for warships and merchant vessels to have 'eyes' to warn them of approaching danger.

At midday on 18 June *U-48* sighted a convoy heading north-west at slow speed. It consisted of about twenty steamers including a tanker. Because the circumstances dictated an attack from the 'land side', *U-48* headed west first to avoid the convoy's forward sweeper.

'UZO to the tower!' The IWO came up and at the UZO took a bearing on the first and second steamers of the western column of ships. Once the first ship grew huge in the optic, Suhren gave the order to fire. Nothing happened. The cable was flooded preventing the UZO data from being transmitted.

'Shoot from tube IV based on the attack computer, Suhren!' The angle

The Battle of the Atlantic: U-48 under New Command

was too great and the torpedo missed. *U-48* had come up close to the last ship of the column whilst waiting to see the result of the second torpedo and had been spotted. A signal 'SSS' had been transmitted. The boat pursued a large curving course away at full speed and escaped an escort which attempted to intercept her. A few deterrent depth charges were dropped but detonated at some distance away. Once this danger had passed, Rösing gave a fresh order.

'The boat will attack. Aim carefully, Suhren! Fire at the 5,000-tonner a thousand metres on the beam!' Suhren indicated with a gesture that he was ready. He had the target in his sights. 'A stern shot for the next one, Herr Kapitän?'

'Very well! After the shot from tube III bear away and fire from the stern at the following steamer.'

The first steamer entered the UZO binoculars. Behind the first Suhren saw a significantly larger ship. If the torpedo missed the first, it might easily hit the second ship, half of which could be seen overlapping.

'Shoot, IWO!' Suhren activated the electrical firing system at the touch of a button. The bow rose slightly but was restored immediately to the horizontal by the control room petty officer flooding the forward tanks.

'Torpedo running!'

At the commander's order to turn away, the battle helmsman in the tower turned the ship's head, and once the changed bearing was sufficient, the torpedo left the stern tube. It missed because in the great haste the angle had not been adjusted. After 114 seconds the torpedo from tube III hit the second steamer, the Norwegian *Tudor*, 6,607 gross tons, which sank at 45°10'N 11°50'W. Looking back at the convoy, Rösing watched as a large number of colourful star-shell lit the night sky. One of the escort vessels drove off *U-48* and contact with the convoy was lost, although a little later the boat returned and found a freighter estimated at 5,000 gross tons.

The convoy commodore ordered a general course change which brought the 5,000-tonner heading straight for *U-48*: the people on her bridge saw the U-boat and 'fired some pretty star shells and red flares'.

'That ship is coming straight for us, Herr Kapitän!' Suhren shouted.

'Fire tube I!'

'Tube I – *los!*' After 75 seconds the torpedo hit the *Baron Loudon*, 3,164 gross tons, and sank her. The escort turned towards *U-48* again, from her forecastle came muzzle flashes, and the shells howled across the dark waters to splash in the sea a little short of *U-48*'s port side.

'Maximum speed ahead both engines – steer zigzag! Everybody hold

95

U-48

on!' *U-48* began to weave at her fastest speed through the waves. Shells pursued her, but could not reach. In side the boat the men braced themselves against piping and struts, loose equipment flying about the compartments. *U-48* escaped the hail of shells thanks to her all-out effort, though some fell very close. The convoy made a 360° turn to starboard, thus preventing *U-48* from making a fresh attack run, but at the third attempt Suhren had a 7,000-tonner in the UZO. A torpedo fired from the stern tube hit this ship amidships after 122 seconds. As the great fountain denoting the hit rose up, the clock showed 0345 hrs. All hell was let loose. The entire convoy fired signal rockets, and the armed ships star shell, in the search for the surfaced U-boat. The casualty was the steamer *British Monarch*, 5,661 gross tons, at 45°N 11°21'W. Although the ships of the convoy had opened fire, and some of the shells fell close to the submarine, Rösing ignored them and turned his attentions to the nearest freighter. This spotted him, turned away and opened fire. The boat made haste to show her narrowest silhouette but when a warship appeared at 0735 hrs and headed directly for him, Rösing dived the boat in some urgency. Three hours later when it was safe to do so he surfaced and signalled the BdU: 'Three ships sunk, convoy dispersed. Am at quadrant BF 7165.'

On the night of 20 June a large ship was sighted sailing independently on a course favourable for an attack. Rösing took the boat to periscope depth and perched in the periscope saddle. Soon the fast ship filled the optic.

'A tanker,' he informed the crew at battle stations. She had a black funnel with the letter 'V' within a white ring. 'Submerged attack, we shall go in close to ensure we sink her,' he announced to everyone. Tube I was flooded: the torpedo petty officer reported the tube ready. *U-48* crept ever closer until the target ship's after structure filled the binoculars. The torpedo leapt free at 350 metres range, striking the tanker 22 seconds later with a devastating explosion amidships. This was the Dutch *Moerdrecht*, 7,493 gross tons, and sank by the stern within two minutes at 43°34'N 14°20'W. Thus the boat found 'prime game' once more.

On 21 June *U-48* turned for home, advising by radio: 'Am at square BE 8121. So far sank eight steamers with 42,860 gross tons. Returning to base, two torpedoes.' 'Only' seven ships had been sunk, and the eighth, *Eros*, torpedoed, but this was a quite outstanding patrol taking into account the difficult conditions under which it was carried out. At 2336 hrs the BdU signalled: 'Bravo *U-48*!'. During the run home the boat was forced to make emergency dives to avoid aircraft on eight occasions in one day alone. On two of these occasions bombs fell very close.

The Battle of the Atlantic: U-48 under New Command

U-48 entered Wilhelmshaven on 26 June 1940 to be welcomed by the BdU. Rösing made his report to the Great Lion the following morning. On 28 June *U-48* met up with *Sperrbrecher 9* at 1307 hrs for the escort to Brunsbüttel lock, and at 2342 hrs that day made fast at the Tirpitz Mole, Kiel upon concluding her sixth successful war patrol. All off-watch crews at the base turned out to greet her.

A little later *U-46*, *U-47*, *U-48* and *U-51*, the most successful boats of 7.U-Flotilla, all went into the yards for major overhaul and refit prior to their next patrols. Of this sixth patrol the BdU commented: 'Excellent operation! Tenacious attack on convoy on 19 June exemplary. Dönitz.' The crew divided into three watches for one week's leave each. The boat was scheduled to sail again in three weeks with Rösing still in command because 'Vaddi' Schultze had still not recovered from his illness.

CHAPTER 8

The Seventh War Patrol: Summer Duel

U-48 left Kiel for her seventh war patrol on 7 August 1940 in company with *U-65*. The two submarines separated on 9 August. Early on 12 August, *U-48* was north of the Shetlands: on 14th at the ordered position in square AL 0316 south west of the Hebrides. The boat dived after sighting a destroyer in the mist; the warship was not seen again.

On 16 August BdU Operations Division ordered Rösing to operate with *U-38* and *U-30* against a westbound convoy detected by the B-Dienst wireless monitoring service. On reaching the new area, from periscope depth Rösing soon saw smoke trails and mastheads coming into view on the horizon; during his stealthy approach he saw that the convoy was made up of forty to fifty ships in four or five columns. At once he transmitted a homing signal to bring up *U-38* and *U-30* for the attack, then infiltrated to the centre of the convoy to and fired at a freighter. The torpedo struck the ship's hull but failed to explode. As a result of the continual weaving of the individual columns of the convoy, which also involved their having to avoid colliding with each other, *U-48* ran almost side by side with the ships on the southern flank.

Three minutes after midday *U-48* fired from tube II at the small Swedish freighter *Hedrun*, 2,325 gross tons, and sank her. The next two torpedoes, fired individually, missed after the convoy suddenly reduced speed. The boat withdrew from the ranks of the convoy astern under pursuit by a submarine chaser and a gunboat. After the boat resurfaced and chased back for the convoy, Rösing came across a straggler. He subjected this ship to a very close observation and noticed a wooden shed on the forecastle which he thought could conceal a gun: there was a similar structure on the poop. Suspecting that this was a Q-ship, he left her at speed.

On the evening of 18 August, IIWO Ites on watch sighted a very fast independent ship bearing 260°.

The Seventh War Patrol: Summer Duel

'He is doing at least 15 knots, Herr Kapitän,' he informed Rösing as the latter appeared on the bridge.

'Give chase. We shall have her,' he replied, raising his binoculars to study the enemy ship. Two hours later *U-48* was still in pursuit of the fast-moving quarry and not an inch nearer. By midnight, however, perseverance had paid dividends, and the target was in the aiming optic. Tubes I and II were ready, Suhren at the UZO. The torpedoes were fired individually with a ten-second interval at 0005 hrs. Both struck after only 40 seconds running time. The steamer sent an 'SSS' signal (I am under attack by a submarine) and lay motionless on the sea. After her crew had taken to the boats she received the *coup de grâce* from the stern tube. The Belgian *Ville de Gand*, 7,590 gross tons, went to the bottom.

After a fresh sighting next morning, *U-57* under Oberleutnant-zur-See Erich Topp was sighted. The two commanders exchanged greetings and agreed to operate separately and parted. The lone ship, zigzagging furiously, escaped. *U-57*, the 'Red Devil' boat, so-called for the dancing red devil painted on the tower, had left Lorient at the beginning of August 1940. She was one of the first boats to operate out of the newly-acquired Atlantic bases on the Bay of Biscay. So far Topp had had no success, and had abandoned an attack on the steamer *Ceramic*, 16,000 gross tons, because of heavy seas – this ship would meet her tragic end at the hands of *U-515* (Henke) two years later. Next Topp had been attacked by an aircraft, the bombs splashing down and exploding so close that a diesel engine foundation tore and the camshaft parted. After a conference with his officers Topp decided not to abandon the voyage even though his maximum surface speed on one diesel was only nine knots: he had little chance of achieving anything at this speed but decided to try anyway.

In the North Channel he had sighted a convoy and fired two torpedoes before being spotted by the escorts. The boat was still diving when the first depth charges came down. Water entered the interior through a breach and *U-57* hit the seabed at 45 metres. The systematic depth-charging continued until shortly before midnight, then the destroyers stopped and listened. Topp escaped at slow speed on the electric motors to finally gain his operational area west of the Hebrides. Here he met *U-48*. He described this meeting thus:

'Commander to the bridge!' The shout of the watchkeeping officer resounded into the interior of *U-57*. Topp was bringing his KTB up to date when he heard the call. He hurried to the tower.

'German U-boat 10° to starboard, Herr Oberleutnant!' the IIWO reported, handing the commander his binoculars.

U-48

'Fire recognition signal.' With a dull report the flare left the signal pistol and exploded in the heavens: within seconds the other boat, its tower already crowded, gave the correct response.

'That is *U-48*, Herr Oberleutnant!' cried a lookout.

The two boats closed to loud-hailer range.

'Commander to commander!' the chief of 7.U-Flotilla called through his megaphone, 'Somewhere nearby the convoy must have crabbed round. Probably a course change.'

'Had any success, commander?' shouted Topp.

'Yesterday sank the *Ville de Gand*, 7,590 gross tons. And a small ship on the 16th. Then I came across a Q-ship. All in the westbound convoy.'

'I have had damn' bad luck, my boat is crippled. But perhaps I can still do something, I have a couple of eels in the tubes.'

'Very good, Topp, but take care, understand?' Rösing could give such a warning without insulting the more junior commander, for he had the experience and success of a flotilla commander behind him.

'I shall certainly watch out, Herr Kapitän!'

'May your mast and hatches break! [*Mast- und Schotbruch* – an old sailing ship greeting wishing bad luck in the hope of obtaining the opposite] Whoever sees the convoy first gives the homing signal, agreed?'

'Agreed – pity your independent has escaped.' After last waves in parting from the respective crews the two boats went their own way. *U-57*, which had transferred her torpedoes from their upper-deck storage into the interior, combed the sea for the reported convoy. Nothing was found on 20 August, but at midday on the 21st while Topp was on the bridge with the duty watch the telegraphist brought him a signal from BdU Operations Division.

'Helmsman! Starboard 10° – new course 255°'

'255° it is,' the battle-helmsman responded. Seconds later the change of course was felt by the men.

'What's up, Herr Oberleutnant?' the IIWO enquired.

'The B-Dienst has decrypted messages from the convoy. Its assembly point has been shifted 50 nautical miles north, therefore we are cruising around here for nothing. We shall find them on the new course.' *U-48* had also been alerted as to the course change and was now steering for the convoy. *U-38* and *U-30* strove to get there too, but were so far off that it was doubtful if they could make it. Probably their best hope was a straggler.

All day the handicapped *U-57* chased after the convoy, and finally at 1120 hrs on 23 August Topp received the first homing signal from *U-48*.

'Rösing has sighted the convoy. It 's almost enough to make you believe

The Seventh War Patrol: Summer Duel

he can sniff one out from a hundred miles away,' Topp remarked to his IWO. An hour later the starboard aft lookout reported: 'Aircraft to starboard, 20° abaft the beam.'

'Smoke columns!' exclaimed the IWO, 'that is the convoy!' Topp could hear depth charges exploding on the far side of the convoy. 'Those are meant for *U-48*. Let us hope Rösing can escape our cousins!'

'Definitely, Herr Oberleutnant, the Korvettenkapitän is a very wily fox. Nothing and nobody can wipe him out so easily.'

U-57 had managed to head off the convoy even at nine knots, and was keeping at the limit of vision: now all that remained was to approach submerged at full revolutions and fire off her remaining torpedoes. The boat rose to periscope depth, Topp ordering the men to battle stations. Now the crippled steel wolf, angling towards the convoy, was ready to bite. Topp raised the periscope repeatedly for a peep at the ships and in search of the convoy escorts, which were bound to be around.

'We shall never make it at this speed, Herr Oberleutnant,' the chief engineer advised.

'E-motors full ahead then!'

The hum grew louder and more shrill. The periscope mechanism hissed. Crouched in the saddle, Topp looked first along the line of travel and then to where the screw noises had been reported by the hydrophone operator.

'Directly ahead a tanker. Prime game. We shall fire a fan of two. Tubes I and III, bow doors open!'

'Bow doors are open, tubes flooded!' the 'mixer' reported.

The tanker maintained a straight course. Topp watches as the range slowly diminished. The low forecastle of the tanker grew larger in the optic, then the midships section, and the tall after-structure.

'Fire tubes I and III!' The boat jolted, the bows rose and were trimmed level at once by the control room engineer by flooding the equaliser tanks.

'Both torpedoes running!' The twin missiles, each armed with a 350kg TNT warhead, headed for the target at 38 knots. Ten seconds before the expected hit Topp raised the periscope.

'Time is up!' called the coxswain. Seconds later two masthead-high columns of fire and water rose up at the ship's sides, and as the thunder of the double explosion reverberated to the boat, gigantic flames were already flaring out of the tanker amidships. The glowing fireball expanded in the blink of an eye to envelop the ship in a dark-red glowing inferno over which a great cloud of black smoke formed. Two minutes after the torpedoes hit the tanker was burning from stem to stern. The men of *U-57* heard huge

U-48

explosions as the boat manoeuvred for a fresh attack. At that instant a second and then third steamer became visible in the gloom.

'Single torpedoes at two steamers each of estimated 5,000 gross tons. Tubes II and IV ready!'

When the boat reached the most favourable shooting position Topp gave the order to fire. Both torpedoes had their individual settings and hurtled for their respective targets.

'Both eels hit!' Jubilation broke out aboard the boat.

'I request silence!' At once it fell quiet.

'One steamer is sinking. He is stopped with an increasing list. The other has lost speed. He should have another torpedo. Reload tube I as soon as you can!'

In the bow room the men began to sweat and slave. The chains of the torpedo hoist, which had to be worked by hand, rattled. The torpedo was lifted from the under-deck storage compartment and manhandled to the tube – much easier work submerged than in a seaway. Topp raised the periscope again. Around the sinking tanker the sea was covered with burning oil. Only the casualty's superstructure could be made out amidst the flames. The first of the two steamers was sinking. The bow had gone under and the propellers, free of the water, continued to revolve for a while before coming slowly to a standstill. Further away, a massive explosion now tore the tanker asunder as the gases in the holds mingled sufficiently with the air to form a highly explosive mixture, tossing deck planking and structural wreckage into the sea. A moment later Topp saw a low shadow flit across the pyrotechnic display, heading directly for *U-57*.

'Alarm dive! Go to 80 metres.' With a rush, water filled the ballast tanks and the boat headed for the depths at half ahead. A touch of the rudder buttons brought her to a new course. She had progressed perhaps 200 metres on this new heading when screw noises became audible to the naked ear. Then the depth charges hammered the sea and shook the boat. A violent depth-charging ensued. A total of eighty heavy and medium-heavy blasts were counted off, and to assist the first escorts two more had joined in. The boat suffered only light damage, repairable with shipboard tools, but contact with the convoy was now lost. The convoy was OB 202. *U-57* sank the tanker *Cumberland*, 10,939 gross tons and in the second attack the freighter *Saint Dunstan*, 5,681 gross tons. The third steamer, *Havildar*, 5,407 gross tons, received a torpedo hit but was able to continue her voyage after emergency repairs aboard. Next evening, 25 August 1940, *U-57* hit the British tanker *Pecton*, 7,468 gross tons, amidships with her last torpedo. She

The Seventh War Patrol: Summer Duel

sank within a few minutes. Having returned to Germany, while waiting to enter the lock at Brunsbüttel, *U-57* was run down by the Norwegian freighter *Rona*, the collision later being ruled a maritime accident by a board of enquiry. Six *U-57* crewmen lost their lives.

Meanwhile, immediately after separating from *U-57*, *U-48* had transferred the torpedoes from the upper-deck store into the interior of the boat. Next day the bosun's mate of the watch sighted a lone steamer. Then came a convoy, from which this ship was evidently a straggler. The boat headed at full speed for an attack position. Night had fallen and while running fast on the surface a corvette appeared, heading directly for *U-48*.

'Everybody off the bridge. Prepare for alarm dive.'

Rösing remained alone on the tower and watched the approaching corvette, clearly visible by her bright bow-wave. The boat was flooded down to enable a 20-second dive, but even this short time could be too long if the people on the corvette had seen the boat. That this was not the case was proved when the corvette suddenly turned away and returned to the convoy on a long, curving course.

'Bridge watch return. We shall attack again. Battle stations!'

U-48 sliced through the waves towards the foe, running through the night. Thick smoke poured from the stacks of the steamers. A rain of sparks from one of the escorts indicated a defective furnace.

'We shall attack two steamers of 4,000 tons and 5,000 tons.'

On the bridge, the UZO was mounted on its column connected to the attack computer below. The individual values were fed in and the attack based on the calculations. The two torpedoes were fired at 0026 hrs and 0027 hrs. A few seconds after the expected running time elapsed two explosions rent the night.

'Destroyer heading directly for us!' came a shout from the aft starboard lookout.

'Alarm dive!'

The watch scrambled through the tower hatch and dropped like ripe plums into the control room below. Rösing was last in and screwed the hatch shut with a single quick turn.

'Hatch closed!'

With the two forward tanks already flooded, and the others filling, the boat headed steeply by the nose for the deep. Suddenly all could hear the harsh Asdic pings, gradually becoming louder, as the escorts searched for the boat.

'Hard to port! Minimum speed!'

U-48

The boat, still turning, lost momentum, became quieter.

'Switch off all unnecessary equipment.'

Astern the sea erupted in turmoil as four depth charges exploded one after another at various depths. The boat was shaken by the pressure of the blasts but recovered quickly, trim being re-established at 90 metres by the chief engineer. The next series fell well wide: the explosions apparently having knocked out their Asdic. Nevertheless the destroyer began another run.

'Port 10°!'

The boat glided to the new heading at creeping speed; the stern of the destroyer passed by 200 metres off the beam and 90 metres higher. Again came the hammer-blows of the destroyer's depth charges, this time to starboard. These pressure waves were more powerful. A couple of lamps shattered. A depth gauge glass fell out. The repairs were carried out immediately. No orders needed to be given.

'Go to 120 metres.'

The depth gauge indicator came near the red line on the scale. The boat seemed to ache in her frames, but withstood the enormous water pressure. The screw noises grew fainter. The next pattern of depth charges fell 600 to 700 metres away. They had survived.

When *U-48* surfaced after a two-hour run submerged, the telegraphist delivered a signal from the BdU ordering Rösing to a new patrol area. The boat reached it west of the Hebrides on the morning of 23 August. The skies were swarming with British aircraft. Twice *U-48* had to dive to avoid seaplanes, and twice to avoid land-based aircraft. At periscope depth after the last of these emergency dives Rösing found the skies clear of aircraft and ordered the boat to surface. Alone on the tower he surveyed air and sea: the boat was alone.

'Bridge watch come up! Turn on fresh air fans!' The ventilators began to circulate fresh air through the narrow hull of the submarine. A short while later columns of smoke were sighted. The lookouts saw the superstructure of the laggards of the convoy trying to keep up.

'Bridge to radio room. Give a homing signal.'

This was the sign for all U-boats in the vicinity that *U-48* had found the enemy and was on his heels. Whoever took a D/F on the homing signal could close in on it directly provided he was in a favourable situation not too far away. At 1130 hrs *U-48* was forced to dive by three aircraft. These called up a destroyer, visible a little later. The bombs dropped by the aircraft fell well astern of the U-boat as she dived, angling to starboard to escape the

The Seventh War Patrol: Summer Duel

destroyer's course. When the destroyer reached the position where *U-48* had disappeared from the surface, it dropped a few scare charges. No Asdic pings were heard. *U-48* ran an hour submerged, and when she resurfaced the fast convoy had escaped.

August 24th was a sunny Sunday, and from early on the commander had allowed men from the diesel compartment to enjoy a smoke on the tower platform. There was an unwritten rule aboard that the men in the interior regions of the boat should have these short breaks to take the air or smoke as they wished. Just as two off-watch men vacated the tower to be replaced by two more from the electric motor compartment a lone tanker appeared.

'This one is damn' fast, Herr Kapitän, we won't get him unless we fire at once!'

'Both diesels maximum speed!'

This time everything was being asked of the 'Jumbos'. The boat cut through the seas at almost 18 knots and began to overhaul the enemy tanker. She was on the enemy's beam one nautical mile away and once favourably placed Rösing told Suhren to fire when ready. The torpedo was a surface runner. The tanker, misidentified from *Lloyd's Register* as the *Lacklan*, 8,670 gross tons, went on her way nonchalantly without changing course.

'Time's up!'

Three seconds later the torpedo struck aft, sending up a huge column of water. The tanker came to a stop after a mile or so and begin to settle slowly. After she went down twenty minutes later, Rösing steered away to the north. The casualty was the British tanker *La Brea*, 6,666 gross tons.

An hour later *U-38* was sighted to starboard. Both boats had a similar heading and closed to semaphore range to exchange experiences. Kapitänleutnant Liebe was keen to operate against this convoy. The two boats separated after five minutes agreeing to operate far enough apart to comb a wide area of ocean. Just after midnight on 25 August the convoy was sighted on the port beam.

'Battle stations! Boat will run opposite course on convoy's port side. Surfaced attack.'

The UZO binocular was passed up and mounted on its pedestal. Suhren took his place behind it. The enemy speed and course, the speed of the U-boat, the speed and depth of the torpedo were all fed in together with the angle of attack. Tubes II and III were ready to fire, the torpedo mate hovered by the manual release switches in case the electrics should fail.

'Tubes II and III, *los*!' The two torpedoes, aimed at a tanker of an estimated 8,000 gross tons, and a freighter estimated at 6,000 gross tons

U-48

were released with a minute's interval between each. At 133 seconds the first hit the British motor-tanker *Athelcrest*, 6,825 gross tons, and after 182 seconds the next struck the British freighter *Empire Merlin*, 5,763 gross tons. Both ships exploded shortly after being hit, and lit up the night sky.

'Good shooting, Suhren!'

As the boat turned away, Rösing saw the two escorts he had noticed previously, and a third which had suddenly arrived on the scene, proceed to where the two merchantmen had sunk. One of these now detached from the little group and headed for *U-48*.

'Flood down bow! Bridge watch into tower!' Before the commander could give the order for a fast dive, the escort turned away and headed off in another direction. Ten depth charges exploded. 'He probably thought we were making a submerged attack and mistook our diesels in the distance for electric motors nearly, Herr Kapitän!'

'Radio room from bridge: transmit contact report and homing signal.'

The order was confirmed and only minutes later other U-boats within range of the convoy, HX 65A, were heading for it. When *U-48* prepared for a fresh attack she was forced to dive by two escort vessels and lost contact. Upon resurfacing at 2224 hrs Rösing had the fans turned on. The sea was empty. No matter how much they swept the horizons with their binoculars there was nothing to be seen. As they hunted along the general course of the convoy, Rösing signalled: 'To BdU: 46,070 tons sunk. Two stern torpedoes. Am going to Lorient to replenish.' The response of the Operations Division Staff came quickly: 'Excellent. Report how many ships sunk.'

'To BdU: sank seven ships including two tankers. Five of the ships from convoys.'

In fact, the boat had sunk only five ships of 29,169 gross tons confirmed. Two others had been torpedoed, but their subsequent whereabouts was unknown. A few minutes after this signal the lookouts heard the detonation of torpedoes and then saw a red glow in the sky.

'One of our boats is cleaning up there, Herr Kapitän,' the bosun's mate exclaimed.

'Right! And we wish him success.'

This was *U-124* (Schulz). During the Norwegian campaign her commander had lost *U-64* from under him and was now commanding the replacement boat he had been given. It was the first patrol of *U-124*. This was a large Type IXB boat attached to 2.U-Flotilla *Saltzwedel*. On board as apprentice commander and watch officer was Oberleutnant-zur-See Reinhard Hardegen, who would later become one of the noted U-boat aces

The Seventh War Patrol: Summer Duel

and win the Oak Leaves to his Knight's Cross on 23 April 1942. After picking up Rösing's homing signals, Schultz had D/F'd the convoy and fired three single torpedoes, all of which hit the target, sinking two ships and damaging a third.

Meanwhile *U-48* was heading for Lorient, the future U-boat base on the French Biscay coast. Escorted in by three R-boats* and a *Sperrbrecher*, *U-48* entered the port at 2245 hrs on 28 August 1940 and moored before the barracks.

The BdU assessed this patrol: 'Short operation, carried out with tenacity and guts, tactically first rate.' On 29 August 1940, Korvettenkapitän Rösing was the tenth member of the U-boat arm to be awarded the Knight's Cross of the Iron Cross. He now had to relinquish command: having already been a successful flotilla commander, Dönitz had another major post for him as liaison officer with the Italian Submarine Command Staff under Admiral Perona. There he would help to instruct Italian submarine captains in what they needed to know about the Atlantic. In exchange, Comandante Sestini came as Italian liaison officer to the BdU Operations Division. 'I sent Rösing, who had already proved himself as a U-boat commander and flotilla chief, to join Perona's Staff.'[1]

Summary of the First Year of War for the U-boat arm

A few days after *U-48* returned from her eighth patrol, the first year of war came to an end. The U-boat arm had achieved some outstanding successes, but suffered a series of bitter losses. It was important however that in the last phase of the first year U-boats had sailed once more and been successful. This enabled the view to be taken that the U-boat crisis had been surmounted.

The victory of the German Wehrmacht over the French released the Biscay ports for the German U-boat arm in the summer of 1940. This reduced the long run to and from the Atlantic operational areas by about 450 nautical miles each way. The British trade routes now passed the doorstep of the U-boat bases. From his HQ at Sengwarden near Kiel, Dönitz arranged that the first U-boats running into French ports should make for Lorient. Workers were seconded to Lorient from Germania Werft Kiel to carry our repair work and refitting. The advance parties of the first French-based flotillas were sent in.

For the first time, Admiral Dönitz saw the chance of a favourable

---

* *Räumboot*: a motor minesweeper. Tr

U-48

outcome to the war. The equipment transports rolled. A few days later the first German U-boat put into Lorient. The transfer of the Operations Staff from Sengwarden to France was being prepared. Dönitz, who realised that nothing could be more important personally than the closest contact to his commanders and crews, arranged for his own transfer to France in mid-June 1940. Provided time allowed, he wanted to receive homecoming U-boats, just as he took personal leave of them when they sailed. Commanders returning from patrol had to deliver their report to the Great Lion on the morning after their arrival at Lorient, and the Admiral Staff would pore over the KTB to identify every peculiarity and examine its value for other boats. In this way Dönitz could understand all worries and emergencies of the U-boat seafarer and take action on justified complaints of whatever nature. Everything he did was deliberately aimed at welding his commanders and crews into a blood-brotherhood.

On 23 June 1940 he went to the Biscay coast. On 7 July *U-30* was the first boat to enter Lorient from the Atlantic to refuel, re-arm and replenish for a new patrol. By 2 August a U-boat repair yard had been set up at Lorient. Henceforth every boat putting out for the Atlantic was spared a whole week's voyage through dangerous waters.

While the BdU Organisation Division under Kapitän-zur-See Friedeburg went to the Baltic with the organisational, technical and weapons staffs, the Operations Division under the former No 1 Admiral's Staff Officer, Korvettenkapitän, later Fregattenkapitän, Godt moved to the Atlantic coast. It was Friedeburg's task, later as Commanding Admiral U-boats, to oversee training on newly-commissioned U-boats, personnel and the technical side, and to resolve all questions arising.

The main concern of the BdU in the second half year of the U-boat War was primarily to press ahead as smartly as possible with large-scale U-boat construction. The fulfilment and forcing through of this aim was the obligation of the newly-created OKM U-boat Office, which would manage and expedite the special wishes of the BdU. On 8 September 1939, a week after the outbreak of war, Dönitz had made his wishes regarding U-boat building known in a memoir to OKM. He wanted at least 300 U-boats for the Front. In his new-buildings programme, which set aside the peacetime planning, in September 1939 Raeder had approved the building of those types of U-boats recommended by Dönitz. With reference to current losses and long-term repair work which had to be seen as additional to the increase in stock, he agreed a monthly production output of twenty-nine boats. Because the time between placing the building contract to delivery of the

The Seventh War Patrol: Summer Duel

finished boat varied from nineteen to thirty months, to which another three to four months had to be added for trials and working up, the BdU had not been able to count on an increase in U-boats available for the Front until June 1941. On 8 March 1940 Raeder cut the U-boat building programme to twenty-five boats per month, but even this reduced schedule could not be maintained. The monthly delivery of U-boats in the first half of 1940 was on average two boats, which was less than the boats lost monthly to enemy action.

On 31 August 1940 when the Operations Division drew up the summary for the first year of the war, the credit side of the balance sheet read: *Sunk*: one battleship, one aircraft carrier, three destroyers, two submarines and five armed merchant cruisers, plus 440 merchant ships of 2,330,000 gross tons.

The members of the U-boat arm who had been awarded the Knight's Cross as at 31 August 1940 was as follows, (unless otherwise stated all recipients held the rank of Kapitänleutnant at the time of the award):

1. Günther Prien (*U-47*) 18 Oct 1939
2. Herbert Schultze (*U-48*) 1 Mar 1940
3. Konteradmiral Karl Dönitz (BdU) 21 Mar 1940
4. Korvettenkäpitan Werner Hauptmann (*U-37*) 9 May 1940
5. Otto Schuhart (*U-29*) 16 May 1940
6. Wilhelm Rollmann (*U-34*) 31 Jul 1940
7. Otto Kretschmer (*U-99*) 4 Aug 1940
8. Heinrich Liebe (*U-38*) 14 Aug 1940
9. Fritz-Julius Lemp (*U-30*) 14 Aug 1940
10. Korvettenkäpitan Hans Rösing (*U-48*) 29 Aug 1940
11. Fritz Frauenheim (*U-21* and *U-101*) 29 Aug 1940

The U-boat losses in the first twelve months of the war totalled twenty-nine. These were:

1939

14 Sep 39 *U-39* (Glattes) Hebrides, destroyer
20 Sep 39 *U-27* (Franz) Hebrides, destroyer
29 Sep 39 *U-35* (Lott) Shetlands, destroyer
8 Oct 39 *U-12* (von der Ropp) English Channel, mined
13 Oct 39 *U-40* (Barten) English Channel, mined
13 Oct 39 *U-42* (Dau) SW of Ireland, destroyer

U-48

14 Oct 39 *U-45* (Gelhaar) E of Ireland, destroyer
24 Oct 39 *U-16* (Weingärtner) Off Dover, mined
4 Dec 39 *U-36* (Fröhlich) North Sea, RN submarine

1940
30 Jan 1940 *U-55* (Heidel) North Atlantic, destroyer
31 Jan 40 *U-15* (Frahm) North Sea, rammed by German T-boat
5 Feb 40 *U-41* (Mugler) S Ireland, destroyer
12 Feb 40 *U-33* (von Dresky) Firth of Clyde, minesweeper
13 Feb 40 *U-54* (Kutschmann) North Sea, mined
23 Feb 40 *U-53* (Grosse) E Orkneys, destroyer
25 Feb 40 *U-63* (Lorentz) Shetlands, destroyer
11 Mar 40 *U-31* (Prellberg) Jade Bay, bombed, later salved
20 Mar 40 *U-44* (Mathes) Shetlands, destroyer
10 Apr 40 *U-50* (Bauer) Shetlands, destroyer
13 Apr 40 *U-1* (Deecke) Stavanger, RN submarine
15 Apr 40 *U-49* (von Gossler) Ofotfjord, destroyer
25 Apr 40 *U-22* (Jenisch) North Sea, mined
31 May 40 *U-13* (Schulte) Off Newcastle, sloop
21 Jun 40 *U-122* (Looff) Missing, Northern Channel
1 Jul 40 *U-26* (Scheringer) North Atlantic, corvette
3 Aug 40 *U-25* (Beduhn) Terschelling, German minefield
16 Aug 40 *U-51* (Knorr) Biscay, RN submarine
21 Aug 40 *U-102* (Klot-Heydenfeld) Biscay, missing

At the outbreak of war there were fifty-seven serviceable U-boats. The commissioning of twenty-eight boats to 31 August 1940 was matched by twenty-eight boats lost (the twenty-ninth being raised, repaired and recommissioned in the first year of war). Nevertheless despite the nominal stock of fifty-seven Front U-boats, the actual number of these available for operations had been reduced by twelve boats because men for the new boats about to enter commission had to learn the ropes on training boats, and boats had to be transferred from the Front for the purpose. Moreover some of the newly-commissioned boats were still undergoing trials.

The fact that despite the outstanding successes of the German U-boat arm so few boats were built was so incomprehensible for the British Admiralty that the questionnaire they obliged Grossadmiral Dönitz to complete at Mondorf in 1945 repeatedly made the same demand: 'Why did the Germans not put everything into U-boat construction after they had tried

The Seventh War Patrol: Summer Duel

and tested the system in the First World War and knew what could be achieved with a large U-boat arm?' 'The laggardly manner in which the Germans intensified their U-boat construction,' Captain Roskill RN concluded in the official British work *The War at Sea*, 'had the most fortunate consequences for Great Britain.' The U-boat arm had proved its ability to strike hard, however, and its golden hour was yet to come.

CHAPTER 9

The Biscay Front

After an advance party of BdU Operations Division moved to Paris on 29 August 1940, the Staff followed from Sengwarden on 1 September. This move was necessary because all naval command centres were concentrated in Paris for Operation *Seelöwe* (Sealion), the invasion of England. The Staff set up in a narrow four-storey house at 18 Boulevard Suchet on the Bois de Boulogne. It was a private residence and Dönitz gave strict orders to make absolutely no changes or modifications to the property anywhere other than in the rooms they had requisitioned for use. The house was large enough to accommodate the entire Operations Division, including the telegraphy unit and military security personnel. All private cupboards were sealed, and no seal was ever broken during the long period of occupation by the Operations Division, or after them by a BdU sub-office located there. The BdU and his Staff were very aware of the need to respect private property.

From this address the Great Lion directed the operations of his grey wolves. It was here that the commanders reported after each war patrol. One of the first to call in to see his Commander-in-Chief was Korvettenkapitän Rösing, to hear from Dönitz that he was being relieved of command of *U-48* for an extremely important post awaiting him, on the staff of Admiral Perona.

'You are going to Bordeaux, Rösing. There you will instruct and encourage the Italian submarine commanders to fill the gaps which exist in their training. They are not yet ready for Atlantic operations.'

'So, to some extent I shall be a nursemaid, Herr Admiral!' Dönitz smiled: he enjoyed these candid remarks from his commanders.

'Beyond that, and above all, there is one thing I intend to achieve: that those twenty-seven submarines which the Italians have placed at our disposal to assist in the U-boat war actually do assist. If you can do that, Rösing, then you will have achieved a great deal. We must not allow ourselves to demand of a foreign nation and its sailors all those characteristics which we believe we have ourselves. The organisation, the

The Biscay Front

way of thinking and the education and training of Italian naval men is different from our own. It is not necessary for those on high to give guidelines on how to go about this. You will handle our Italian comrades in such a way that they will eventually "realise to a certain extent from within themselves" what is to be done and what left aside.'

'And where should the Italian boats operate, Herr Admiral?'

'I think that they should gain their experience around the Azores. After that they will work together with our boats west of the North Channel on the main convoy routes.'

In conclusion Dönitz expressed his gratitude to Rösing, which extended also to *U-48* and her crew: 'You commanded *U-48* on her sixth and seventh war patrols in an exemplary manner. Your successor will find it difficult to follow you. Perhaps you should discuss with him the quirks of the boat and crew. It serves no useful purpose if he is left to make his own mistakes.'

'Thank you, Herr Admiral. And who is the lucky man who will command *U-48* on her eighth and on possibly many more war patrols?'

'It is Kapitänleutnant Bleichrodt. You already know him.'

'Of course, our Ajax.'

Now Dönitz smiled broadly, rising to offer Rösing his hand. '*Mast und Schottbruch*, Rösing!'*

Just as he received Rösing, Dönitz received all commanders putting in from sea in those first days of September 1940. On the 5th, Oberleutnant-zur-See Endrass arrived and received the Knights' Cross from his Commander-in-Chief. He was followed by Günther Kuhnke on 19 September and Kapitänleutnant Schepke on the 29th.

Each morning, Korvettenkapitän Werner Hartmann delivered the U-boat Report in the situation room. On 9 May 1940 he had been the fourth U-boat commander to receive the Knight's Cross and now as No 1 Admiral's Staff Officer he collated the events of the previous day and night and the very latest signals from U-boats at sea. From 18 Boulevard Suchet, Dönitz directed each individual boat, arranged for packs to assemble in picket lines and set individual boats on known or reported convoys. Together with his Chief of Staff and the Admiral's staff officers, the attempt continued daily to find the best operational area for the boats and deploy them from these positions on the basis of the B-Dienst wireless monitoring reports. If Admiral Dönitz had had *at this time* that fleet of U-boats which he had

---

* Hans-Rudolf Rösing ended the war as FdU West/Norway in the rank of Kapitän-zur-See. Born in Wilhelmshaven on 28 September 1905, he died in Kiel on 16 December 2004 at the age of 99 years.

U-48

calculated would be necessary and had requested before the war started, the enemy would certainly have been in the direst straits and perhaps worse, as their experts have made known.

In October 1940, the BdU Operations Division finally transferred to the French coast. Operation *Seelöwe* had been shelved, and the continuing presence of the Staff in Paris was no longer justified. In any case, Dönitz wanted to be closer to his U-boat bases on the Atlantic coast to be on hand when U-boats sailed and arrived. Now the BdU and his Staff occupied the empty villa of a French sardine merchant at Kerneval near Lorient. The radio and telex offices, accommodation and dining rooms, the situation room and officers' mess were located in adjacent buildings. This villa was situated close to the Atlantic in the centre of an ancient park with many trees– so close that the crash of the incoming surf could always be heard from the villa, which gave a wide view out to sea. Dönitz could be on the quayside very quickly when an incoming boat was reported, and he missed welcoming nobody unless pressing circumstances made it necessary, either by the need for him to be in Berlin or making an inspection at another base.

It was from Kerneval that he planned the great U-boat battle which was to go down in U-boat history as the 'Knight of the Long Knives'. One of the boats involved in this fierce convoy battle was *U-48*. The boat had transferred direct to Brest with 1.U-Flotilla, and Heinrich Bleichrodt, a naval officer of the 1931 entry who had not originated in the U-boat arm, would not find it easy to follow in the footsteps of the two previous highly-experienced commanders aboard this successful boat. The two watchkeepers, Suhren and Ites, had already completed seven war patrols under these two commanders aboard *U-48* and knew their trade inside out. This led to some difficult situations during the eighth war patrol, for which *U-48* sailed on 8 September 1940.

CHAPTER 10

U-48 and Her New Commander: Convoy SC3

The boat sailed from Lorient on her eighth war patrol under her new commander Heinrich Bleichrodt. At about the same time *U-99* (5 September) and *U-59* (7 September) had also put to sea. A few days after *U-48*, *U-43* had sailed on patrol from Germany and was still in the North Sea when *U-48* was already in her operational area south-west of Ireland.

On 14 September a destroyer was seen for a short time but then disappeared quickly. The boat had been 36 hours on station. That night there occurred a situation which Teddy Suhren described in the book he co-authored:

> The night was pitch black when Otto Ites relieved me at the change of watch. Instead of exercising caution we had a chinwag and before we knew it we were surprised to find ourselves ahead of the central column of a convoy. I put the rudder hard over and ran the engines flat out to put the boat on the beam. As usual we shouted, 'Commander to the bridge!'
>
> A gap had opened ahead of the boat through which it could have passed and then been able to fire, certain of a hit, into the convoy from outside it. Bleichrodt, groggy from sleep, saw only the side of a ship towering as high as a house above us, misunderstood the situation and shouted in horror: 'Alarm dive!'
>
> This destroyed all our chances of attacking and dragged us away from the window of opportunity. As we went inside, lightning fast, Otto Ites fell most of the way down into the control room and in a loud voice began to revile the commander, who was closing the tower hatch above us. I grabbed Otto by the collar and hissed: 'Shut your mouth! Are you crazy? You want to wreck the boat? When the confidence of the crew in a commander receives a shaking, you can never foresee the result.'[1]

U-48

This occurrence, described by both authors in *Nasses Eichenlaub*, resulted from the inexperience of the commander, who afterwards learned the ropes very quickly, and for that reason was eventually very successful on his first war patrol and brought the boat back safely. That the two watch officers on the bridge allowed a ship to approach so close that it 'towered as high as a house above the conning tower' was a 'matter for court-martial', as one of the lookouts commented. Because the crew got wind of some of this, it soon spread everywhere and led to an investigation by the flotilla chief. Suhren played it down and remarked in the book that Bleichrodt gradually got wise 'to what was important'.

Back to the events at sea during the eighth war patrol. After resurfacing, *U-48* closed in on Convoy SC3 and transmitted homing signals for other U-boats in the vicinity. During the afternoon of 14 September, the boat lurked at the limit of visual range on the convoy's southern flank and on a parallel course awaiting nightfall to move in. When it grew dark the boat had already come up on the leading ships of the convoy.

'Battle stations! We shall attack on the surface!'

The UZO was placed on its column and manned. All tubes were reported ready to fire as Suhren aimed the optic at the most favourably placed steamer, and fired. As the torpedo set off, the low shadow of a warship appeared, heading directly for *U-48*. The high foaming bow-wave could be seen distinctly.

'Escort coming for us.'

A glance confirmed for Bleichrodt that it was too late to dive. In this first great test of his mettle aboard *U-48* he did what was the only correct thing to do in the circumstances.

'Rudder hard over and full ahead both!'

As the boat was making her turn he ordered Suhren at the UZO: 'Keep on the escort and fire!' The escort was seen in the optic apparently intending to ram. The data was fed into the UZO at lightning speed, and a minute after the first torpedo was released, the second headed for the sloop, now only 900 metres distant. Meanwhile the first torpedo struck the Greek freighter *Alexandros*, sending up a column of fire and water, and a few seconds later the second torpedo hit the sloop astern. Immediately the depth charges stacked there exploded in an inferno, and HMS *Dundee* was torn apart.[2]

As they ran off at high speed, the men on the tower watched the Greek freighter sinking.

'Reload! We shall attack again!'

U-48 returned to the convoy's mean course. Two tubes were ready, another two needed thirty minutes more. A second small warship ahead of the convoy turned aside and crossed the wake of *U-48* but failed to sight her. Bleichrodt had already flooded down and so avoided the need to dive. He was now heading the boat closer to the port side column of the convoy as the reloading was reported finished by the bow room.

'We shall go for the steamer of about 6,000 tons forward and the one of about 7,000 tons behind it. Have you got both, IWO?' Suhren at the UZO confirmed that he had. The date was fed into the UZO, which was able to calculate for six targets at the same time. When the steamers were at 1,000 metres, the operator reported 'Solution!' Suhren let the targeted ships come a little closer before firing the first torpedo.

'Torpedo running!' shouted the 'mixer'.

'Corvette coming directly for us!'

'20° starboard, full ahead both!'

U-48 turned away, the diesels hammering so furiously that the boat trembled as she picked up speed. The corvette ran past, leaving them with the opportunity to stay on the surface and keep at the convoy. When the corvette dropped a few deterrent depth charges proving she had not sighted *U-48*, Bleichrodt reduced speed a little and turned on a parallel course.

'Reload tube III, we shall try once more!'

In the convoy the torpedoed steamer *Empire Volunteer* had still not sunk, but was listing heavily with the bow rising slowly above the surface. Two auxiliaries were apparently attempting to pick up the crew.

'Boat will attack again. Tubes I and II ready for surface attack.' The UZO had been returned to the tower and reinstalled on its pedestal. At 0300 hrs the next torpedo struck the British freighter *Kenordoc*, 1,780 gross tons, which sank at 57°42'N 15°02'W. After this *U-48* was finally driven off and forced to dive. At creeping speed on the E-motors the boat turned aside and the depth charges all fell wide.

Heinrich Bleichrodt had proved himself a worthy successor to the previous commanders in his first major operation with the boat, thanks to the assistance of his two watch officers, and had sunk three steamers and one sloop. The boat continued her patrol. In the early hours Bleichrodt reported his success against Convoy SC3 in a short signal, then headed west on the surface.

The BdU signalled to all boats: 'Off the North Channel, *U-48* attacked and broke up a westbound British convoy.' The radio operators noted other signals from boats in the vicinity: for example *U-99* (Kretschmer), who early on 16 September north-east of Rockall Bank sank his first victim, the

U-48

Norwegian *Lotos*, 1,327 gross tons, and a second ship one day later. On the afternoon of 17 September, *U-65* (von Stockhausen) reported sinking a 5,000-tonner.

'Keep a 100 per cent alert lookout, men!' Bleichrodt exhorted the watch when coming to the bridge for a breath of air. An hour later mastheads were reported, then ships. It was apparently an independent ship to which a few others had attached themselves on account of the mutually convenient speed. That a destroyer was present was not recognised until a little later.

'The boat will make a surfaced attack!'

U-48 headed north-north-east to reach the attack position against this westbound convoy. This was successful with both diesels at full ahead, and by 2300 hrs the leading ship could be made out clearly.

'That is a very fat tub, Herr Kaleunt,' the bosun's mate of the watch whispered, 'at least 10,000 tons.'

'Good estimate, I think she is at least that.' The boat glided ever closer. Two torpedoes were ready for a fan of two, the 'mixer' waiting for the order to fire.

'Fire fan, tubes I and II.

Both torpedoes were expelled by compressed-air cartridge and then ran under their own battery power through the sea towards the 10,000-tonner. It was 0001 hrs on 18 September 1940. The bow lifted following the loss of ballast caused by the loss of the torpedoes' weight.

'Now the steamer behind her. He is about 5,000 tons, see him, IWO?'

'I see him, Herr Kaleunt. Single shot from tube IV at the second steamer.'

While the new data was being fed into the angle calculator, the coxswain kept an eye on the stopwatch in his hand. Ninety seconds had passed.

'Time is up!' Four seconds later a great geyser reared up from a hit amidships on the bigger steamer, and a couple of seconds later the second torpedo hit astern.

'Steamer sending SOS. Name is *City of Benares*. In *Lloyd's Register* she is 11,081 tons.'* A roar of delight went through the boat

'Absolute silence please,' 'Ajax' called out, and the jubilation fell away. *U-48* moved closer to the selected second steamer. A corvette in the vicinity

---

* In 1945 Bleichrodt was detained as a war criminal and accused by the British Admiralty of having 'secret orders' to search out and sink the *City of Benares* because she had a number of Jewish evacuee children aboard, seventy-seven of whom lost their lives. When the only evidence available was found to be a BBC propaganda broadcast from 1941, the charges were dropped and Bleichrodt released. The case was probably brought to cover up the fact that the *City of Benares* should have been declared a hospital ship and not sent across the Atlantic in a convoy. The entire responsibility for the loss of the ship rested with the British Admiralty. Tr

U-48 and Her New Commander: Convoy SC3

of the U-boat turned away to render assistance to the *City of Benares* and her passengers.

'Steamer is sinking quickly. The boats are being lowered,' Bleichrodt shouted below.

'Tube IV clear to fire,' reported the 'mixer'.

'How does it look, IWO? Do you have him?'

'Steamer is just coming into the optic, Herr Kaleunt,' Suhren said from his position at the UZO, confirming that the commander, who conned the boat during surface attacks, had manoeuvred *U-48* well.

'Solution! Solution! Solution!' shouted the operator below.

'Tube IV, fire!'

This time the bow hardly rose at all – the control room petty officer had flooded the equaliser tanks at precisely the right time.

'Eel running,' the mixer stated.

At that moment, while the second torpedo was running towards the target, the *City of Benares* sank. The wreck creaked and knocked and groaned in her death plunge.

'Hit, bow forward!' Bleichrodt reported as he saw the column of water rise up at the forecastle of the second steamer.

'Ship is stopping, speed dropping off. Another ship astern is avoiding her. We shall have this one too and . . . Alarm! Diving stations!' Out of the corner of his eye the commander had spotted the glittering bow-wave of an escort in the pale light of the moon. The warship was heading directly for *U-48*. The tower watch disappeared through the hatch and dropped down into the control room. Bleichrodt was last down, turning the handwheel of the hatch cover tight and reporting the hatch shut to the chief engineer. Zürn then flooded the ballast tanks to send the boat in a precipitous dive. The second ship hit was the *Marina*, 5,088 gross tons. She sank at 56°46'N 21°15'W. At 30 metres the propellers of the pursuers thrashed overhead very loud.

'Hard to port!'

The diesels had long-since stopped, the E-motors hummed and with the rudders hard over *U-48* escaped a series of five depth charges, although the boat was rattled by the explosions in the wake to starboard.

'Screw noises diminishing,' reported the hydrophone operator.

'Two patrol boats at 170°,' he called out a minute later.

'Go to 70 metres.' Bleichrodt was at the chart table in the control room. His face looked drawn as he wrestled with the new job of extracting the boat from the grasp of her pursuers, and surviving.

U-48

'Starboard 10°.' The battle helmsman in the tower confirmed the order.
'Creeping speed.'

At the slowest possible revolutions *U-48* came away from the course of pursuers.

'How does it look now, hydrophones?'

'Pursuer keeping to his old course – no, wait – turning towards us now – direct for us!'

'Hard to port!'

This cat-and-mouse game in which they were the mouse was brought home to them a little later when the escort vessel passed by and then came back to confront the submerged U-boat. He was almost beyond them when the depth charges suddenly roared like thunder, lifting up the bows and hurtling the boat 10° off course. Light bulbs popped. In the boat darkness fell.

'Turn on emergency lighting!'

'Exhaust valves leaking!' came from the engine room.

'Check all outboard vents.'

'Leak has stopped.' Seconds later the main lighting came back on.

'Hydrophone room to commander: second attacker is destroyer. First escort vessel is leaving. New propeller noises coming up from astern.'

'They are marking our position for the third boat to crush us,' Bleichrodt remarked to the chief engineer.

'Both motors absolute maximum ahead.' The E-motors whirled the propellers, pushing the boat forward at eight knots, curving to starboard. It outfoxed the enemy, who dropped two series of five depth charges each where he thought the submarine should be, according to his calculations.

'Think of it as a penance,' Bleichrodt said genially. The pattern of ten did no damage. *U-48* now proceeded at her fastest possible submerged speed. Bleichrodt, having escaped the encirclement, turned the boat on the general course and came to periscope depth once the propeller noises had faded.

'Boat is hanging on the periscope,' the chief engineer reported. From the saddle, Bleichrodt had a quick peep ahead, then pedalled around the periscope column. The night was now black as pitch.

'Bridge watch ready in the tower. Surface!'

Bleichrodt unwound the hatch wheel, threw open the cover, heaved himself through and looked around. A reviving stream of fresh air entered the boat, wafting over the battle helmsman. Then the fans whirled it through the interior.

The *U-47* crew at Kiel after their return from Scapa Flow, October 1939.

The *U-47* crew after the award of decorations.

The battleship *Scharnhorst* seen from *U-124*, 10 March 1941.

Weapons exercise aboard *U-124*, South Atlantic, March 1941.

U-124 assists survivors from a sunken ship.

Survivors come aboard *U-124* to allow their upturned lifeboat to be righted.

In the Atlantic – hit amidships!

A steamer takes her final plunge.

Kapitänleutnant Schultz, commander of *U-124*, after receiving the Knight's Cross.

U-103, with this boat Korvettenkapitän Schütze won the Oak Leaves.

Reinhard 'Teddy' Suhren, IWO aboard *U-48* on nine war patrols.

Otto Ites, IWO and IIWO aboard *U-48*, IWO from September 1940 to March 1941.

Otto Ites won the Iron Cross First Class while still a watchkeeping officer.

The crew of *U-48* after the mention in the Wehrmacht Report.

Heinrich Bleichrodt, third commander of *U-48*.

A burning tanker adrift in two sections.

U-48 after sinking 115,000 gross tons. Weest Bescheed = 'He knows his way around'.

Kapitänleutnant Suhren being greeted after his return from a war patrol.

In the foreground Gerd Schreiber's *U-95*, behind her *U-124* under Wilhelm Schultz.

The *U-96* cook in his pantry.

Mealtime in the torpedo room.

A view through the hatch into the *U-65* control room.

The stern diesel room.

The *U-124* medical officer rows his rubber dinghy across to *U-107*.

Dönitz greets the crew of *U-37* on their return from a patrol.

Hans-Rudolf Rösing.

Heinrich Bleichrodt.

Erich Zürn.

Herbert Schultze.

Willy Kronenbitter, tried and tested *U-48* coxswain.

U-48 and Her New Commander: Convoy SC3

'Bridge watch come up!'

The lookouts assumed their quadrants and raised their binoculars. Each of the men had a 90° sector to cover. If a ship was not reported before the truck of her mast became visible, that was a serious disciplinary matter.

'We'll hang around and hope to have another shot at them.'

The boat coursed through the darkness: when the sun rose, the first columns of smoke were ahead to port.

'We'll advance on them at the limit of vision and aim to make a submerged attack as soon as it is dark and can turn in on them.' *U-48* headed eastwards at full speed, along the track towards England that the convoy would have to take.

On 18 September 1940 a new big convoy was sighted in grid square AM, which stretched from 59°N 13'W to 57°N 11'W, and had been reported by the B-Dienst five hours previously. Dönitz had already sent his nearest sea wolves to intercept. That morning Bleichrodt telegraphed his two sinkings. On the night of 19th he would send another announcing the demise of the *Magdalena*, but that lay in the future. When the boat gained on the convoy's head during the afternoon, the sweeper came up from astern and forced *U-48* to dive. She stayed down for an hour, then made up for it on the surface. At the right juncture for a submerged attack, the boat went to periscope depth, curving gently towards the convoy until the sweeper blocked her path for a while. Once the sweeper resumed its position the attack began.

'Submerged attack, tube I.'

'Tubes flooded, bow doors open.'

Bleichrodt ensured that the boat remained in the correct shooting position by frequent economic checks through the periscope. The targeted steamer had been in the UZO for some time. Another slight correction, then came the automatic report: 'Solution!' But Bleichrodt wanted to be certain. The boat crept ever nearer.

'Tube II – *los*!'

The bow tipped up a little, was trimmed level and departed slightly from the attack course. Precisely when the running time was up a flash was seen at the steamer's side. The victim stopped as flames curled up from her stern.

'Ship is lying stopped, has begun to burn. Crew taking to the boats.' He retracted the periscope. *U-48* bore away, and the next time Bleichrodt looked at the casualty he saw raging flames rising from within the ship. No enemy warships were about.

'Surface!' Immediately after the chief engineer reported 'Boat is through!' the radio crew picked up the steamer's distress message on the 600-metre frequency.

'SSS from *Magdalena*, torpedoed by German submarine, burning overall, sinking quickly, help!'

'Steamer is called *Magdalena*, 3,118 gross tons in Lloyds Register,' the radio petty officer reported. Escort vessels now appearing forced Bleichrodt to turn away, and once the boat had lost sight of the convoy to the south-east, tube I was reloaded.

Early next morning the upper-deck torpedo were transferred down. This was a very dangerous procedure, for when the torpedo hatch was open and the eel was being let down into the interior, the boat was defenceless: if an enemy ship came by it would be curtains. When the torpedo hatch was finally sealed down, Bleichrodt breathed a great sigh of relief. 'Check over the torpedoes immediately,' he ordered the 'mixers'. The radio crew put on a new gramophone record which was relayed to all compartments through the boat's intercom and *U-48* headed north-west on the diesels at slow speed.

The BdU decryption service had identified the rendezvous for a convoy arriving from North America with its naval escort from Britain very early in September and four days in advance of the rendezvous. *U-47* (Prien) had already expended the entire stock of torpedoes at this convoy, SC2. Because he had no torpedoes but plenty of fuel, the Great Lion had put him west of the 23rd parallel of longitude as a 'weather boat'. From there twice daily *U-47*'s radio operator would report the weather for the Luftwaffe. On 20 September 1940 whilst in this position the *U-47*'s lookouts sighted Convoy HX72 out of Halifax, Nova Scotia. Prien reported it at once and kept abreast of the convoy. Dönitz ordered five boats to converge on it: *U-99* (Kretschmer), *U-100* (Schepke), *U-32* (Jenisch), *U-47* (Prien), who could only attack with his deck gun, and *U-48* (Bleichrodt).

Upon receiving a copy of the signal, Bleichrodt grabbed his cap and binoculars and, with a warning shout, a glance at the compass and a nod to the battle helmsman he climbed up. The boat was heading to where the *U-47* homing signal had been D/Fd, the intention being to intercept the convoy on the evening of 20 September. Shortly before midnight the D/F loop was used again when Prien advised his position, course run and the speed of the convoy. Immediately afterwards BdU Operations Division signalled, 'Search line disbanded. Each boat should attack convoy after own assessment.'

U-48 continued to run directly towards Prien's homing signal. Bleichrodt remained on the tower. The radio petty officer handed him the copy of a

U-48 and Her New Commander: Convoy SC3

short signal just received from *U-138* (Lüth) reporting having torpedoed three ships from Convoy OB216, amongst them the modern British tanker *New Sevilla*, 13,801 gross tons.

'This name Lüth,' Bleichrodt said to his IIWO Ites, who had taken over the watch, 'is one to look out for'. Later he would discover that his feeling for coming events was exactly right, for Wolfgang Lüth would become one of only two U-boat commanders to receive the Oak Leaves with Swords and Diamonds (commander of *U-9*, *U-138*, and *U-181*, awarded 11 August 1943). Precisely five hours after his three sinkings within six minutes, at 0227 hrs on 21 September *U-138* sank a fourth steamer from Convoy OB216, the *City of Simla*, 10,138 gross tons. The bridge watch confirmed that on hearing the victim's tonnage, Lüth said to the radio petty officer, 'I fear your scoundrel has given me an extra 138 gross tons. Bring the book up!' *Lloyd's Register* was produced and Lüth saw that the tonnage actually was 10,138 tons, an omen for him because the final three digits were also the number of his boat.

U-99, nearest the convoy, got so close to it on the night of 20 September that the lookouts could hear the screw noises. Next morning there was an acid 'conversation' between the commanders of *U-99* (Kretschmer) and *U-47* (Prien). Having spotted *U-47* in the darkness, Kretschmer ordered a textbook practice attack on the other boat. Not until he was close enough to ram did the *U-47* lookouts see him. *U-47* went to full ahead then sent the recognition signal with the blue lamp filter, to which *U-99* replied with the correct answer for the day. Prien had his typhoon-megaphone charged and called to Kretschmer, 'Otto, this damn stroke would not have been successful if I had been on the bridge myself.'

'Take care, Günther, you are in sore need of new lookouts, that is all,' Kretschmer replied. After a brief conversation the two boats parted. Prien had pointed out to Kretschmer a big tanker which was straggling. Kretschmer decided to attack. A little later the tanker hove into sight and the torpedo hit at 0312 hrs. The British *Invershannon*, 9,154 gross tons, sent an SOS. *U-99* moved off lateral to the convoy to avoid a destroyer racing forward. The convoy fired star shell, but Kretschmer was tenacious and an hour later fired at another steamer from 800 metres. This was the ammunition ship *Baron Blythswood*. Hit amidships, explosions tore her apart with a minute, and she sank at once.

U-48 was still well short of the convoy. 'There's a few more over there, Herr Kaleunt!' the bosun's mate told Bleichrodt.[‡‡] The commander nodded. Raising his Zeiss he saw the flames licking up from the stricken tanker.

123

U-48

'The convoy is before us. We must reach it as soon as possible.' He lowered his binoculars. 'Both diesels full ahead.' The piston arms worked furiously to push *U-48* more urgently through the sea. Running alongside the starboard flank of the convoy towards its leading ships a half later, they passed the spot where Kretschmer's tanker was sinking, where two escorts were still searching for survivors. *U-48* sailed around them.

When the second hit resounded through the night and the pyrotechnics of *Baron Blythswood* lit the sky, *U-99* closed in to attack a third ship. This time *Elmbank* was hit, but kept going, if much slower, until finally forced to stop. Seconds later she morsed: 'SSS *Elmbank* torpedoed help.' Rocket flares rose up from the convoy and star shells drew a dazzling trail across the night. Foghorns trumpeted wildly. *Elmbank* was a tough nut. Because she would not sink, Kretschmer attacked with the 88mm deck gun, and let her have eighty-eight rounds, which she survived. Kretschmer left the *Elmbank* to finish off the *Invershannon* with a torpedo, and after this broke the tanker's back he returned to *Elmbank*. Before he could resume his bombardment of the ship, *U-47* came up from astern and Prien begged his colleague to allow him 'a few rounds at the refractory object'.[3] Kretschmer told Prien to help himself and now both submarines shelled the long-abandoned wreck. When Prien had expended all his ammunition he left, and Kretschmer finished off the *Elmbank* by setting her afire with phosphorus rounds. Soon afterwards she went down, enveloped in flames. The sea hissed and seethed to lament her departure.

Now back to *U-48* which had stolen ahead of the convoy at full speed and was now in a position to attack.

'Battle stations! The boat will attack a steamer estimated at 5,000 tons!'

It was 0614 hrs on this 21 September when a single torpedo fired from tube II ran for 71 seconds and hit the British *Blairangus*, 4,409 gross tons, which stopped at once and sent an SOS. One of the destroyers on the starboard flank came rushing to the U-boat's assumed location, and her commander was not far wrong. *U-48* dived at full power on the E-motors in an effort to shake off the destroyer which, fortunately for Bleichrodt, was not equipped with Asdic. The hunt lasted three hours and on occasions the depth charges fell unpleasantly close, but once again the boat escaped

---

‡‡ Although never named, this bosun's mate was almost certainly Berthold Seidel, who sailed with Bleichrodt on every one of his voyages aboard *U-48* and *U-109*. Seidel had completed so many U-boat voyages that it was believed no U-boat on which he was serving could be sunk. In September 1942 Bleichrodt recommended him for the German Cross in Gold on the basis of his having completed fourteen war patrols totalling eighty weeks at sea. The decoration was awarded. Tr.

U-48 and Her New Commander: Convoy SC3

unscathed. At first light *U-48* surfaced, but was forced to submerge again after thirty minutes on the surface.

Schepke at Convoy HX72

The boats attacking Convoy HX72 pursued it all day though repeatedly driven off and forced under water by the escorts. Not until evening could they surface to make an attack from astern. *U-100* (Schepke) was the first to shoot. This time the 'one-torpedo specialist' wanted to sink four steamers with four single torpedoes.

'We shall fire singly at four units including a large tanker estimated at 10,000 tons,' Schepke announced into the boat, while his Torpedo Officer lined up the UZO binoculars. Taking his opportunity when the moon was hidden by thick cloud, Schepke came in extremely close to the convoy while the IWO fed the individual data into the attack computer. As the column of ships came plodding along, the four targets were favourably placed for the attack, and one after another the four torpedoes were ejected by their compressed-air cartridges and ran fast for their respective objectives: at 2310 hrs the first and second, at 2311 hrs the third and at 2313 hrs the fourth. Once all four were running, *U-100* turned away and Schepke ordered the tubes reloaded. One minute later the sea became an inferno as the torpedo hits spouted high, and then the distress messages rent the ether. The convoy commodore signalled all ships to turn to a new heading. Colourful star shell, red signal rockets and distress flares were fired up and lit the night in various colours. Random depth charges were dropped as a deterrent. The first casualty, *Canonesa*, 8,286 gross tons, lay stopped and listing. The motor tanker *Torinia*, 10,364 gross tons, was hit and burning. The steamer *Delcain*, 4,608 gross tons, stopped and then sank. Only the fourth ship, although hit, managed to escape, heading north west through the north-headed columns to disappear from view and lick her wounds. Two destroyers forced Schepke to dive and passed overhead without dropping depth charges. Trimmed at 80 metres, a half hour later the 'mixers' had reloaded the four bow tubes and *U-100* was ready to resume the chase.

U-48 had witnessed the success of *U-100* and ran towards the stern of the convoy to attack. The destroyers, occupied with finding the boat which had fired, left the convoy in search of it. This gave *U-48* her chance. At 2328 hrs *U-48* torpedoed the *Broompark*, 5,136 gross tons. The ship did not sink, however, and *U-48* was seen and forced to dive. She crept free of the subsequent depth-charge pursuit. When Bleichrodt surfaced after ninety minutes of being the hunted, he found that the convoy had moved on, but

U-48

he was forced below again. *U-100* sank two more ships from HX72: early on 22 September a large tanker, the British *Frederick S. Fales*, which sank after being hit by two torpedoes, and at 0214 hrs the same morning the Norwegian *Simla*. This exhausted Schepke's stock of torpedoes. Convoy HX72 had been depleted by seven ships within five days.

On 24 September 1940 the BdU signalled: 'Schepke. In recognition of your recent success in the battle against convoys, the Führer awards you the Knight's Cross of the Iron Cross.' Within an hour *U-100*'s mechanics had fashioned a gigantic Knight's Cross in sheet metal for him which they presented to Schepke on the run home.

U-48 had also received orders to return to port after her last signal. She had sunk several ships and damaged another from Convoy HX72. The convoy lost twelve ships of 72,727 gross tons sunk, and three of 18,022 gross tons torpedoed and damaged. Dönitz noted in his KTB: 'The attack on HX72 has shown that the principles relating to the use of radio-telegraphy at the Front, and U-boat training for attack, were correct.'

On 25 September when *U-48* returned to Lorient after a short but successful patrol, nine pennants each representing a claimed sinking fluttered from the periscope mast. The total tonnage of these casualties was 41,334 gross tons. Later when it was known that *Broompark* had survived, the figure was revised downwards by 5,136 gross tons. On his first voyage with *U-48*, Heinrich Bleichrodt had proved his special abilities as a U-boat commander.

This offensive against Convoy HX72 was a great success, but only a month was to pass before it was cast into the shadows by a real wolf-pack offensive which would go down in U-boat history as 'The Night of the Long Knives'. In order to portray this great battle one must first describe the events which made the formation of a strong U-boat pack possible. This battle made October 1940 one of the most noteworthy months of the almost four-year Battle of the Atlantic.

CHAPTER 11

The Duel with Convoy SC7 – 'The Night of the Long Knives'

After a short refit and crew leave, *U-48* left Lorient on her ninth war patrol on 6 October 1940. The patrol was the second for Bleichrodt as commander. He had been accepted by the men, and not least thanks to his outstanding crew he had made himself a good replacement for 'Vaddi' Schultze.

As the boat cast off, Bleichrodt gave a wave to his colleagues on the quayside and then turned to face forward as was his custom. He would never look back. Three days previously *U-58* (Schonder) and *U-59* (Jürst) had sailed, and on 8 October *U-138* (Lüth) followed. *U-48* set out to cross the Bay of Biscay at high speed. The test dive was carried out to the satisfaction of commander and chief engineer, a small leak in the tower being repaired with shipboard tools. Part of the Biscay crossing was made submerged mainly due to being forced under upon sighting land-based aircraft and Sunderland flying boats: minor damage was inflicted, and repaired aboard.

On 9 October *U-58* reported by burst-signal that she had sunk a British steamer. The *U-48* coxswain, IIIWO Obersteuermann Herbert Engel, saw from the chart that Schonder had left before them but was significantly farther south. Next day *U-48* had reached the operational area when a signal was picked up in which Viktor Schütze (*U-103*) reported that he had sunk two steamers the previous night further south.

'We are on the right track, Herr Kaleunt,' opined the bosun's mate as Bleichrodt read the signal, and concluded, 'Soon we shall have something in front of the tubes and then we'll go to town.'

'Let's hope so,' the commander replied and looked along their course. A little later they received more reports of successes. Schütze in *U-103* and Moehle too, in *U-123*. He had sunk the *Graigwen* after Schütze had torpedoed her the day before.

'100 per cent sharp watch men!' Bleichrodt told the lookouts, 'We are now very close'.

U-48

Eight hours later the lookouts reported smoke. The commander was summoned to the tower and shown the upperworks of the leading steamers on the horizon.

'We shall head south and run a course parallel to the convoy.'

The boat cruised at the limit of visual range. The sweepers protecting the stern of the convoy came well south of it while running from astern to forward, forcing *U-48* to withdraw, but the boat was not spotted. When dusk fell, *U-48* moved in. At 2115 hrs Bleichrodt ordered: 'Battle stations. We shall attack the convoy.'

This would be a surfaced attack, for night had fallen and the moon was hidden by thick banks of cloud. The following sea was high and rough, the wind at storm force, pushing the boat quickly forwards; when *U-48* turned towards the convoy, the UZO was already installed on its pedestal, Suhren awaiting his orders.

'There's a tanker in the second column,' Bleichrodt shouted to him above the fierce wind, 'I'll bring us in closer!'

The boat crept up on the columns of ships. Suhren had seen the tanker. 'She's at least 8,000 tons, Herr Kaleunt.'

Bleichrodt nodded. 'Also aim at the steamer obliquely astern which looks even bigger, and the bucket of 5,000 tons running ahead of them.'

The boat glided nearer. A single torpedo for each of the three ships was readied. It was 2150 hrs on 11 October when the first hit the fat steamer, throwing up a huge column of fire. As Bleichrodt moved the boat's head to bear a few degrees closer to the tanker, the latter zigzagging to avoid the torpedoed steamer.

Don't fire yet, IWO.' Whilst behind them the steamer lay burning and sending out distress messages, and signal rockets and red bundles of flares advertised the U-boat attack, *U-48* cut through the high seas for the tanker. At 2209 hrs the second and third eels were fired. Both hit: first the Norwegian freighter *Brandanger*, 4,624 gross tons, then the much larger British motor ship *Port Gisborne*, 8,390 gross tons, also began to call for help. The torpedoes hit amidships and aft respectively. Suhren missed the tanker.

'Destroyer to port, approaching quickly,' the lookouts reported. Bleichrodt turned swiftly, saw the warship's foaming bow-wave and the tracer which hissed down a half-mile ahead of her bows.

'Both engines slow, 10° to starboard!'

'10° starboard it is,' the battle helmsman confirmed from within the tower. The boat heeled and the destroyer lost the scent, though still firing tracer.

The Duel with Convoy SC7 – 'The Nght of the Long Knives'

An hour later *U-48* returned to the convoy and the tanker. By midnight the boat was ideally placed, a textbook attack followed. At 0014 hrs the torpedo was fired and hit after a 97-second run. The tanker began to burn at once.

'Torpedoed by German submarine, help,' broadcast the Norwegian *Davanger*, 7,102 gross tons. That night Bleichrodt sank three ships of 20,116 gross tons. Convoy HX75 was the victim of this blood-letting.

For ten minutes the commander watched the tanker, burning from stem to stern, noticing how quickly she began to settle. The gases building up inside her ship tore out the deck planking as they exploded and flames stabbed out along her length. A mile-long thick carpet of oil, also in flames, trailed out behind astern of her. Two escorts were trying to get to the crew in the boats. A third vessel, identified as a destroyer, dropped some depth charges as a deterrent, far enough away from the lifeboats as not to endanger them by the blast, then turned towards *U-48*. Increasing speed quickly the destroyer, bow high out of the water, had seen the boat.

'Alarm dive!'

The bridge watch tumbled down into the control room, the commander landing last after sealing the hatch and advising the chief engineer that he had done so. Zürn ordered the two forward ballast tanks flooded to give the boat bow-heaviness for the plunge, and the diesels continued to run until the boat went under. Then the E-motors cut in and at an order to the helmsman the boat moved off the destroyer's line of approach. The first depth charges hammered down to port and astern.

'Go to 100 metres.'

The boat was trimmed when the depth gauge showed this depth.

'Screw noises growing louder. A second destroyer is turning towards us from astern,' reported the hydrophone operator. Suddenly they heard a bright chirping sound, louder by the second.

'First destroyer searching with Asdic, Herr Kaleunt.'

'Hard to starboard, go to 120 metres.'

The boat's head changed as she fell another 20 metres. The noise of the destroyer's screws, once fainter, now returned to their original volume and then doubled: there were destroyers astern and to port. Bleichrodt attempted to deceive them as to his position by very slow speed and sudden course changes. Depth charges were dropped in four groups at short intervals, twice astern and then one on either beam. This forced *U-48* deeper. The chief engineer halted the dive at 156 metres. Seconds later the second destroyer, which had been waiting for the eruptions to tail off before attacking, dropped her own series which hurled the boat yet deeper and to one side. Bleichrodt felt his stomach contract.

'Boat is down 10° by the stern,' the chief engineer reported. Somewhere water was coming in, and a compressed air pipe had fractured. An injured man was crying out.

'Port E-motor out of action!' the E-room artificer reported.

The boat turned a full circle and ran below the destroyers. The explosions had knocked out their Asdic. The screw noises droned loudly as *U-48* passed at creeping speed below the two destroyers. All depth gauges read 160 metres. The chief had got the boat horizontal again. The sound of hammering resounded through the boat from the E-motor room.

'Quiet, the enemy ships will hear us,' Bleichrodt called out imperturbably.

'Port E-motor repaired!'

'Full ahead both!'

While the two Asdic-less destroyers now dropped their depth charges by guesswork, *U-48* headed south-south-west. One after another the reports of completed repairs flowed to the control room. Bleichrodt ordered the boat up to 120 metres. Compressed air began to force the seawater from the tanks until the ordered depth was reached.

'That was a close shave,' the control room petty officer remarked. During attacks on the boat he kept a small blackboard on which he chalked up the depth charges he counted. When the boat went to periscope depth three hours after the alarm dive, Bleichrodt circled the head of the instrument cautiously. The sea was empty. Convoy HX75 had sailed away leaving a few of its participants on the seabed as a prelude to Bleichrodt's second patrol as commander.

'To BdU: from convoy eastbound with strong escort sank two steamers and one tanker. Total 20,116 gross tons. Plan squares AL 0378 and AL 0381. Depth charged. Bleichrodt.'

Ten minutes later the BdU signalled: 'Bleichrodt. Well fought. Carry on. You are on a good arterial track.'

U-48 was unable to confirm this 'good arterial track' over the next few days, and although the radio room copied down reports of successes from Schütze, Korth and Wolfgang Lüth, they had all scored west of *U-48*. Though heading in that direction at slow cruising speed, the lookouts saw nothing, and the hydrophone operator heard nothing. On the evening of 15 October when *U-103* (Schütze) reported a sinking, the bosun's mate on watch observed: 'He's obviously after the Swords!'. Viktor Schütze had

The Duel with Convoy SC7 – 'The Nght of the Long Knives'

been awarded the Oak Leaves to his Knights' Cross on 14 July 1940, the twenty-third German serviceman to receive it, and it looked as though 'Fatty', as he was known secretly, was not done yet.

In the early hours of 16 October 1940 in square AL 2876, after *U-124* sank the steamer *Thistlegarth*, new hope was born in the *U-48* crew that soon they would find another victim, and they were not disappointed, for late that afternoon the bridge watch reported mastheads. By the time Bleichrodt arrived on the bridge, the upperworks of the convoy were visible. A mass of smoke trails decorated the distant horizon.

'Convoy, Herr Kaleunt!'

'10° to port.' This was to avoid the chance of being seen by the leading sweepers. Once off the parallel course he awaited his opportunity to turn in towards the convoy. Meanwhile it could now be seen in its entirety.

'To BdU: convoy sighted. Thirty ships west of Rockall Bank in square AL 3380. Still no escort from the east. Bleichrodt.' Immediately the BdU responded: '*U-48* stay with convoy and transmit homing signals. *U-46*, *U-99*, *U-100*, *U-101* and *U-123* operate against convoy.'

Shortly afterwards the bridge watch sighted four stragglers and finally the escort for the convoy, which had come out from the direction of England. These were the sloops *Scarborough* and *Fowey* and the corvette *Bluebell*. All that night *U-48* kept track of the eastbound Convoy SC7 (Sydney–Nova Scotia–England). The boat was forced away twice before reaching the correct attack position on the morning of 17 October.

'Battle stations. We shall attack the convoy.'

All four forward tubes ready, the boat headed through the darkness towards the merchant armada. Two torpedoes were intended for the big tanker in the southernmost column, a good target together with freighters of an estimated 5,000 and 6,000 tons respectively.

'Solution!' the attack computer tracker reported. The commander let the boat get closer, then the Torpedo Officer raised his hand as a signal that he was ready to fire.

'Tubes I to IV – *los*!'

'All torpedoes running.'

After 87 seconds the first two hit the tanker. Four seconds later came the third explosion and nine seconds after that the fourth.

'All four torpedoes hit!' Bleichrodt called down into the boat. 'Tanker is stopping, on fire amidships and astern!' *U-48* moved off to the south as slow speed as a sloop came on a direct course for her but then turned away to attend to the second steamer which lay stopped and firing red signal rockets.

U-48

'Tanker is *Languedoc*, by *Lloyd's Register* 9,512 gross tons. Steamer *Scoresby* also sending distress message. Is 3,843 gross tons.'

'What happened to the third ship?'

'Have heard nothing,' the telegraphist replied.

'We certainly hit him, perhaps he hasn't realised it yet.'

'Aircraft coming from ahead!' shouted the bosun's mate. Bleichrodt lifted his binoculars: through the gloom of the early morning he made out the massive fuselage of an approaching Sunderland flying boat.

'Starboard 20°!' The boat heeled: the commander watched to see if the Sunderland reacted. It banked.

'He's seen us. Alarm dive!'

U-48 sought the depths quickly. The flying boat misjudged it: bombs were dropped, but well astern.

'Go to 70 metres.' The boat levelled out before running parallel to the assumed course of the convoy full ahead on the E-motors. In the bow room the 'mixers' were reloading the tubes feverishly. This was no easy work with only muscle-power and a hand-operated pulley, but ninety minutes later the job was done and Bleichrodt brought the boat to periscope depth. The sea was deserted. Even the skies were empty.

'Watch ready in the tower. Surface!'

'Boat is through!' the chief engineer reported. Bleichrodt threw open the tower hatch. An ice-cold gust of morning air lashed his face. From the tower he spied on the port beam a dark point closing quickly above the surface of the sea, gradually growing in size, gradually assuming the shape of an aircraft. She dropped bombs, woefully wide, but Bleichrodt dived the boat just in case. Now that the presence of U-boats had been confirmed, the convoy commander Allen reported it, and the Admiralty ordered him to change course to the north-east.

Four hours after *U-48*, *U-38* (Liebe) had found SC7 and sunk a Greek steamer. In the early hours of 18 October 1940 he torpedoed the *Carsbreck*, 3,670 gross tons. Although Liebe transmitted homing signals these were not received. The BdU Operations Division signalled *U-48*. requesting homing signals: they received no reply, and when the boat surfaced hours later, Bleichrodt informed them that he had lost contact with the convoy. He warned the BdU and U-boat commanders of the flying boats which were apparently circling the convoy in large numbers.

Dönitz now ordered the boats to form a north-south patrol line well to the east of the last known position of the convoy. This would enable all available boats to arrive in good time. Most important of all was that the

The Duel with Convoy SC7 – 'The Nght of the Long Knives'

patrol line should lie ahead of the convoy's path, preferably so that the boats would sight the convoy on the morning of 18 October. Dönitz's calculations paid off. Early on the 18th all boats were in position and keeping a sharp lookout for the convoy. *U-48*, which was surfaced and had gone ahead, came across its starboard flank and twice sent homing signals with her location. It was 0930 hrs when Bleichrodt dived the boat and, seeing a very favourable target, prepared to attack.

'Torpedo room, tube I clear for submerged attack.'

'Tube flooded, bow cap open.'

U-48 crept close to the objective, then fired off the torpedo. The periscope came free for a few seconds while the chief engineer wrestled the boat level: after the running time elapsed the torpedo struck and set aflame the British steamer *Sandsend*, 3,612 gross tons, which had apparently detached from SC7. Ten minutes later she had gone down.

Convoy SC7 did not encounter the patrol line of U-boats until that evening. *U-123* (Moehle) opened the attack with a torpedo at 2020 hrs which was a prelude to the massacre. The casualty was the British freighter *Beatus*, 4,885 gross tons. She sank at 57°31'N 13°10'W. Fifty minutes later *U-46* (Endrass) fired at three ships beyond the escorts. *U-101* (Frauenheim) had joined *U-46* almost at the same time and fired a little later. As a result of these twin attacks the small Swedish ship *Convallaria* was sunk. *Shekatika*, 5,458 gross tons, torpedoed by Frauenheim stayed afloat to be torpedoed again by *U-100* (Schepke) two and a half hours later but still she refused to founder: finally Moehle in *U-123* managed to sink her the following day from very close range. The solution to the mystery was revealed by her cargo when she broke up: *Shekatika* had been kept afloat by her cargo of timber.

Meanwhile the ships of the convoy had run into the patrol line and were being attacked from all directions. *U-99* (Kretschmer) got into the midst of the convoy and fired almost simultaneously with *U-100* (Schepke) and *U-101* (Frauenheim). The three escorts were no match for the number of submarines present, and ran helplessly hither and thither between the various casualties. The wolf pack surrounded the convoy. In the early hours of 19 October *U-123* (Moehle) joined the trio, and then they alternated in groups. By the forenoon Convoy SC7 had lost seventeen ships sunk plus three damaged. Torpedoes were fired at thirty-three ships. That same morning *U-99*, *U-101* and *U-123* headed for home having expended all their torpedoes.

All other boats remained with the convoy: on the way to join them *U-47* (Prien) came across the England-bound Convoy HX79 west of Rockall. The ocean escort of this important convoy had been weakened after the early

U-48

departure of the armed merchant cruisers *Montclare* and *Alaunia*, and the new escort had not attached itself until the morning of 19 October after leaving westbound Convoy OB229. This was the escort group which the British said would be of the maximum effectiveness against the German U-boats. It consisted of the destroyer *Whitehall* under the highly respected Lieutenant-Commander Russell, the destroyer *Sturdy*, the minesweeper *Jason*, corvettes *Hibiscus*, *Heliotrope*, *Coreopsis* and *Arabis*, the naval trawlers *Lady Elsa*, *Blackfly* and *Angle*, and the submarine *O-21*. The convoy consisted of forty-nine ships, all fully loaded with material for Britain. It had weighed anchor at Halifax and it was hoped that with the powerful escort, the U-boats having vented their fury and resources against SC7, it would have a clear run home. In this they were to be disappointed.

U-47 sailed on 12 October 1940 after only seventeen days' lay-up and refit. Prien had headed for Convoy OB228 reported by *U-93* (Korth) on 16 October. but when Korth lost contact, Prien lacked an objective until *U-48* sighted and reported SC7 late that same day. It was Prien's eighth war patrol and he was looking for more success. As *U-47* ran at full speed for the action, the bridge watch could already hear the distant grumble of exploding torpedoes. Forced below by the escorts, by the time Prien eventually regained the surface on the morning of 19 October, contact with SC7 had been lost, and by evening its remnants were long gone. Shortly afterwards he was rewarded when his IWO sighted another convoy, the size of which gradually became apparent.

'To BdU: plan square AL 0372 sighted convoy at least forty ships. Strong defences. I am remaining with it and will give homing signals on request. Prien.'

Dönitz directed *U-46*, *U-48* and *U-100* to this new convoy, HX79. Although these boats had taken part in the convoy battle of the previous two nights, they all still had torpedoes. He also ordered *U-38* (Liebe) and *U-28* (Kuhnke) to attend, but *U-28* at least was so far away that it seemed doubtful Kuhnke could get there.

By the evening of 19 October, *U-47* at the convoy transmitted a homing signal several times and having overhauled the leading ships turned towards them to attack. Immediately after ordering his crew to battle stations, two torpedoes exploded on the far flank of the convoy, the sound of the detonations being borne to them on the wind.

'Someone else is attacking over there, Herr Kaleunt,' observed Prien's new IIIWO, Oberleutnant-zur-See Stephan. This was the arrival of Liebe in *U-38*, who sank the first two steamers of HX79 with torpedoes fired at 2213

The Duel with Convoy SC7 – 'The Nght of the Long Knives'

hrs and 2219 hrs. The casualties were *Matheran*, 7,653 gross tons, and the British *Uganda*, 4,966 gross tons. As more shadows appeared in the darkness to port, Prien had his torpedo tubes cleared for surface attack. His Torpedo Officer, Oberleutnant-zur-See von Varendorff at the UZO took bearings on the steamers ordered by his commander. The first torpedo was released at 2227 hrs, stopping the *Bilderdijk*, which began to list very quickly. A distress message was sent giving the ship's identity. She was a steamer of 6,856 gross tons according to *Lloyd's Register*.

'Now the tanker, Varendorff!' Prien himself gave the new heading to the helmsman in the tower. *U-47* reached the most favourable firing position. The tracker had been showing 'Solution' for some time. The torpedo was fired at 2331 hrs and hit the motor tanker *Shirak*, 6,023 gross tons. Contrary to Prien's assumption she did not sink but fell behind the convoy to be finished off by *U-48* on the early morning of 20 October. The tonnage sunk was credited to Bleichrodt even though it had been Prien who had crippled the tanker. This left *U-48* with two torpedoes. Despite all efforts she was unable to catch up with the convoy.

At 2346 hrs *U-47* had sunk the British freighter *Wandby*, 4,947 gross tons: *U-46* (Endrass) had fired two torpedoes with a one-minute interval, the first hitting the wreck of *Wandby*, the other sinking the British steamer *Ruperra*, 4,548 gross tons. *U-47* had four torpedoes aboard with which Prien sank *La Estancia*, 5,185 gross tons, *Whitford Point*, 5,026 gross tons and seriously damaged the British tanker *Athelmonarch*, 8,995 gross tons, although she managed to resume her voyage three hours later and was finally towed home.

Schepke, another of the aces attacking HX79, sank three steamers of 19,900 gross tons aggregate, two of them tankers. The total immediate loss to Convoy HX79 was twelve ships of 71,069 gross tons sunk and three torpedoed, two of these being sunk later. Only *Athelmonarch* was hit and survived. Once the convoy was close to English waters and the U-boats were being constantly forced to dive, Dönitz called off the operation and ordered a new search line farther west. *U-48* and *U-47* headed for France, as did *U-100* and *U-99* after reporting themselves out of torpedoes.[1]

After her short patrol *U-48* reached Lorient on 27 October 1940 with seven pennants representing 43,106 gross tons sunk, fluttering from her extended attack periscope. An eighth ship had been torpedoed and damaged. Dönitz also congratulated *U-47* on the special success. After Prien's last success report on 20 October he received from the BdU this signal: 'As the fifth serviceman of the German Wehrmacht and the first commander of the

U-48

U-boat arm, Kapitänleutnant Prien is awarded the Oak Leaves to the Knight's Cross of the Iron Cross. Adolf Hitler,' to which Dönitz had added: 'Well fought, bravo *U-47*, congratulations Prien.'

A few days later on 4 November 1940 Kapitänleutnant Otto Kretschmer became the sixth German serviceman, and on 1 December Joachim Schepke the seventh, to be awarded the Oak Leaves. These were proud successes for the U-boat arm and the *U-48* crew also received decorations for their resolute commitment. Dönitz recorded in his KTB:

> Within three days, thirty-eight ships from three convoys were sunk by eight U-boats almost exclusively in night attacks. In these battles no U-boat was lost. From these facts I derive the following conclusions:
> 1. The operations prove that the principle laid down in 1935 for the development of U-boat tactics and training to concentrate U-boats to attack enemy ships in convoy, is correct. Concentrating boats had been made possible by the advances in wireless telegraphy since the Great War.
>
> 2. This kind of attack on convoys is only possible with commanders and crews who have had a thorough training. There is a need for a comprehensive and long training period in a large sea area. This training would not be possible if we did not keep the Baltic free of enemy activity.
>
> 3. The performance of such operations will occur more frequently the more boats we have in the areas of operations and the greater the probability of discovering more convoys by means of more eyes, i.e. more boats.
>
> 5. More boats also means that the approaches to England will not become temporarily empty of U-boats after such attacks because, as happens now, nearly all boats have to return to port after firing off all torpedoes.
>
> 6. We cannot always expect successes as in the operations described: fog, heavy weather and other circumstances can reduce the prospects for success temporarily to nil.

'The ability of the commanders, however, will always be decisive,' he concluded, and named all commanders who had been put to the test in this regard in this phase of the Atlantic battle: Prien, Herbert Schultze, Kretschmer, Schepke and Bleichrodt, Endrass, Liebe and Lüth, Frauenheim,

The Duel with Convoy SC7 – 'The Nght of the Long Knives'

Wohlfahrt, Oehrn and Jenish, and a list of others who not until months later would become strong enough to attack and sink as the Great Lion had ordered in the wolf pack battles of the long Battle of the Atlantic.

What remains to be seen is how the other side faced up to the wolf packs. When the British Admiralty went on the offensive at high pressure to combat the German U-boats, and gradually devised, developed and introduced increasingly better weapons and equipment for their destroyers, aircraft carrier groups and aerial defences, only the U-boat pack system was in a position to pull the fat out of the fire.

CHAPTER 12

British Anti-Submarine Developments

News that war had been declared swept through the streets of London at 1100 hrs on 3 September 1939. Merchant vessels at sea bound for British ports received the signal 'Total Germany' from radio station 'Rugby'. From Whitehall. the nerve-centre of the Royal Navy, the British Fleet was put on a war footing with the same two words, and the great maritime struggle began. It consisted in principle of a duel between German U-boats, and British merchant vessels and their escorts.

On 4 September 1939, Winston Churchill, First Lord of the Admiralty, summoned a conference in Whitehall. Chairman was the First Sea Lord and Chief of the Naval Staff, Admiral Dudley Pound. Also present were Admiral Sir Charles Little, Second Sea Lord and Chief of Naval Personnel: Rear Admiral Fraser, Third Sea Lord, responsible for scientific research in naval construction: Vice Admiral Sir Alexander Ramsay, and Rear Admirals Arbuthnot and Philipps.

This Board of Admiralty headed by Churchill agreed that the Admiralty should be located in Admiralty Arch at the end of The Mall nearest Trafalgar Square. The War Room, measuring about eighteen feet by fifteen, was from now on to be the venue where the fate of the Empire would be decided. The first conference after the outbreak of war was also attended by the Prime Minister, Neville Chamberlain, and the Cabinet ministers Clement Attlee, Lord Halifax and Arthur Greenwood. A map, 'World of Mercantile Navigation' hung along one of the long walls.

Merchant shipping, as all in the room were aware, was the decisive factor for the supply of Great Britain. Another map, showing the Atlantic, was intended for the operations now to be expected: the German U-boat offensive against British merchant vessels either sailing singly or in convoy. The Map Room was located in an adjacent office. Here four officers of the three services and the security service received signals not only from British land and air forces, but also from ships at sea and naval bases around the globe. Incoming documents were placed in concertina-files marked 'Secret', 'Top Secret' or 'For the King'. In this room were hung those maps which showed the positions of ships by means of pins with coloured heads. Pins with blue heads marked the locations of German U-boats.

Next to these two rooms was the telephone exchange with fourteen extensions linked by automatic dialling. Churchill later had a separate suite set aside for himself with a direct telephonic link to the US President and later Stalin. The first war conference held on the night of 4 September 1939 considered primarily whether Japan would remain neutral during the opening phase of the war, and whether the convoy system should be reintroduced. The general feeling was that Japan would not become involved yet and that convoys were essential. Churchill wrote in his diary: 'The convoy system is merely a defence against U-boats. The questions of German merchant raiders and major warships are not treated in the documents before us.' Thus the First Lord of the Admiralty came to what would become a major theatre of war during the next few years: the Atlantic.

Next morning the decisions agreed upon by this session were put into effect, determining convoy routes and assembly ports, finding convoy commodores and searching for convoy escorts. Every merchant ship which from now on left any foreign port for Great Britain was to be under the control of the British Admiralty from the beginning to the end of its voyage. Above all, every merchant ship had to be armed as soon as possible, for Churchill had ruled that all merchantmen should open fire on, with the intent of destroying, any U-boat which came within range. Gun crews had to be found for these ships. The trade depots would be responsible for supplying the weapons, smoke installations and gas masks. The Defensively Equipped Merchant Ship Section handled all matters pertaining to their usage. Many veteran RN reservists were called up to serve these guns, and another 24,000 seamen trained in ship defence. During the war this figure rose to 150,000 men. Convoy operations were under the control of the Plans Division, whose head co-operated closely with the Joint Planning Committee. The Operations Division was responsible for all warships attached to convoys, and the Operational Intelligence Centre had a special section for anti-submarine operations. The section worked in the Submarine Tracking Room, where small models representing U-boats, convoys and escorts were placed on horizontal maps and moved to the most recent known position as and when each correcting report was received. It was clear to everybody that this would not be adequate for convoy defence, and both Coastal Command and RAF Fighter Command were on 24 hours notice from the Submarine

U-48

Tracking Room. This switching centre was headed by Lord Winn, one of the Lords of Appeal, and under the overall command of Vice-Admiral Norman Denning.

As a defensive measure against U-boats, it was believed in Britain that Asdic, which had priority for installation in convoy escorts, and primarily destroyers, would detect any U-boat submerged in the vicinity of the escort, enabling depth-charging to impede any attack and possibly result in the sinking of the U-boat. One of the admirals involved in its development said of it in 1937: 'Never again will a U-boat present us with the same problems as we had to overcome in 1917.' By the outbreak of war, the Royal Navy had installed about 2,000 Asdic sets on ships of all kinds, but only 150 sets aboard destroyers, the ships which were actually designed to locate and destroy U-boats. This could not be said of naval trawlers, sloops and corvettes.

The depth charges in use at the beginning of the war were simple metal cylinders weighing 186kg, of which 179kg was the explosive charge. They sank at three metres per second and had a lower depth limit of 60 metres, which meant that the deeper the U-boat, the better its chance of avoiding damage or destruction. Improvements were introduced very quickly and culminated in multiple launchers, 'Hedgehogs' which could throw up twenty-four depth charges simultaneously, each with an individual depth setting.* Depth charges could not be used against surfaced U-boats because the Asdic – an echo-sounding device – did not reflect above water and the first Type 284 radars would not be ready for service until much later.

RAF Coastal Command, responsible in part for the protection of incoming and departing convoys, naturally lacked experience in tackling submarines either surfaced or submerged. At the outbreak of war it had 200 Anson aircraft with a range of 500 nautical miles and a speed of 190 kms/hr. Their payload was two 50kg bombs. It was recognised early on that even land-based reconnaissance aircraft could be dangerous for U-boats. They frequently sighted U-boats heading for the open Atlantic by the north-about route, and in November 1939 Churchill ordered that aerial attacks on German U-boats had equal priority with flying reconnaissance over the sea. Churchill and his admirals thought initially that it must be fairly easy for a fast, low-flying aircraft to overtake and bomb a relatively slow U-boat before it had a chance to reach a depth sufficiently great for safety. This

---

* In fact, Hedgehog fired contact-fused bombs, not depth charges, which exploded only if they hit a U-boat. Ed

British Anti-Submarine Developments

proved very soon not to be the case, and when an aircraft succeeded in dropping a bomb close to a U-boat in the act of submerging, it was obvious to aircraft crews that bombs were not a suitable means of combating U-boats. The first successful such attack was not recorded until 30 January 1940 when a Sunderland sank *U-55* in co-operation with convoy escorts. The ineffectiveness of bombs against submarines saved at least four RN boats when attacked by RAF aircraft in error, however. Not until the spring of 1940 did the RAF receive its first issue of depth charges, and it would be a whole year before depth charges specially developed for aerial use would be delivered to front-line aircraft.

With respect to the arming of merchant ships the major shortage was anti-aircraft weapons, even though Britain had eagerly ordered 20mm Oerlikons from Switzerland since 1937. It would be March 1941 before the Admiralty had armed 3,434 merchant vessels with anti-aircraft weapons and 4,431 other British and Allied ships with one or more such weapons for defence against low-flying aircraft.

The first convoy of the Second World War left Gibraltar for Cape Town on 2 September 1939. Others followed very quickly. They ran from Great Britain to the United States or Freetown in West Africa. Ships able to make more than 15 knots, or not able to make 8 knots, were not eligible for inclusion in such convoys. This meant that convoys always sailed at between 8 and 15 knots while slower and faster ships had to make their own way to wherever they were headed. Because there were insufficient naval escorts to shepherd the rapidly increasing number of convoys the whole way from the port of departure to destination, a convoy would only have an escort from Britain for the first 200 nautical miles west. This meant that to find undefended convoys, German U-boats had to operate west of that limit.

From the important departure ports for Britain such as Halifax, Gibraltar and Freetown, convoys would have a weak escort for the first 200 to 300 nautical miles outwards, and then an aircraft carrier or armed merchant cruiser on the eastern side. Only those convoys bringing Empire troops from Canada, Australia or New Zealand to Europe or North Africa were given a strong escort. By the end of 1939 the entire 1st Canadian Infantry Division had been transferred to Europe in this manner. More transports came to Europe from Bombay bringing Indian troops. Australians and New Zealanders were shipped mainly to Africa aboard the fast liners *Queen Mary* and *Queen Elizabeth* across the world's oceans and all arrived safely.

At the beginning of September 1939 there were several thousand British merchant ships at sea. Many of them put into the nearest port to receive their

U-48

Defence of Merchant Shipping Instructions insofar as these were not included in their standing orders. These orders contravened the London Protocol of 1936 and the Prize Regulations which the U-boat arm observed. The Prize Regulations, as explained earlier with regard to *U-48*, were followed strictly by U-boat commanders even when to do so, as was often the case, posed a serious threat to the safety of the boat. Not until long after the realisation that British merchant ships were armed and had no compunction about using their armament to attack U-boats were the Prize Regulations lifted for the U-boat arm.

As the British counter-measure against German U-boats *and* as a means of blockading Germany, British submarines were deployed alongside the Home Fleet and other naval units. On 3 September 1939 when war was declared and the blockade of Germany began, the Royal Navy instituted its system of contraband control. British submarines patrolled off Horns Reef and the estuaries of the Elbe and Jade. No German merchant ships were sighted, only U-boats. Off Terschelling and in the Narrows between Shetlands and Norway there were a number of attacks by British submarines on 'U-boats'. Errors of identification resulted in British submarines being torpedoed. On 10 September 1939 HM S/M *Triton* attacked and sank a 'German U-boat' which turned out to be HM S/M *Oxley*. On 14 September HM S/M *Sturgeon* fired a torpedo at a 'German U-boat' and narrowly missed HM S/M *Swordfish*. On 20 September the Admiralty took the hint and withdrew all their submarines from the Shetland Narrows.

On 3 September 1939 the Humber Force consisting of the cruisers *Glasgow* and *Southampton* and eight destroyers weighed anchor with orders to capture the German passenger liner *Bremen*, returning to Germany from the United States. It was nowhere to be found, having sought refuge in the secret *Nord* base near Murmansk. As the result of a false report that German heavy units were putting to sea, the British had units of the Home Fleet patrol north of the Orkneys for three days. After that from 6 to 10 September the Home Fleet (Admiral Forbes) searched for blockade runners along the Norwegian coast. The principal capital ships were the battlecruiser *Hood*, the battleships *Rodney* and *Nelson*, the cruisers *Sheffield* and *Aurora* plus ten destroyers. Between 7 and 12 September *Hood*, *Renown*, the cruisers *Edinburgh* and *Belfast* with four destroyers roved the Iceland–Faroes Narrows. The Northern Patrol, formed on 6 September from the 7th and 12th Cruiser Squadrons had units stationed permanently between the Shetlands and Iceland. That month they stopped 108 merchant ships of which twenty-eight were sent into Kirkwall for contraband control.

British Anti-Submarine Developments

Submarines of the Home Fleet (Commanding Admiral, Rear-Admiral Watson) operated in the North Sea and as far as Norway in search of German heavy units. An operation by the Home Fleet with the 2nd Cruiser Squadron and six destroyers into the North Sea to retrieve the seriously-damaged submarine *Spearfish* was protected by two battleships, two battlecruisers, the aircraft-carrier *Ark Royal*, three cruisers and destroyers. These operations led to the first encounters with German naval forces, but no meeting occurred between capital ships of the respective fleets.

Despite all the measures taken, the British Admiralty was unable to reduce the U-boat threat. On the contrary, 1940 saw one U-boat attack after another on the oceans and the only chance of surviving did not lie in the defence against U-boats but in the fact that Germany had built too few of them. Dönitz knew better than anybody that victory or defeat rested on sinking merchant ships quicker than the enemy could replace them. That Hitler did not recognise this and failed to build U-boats to the fullest capacity of his shipyards at the latest by 3 September 1939 was highlighted later as the tragedy of the German U-boat arm. Captain Roskill, the official British naval historian wrote of this in confirmation: 'It is no exaggeration to say that victory or defeat for the Allies in all theatres of war depended in the final analysis on the outcome of that battle which was now being fought out in the expanses of the North Atlantic. Had Great Britain had success torn from her grasp there, in a very short time she would have been facing the final catastrophe.'

At the end of 1940 there were between four and six operational German U-boats at sea at any one time. This meant that the naval war against Britain was being fought at any particular moment in time by no more than about 400 German sailors.

CHAPTER 13

The Grand Finale – *U-48*'s Tenth War Patrol

After Bleichrodt's signal reporting the sinking of the British tanker *Shirak*, he had sunk over 100,000 tons of enemy shipping counting the sloop HMS *Dundee* together with the two freighters *Broompark* and one unknown ship he had torpedoed. He therefore qualified for the Knight's Cross. Bleichrodt's two patrols were *U-48*'s most successful as respects the number of ships sunk and tonnage, and accordingly Admiral Dönitz recommended him for the award.

On 24 October, immediately after it became known that Hitler had approved the decoration, the BdU sent Bleichrodt a signal advising the fact. When shown this signal, Bleichrodt shook his head in surprise, and replied to the BdU Staff. 'Who is the Knight's Cross for?' After the boat returned from patrol, and Bleichrodt was about to receive the decoration, he astonished Dönitz by telling him that he could not accept it: 'If IWO Suhren also receives the award as my torpedo-aimer I shall wear it, otherwise not.' Dönitz turned to Kapitänleutnant Endrass and asked him, 'Well, Bertel, what do you say to that?' Endrass replied in his thick dialect, 'I shall tell thee, Herr Admiral. Why not give Suhren the Knight's Cross? I am thinking he should have it.'

'But he is only a watch officer on the boat and should not receive this decoration until after his first patrol as commander,' Dönitz countered.

'In the meantime he talk out of turn, that is the end of his Knight's Cross and he get nothing.'

'Very well,' Dönitz agreed, 'he shall have it.'[1]

Dönitz enquired of his office how many sinkings Suhren had been involved in as IWO of *U-48*. The statistics showed that over the period when *U-48* had had her three commanders Schultze, Rösing and Bleichrodt, Suhren had been the Torpedo Officer at the UZO during surfaced attacks and as torpedo aimer could claim 200,000 tons of enemy shipping sunk. On 3 November 1940, *U-48* was in the yards for overhaul when the award of

The Grand Finale – U-48's Tenth War Patrol

the Knight's Cross to Suhren was approved and he received it from Dönitz next day 'for playing a decisive role in sinking 200,000 gross tons of enemy shipping. Thus Reinhard Suhren became the first and penultimate watchkeeping officer of the U-boat arm to receive the Knights' Cross: the other exception was the IIIWO of *U-181*, Leutnant-sur-See Johann Limbach. Suhren's brother Gerd, chief engineer of *U-37*, was the first U-boat engineering officer to be so distinguished. Suhren observed: 'All in all, these decorations did not just fall in our lap. We had much to do to get the boat into a firing position. Many dogs mean the death of the hare. Since the outbreak of war a great number of our boats remained out there.'[2]

Suhren was not yet twenty-five: after his transfer out of *U-48*, the Deputy Admiral U-boats, Hans-Georg von Friedeburg, hung the decoration around his neck aboard the accommodation ship *Erwin Wassner* at Kiel. Gerhard Suhren eventually took over *U-564* as commander. With this Type VIIC boat he would become a famous name amongst the aces.

'Vaddi' Returns

On 16 January 1941, after completion of her refit, at Germania Werft from 1 December 1940, *U-48* sailed for a test run and the obligatory trial dive off Heligoland. To replace Bleichrodt, a new commander came aboard during the run west through the Kiel Canal – Herbert Schultze. His health recovered, he had requested Dönitz for permission to sail again with *U-48* and this had been granted.

From Heligoland the boat put out in company with *U-107* (Hessler) on 20 January 1941 on her tenth war patrol. An icebreaker was needed for the North Sea crossing. On the bridge 'Vaddi' Schultze wore his tall fur cap. The former watchkeepers Suhren and Ites had been drafted out to prepare to take over their own commands and were placed by Oberleutnant-zur-See Peter Schrewe as IWO and Oberleutnant-zur-See Atzinger as IIWO.

On the way out on 20 January Schultze was ordered to square AM 15/16 west of the Northern Passage between the Hebrides and Iceland. He reached it on 1 February. The sea was very rough with storm force winds. A steamer was sighted.

'The boat will attack this steamer.'

Schrewe as IWO took his position at the UZO. The first two attack runs were not good, and it was not until the evening when *U-48* could get in close to the enemy ship that the first torpedo was fired. It missed: the seas were so tumultuous that it was almost impossible to obtain a hit. Nevertheless Schultze would not give up, and at 2125 hrs a torpedo finally struck the

U-48

Greek *Nicolaos Angelos*, 4,351 gross tons, and sank her in grid square AL 3616. Schultze had not lost his touch, and even after a year's absence he brought the boat in close to the enemy and obtained a success in fearsome winter seas. After that his luck was out. In the next few days three steamers were sighted but the sea conditions with hurricane force winds prevented any attacks, and eventually *U-48* submerged for safety.

On 4 February *U-48* assembled in the operational area west of the Northern Passage with *U-52*, *U-93*, *U-94*, *U-96*, *U-101*, *U-103*, *U-107* and *U-123*. These were all boats which had been successful and had the most dedicated commanders. In this phase of the war, Kapitänleutnant Günther Hessler[*] had distinguished himself especially. He was not from the U-boat arm, but during his service aboard the torpedo boats *Greif* and *Falke* had learnt to fire torpedoes, an important requirement for a U-boat commander. Hessler had sailed from Heligoland on his first war patrol in command of *U-107*. At sea he exchanged signals with *U-48*, when Schultze had offered his advice should the younger commander require it. On 31 January 1941 *U-107* had had to cope with Force 10 winds. The very high swell and rough seas made an attack impossible, but on 3 February, after two unsuccessful attempts, he had hit the *Empire Citizen*, 4,683 gross tons, from only 500 metres range and finished her off with a torpedo from the stern tube, the ship going down by the bows. The same evening he found a small convoy and sank the RN ocean boarding vessel *Crispin*, escorted by a destroyer. On 4 February when Hessler reported his successes by signal to the BdU, Schultze remarked: 'All hail to Hessler, not only has he snapped up the Great Lion's daughter, but he fires his eels well too.'

On 6 February *U-107* sank a third ship: on 9 February *U-48* moved into square AE8896 but was seen by an enemy ship. The enemy's message had been intercepted by the B-Dienst, and Dönitz ordered *U-48* away from the area to avoid attack by anti-submarine groups. Schultze reached the new operational square AE8594, a sector 39 nautical miles long adjacent to AE7932, on 16 February. Three days later the BdU signalled: 'Convoy. *U-73*, *U-107*, *U-48*, *U-96*, *U-69*, *U-103* on 20 February 1200 hrs form patrol line in grid squares AM2111 to AM1277. Depth six nautical miles.'

U-48 forged ahead with the other boats through the tempest, but most failed to reach the convoy, which was steaming 60 nautical miles farther north than expected. Only *U-95* and *U-96* managed an attack, and on 23 February *U-96* (Lehmann-Willenbrock) sank the steamer *Huntingdon*,

---

[*] Dönitz's son-in-law. Ed

The Grand Finale – U-48's Tenth War Patrol

10,946 gross tons, while *U-95* torpedoed three ships of which two sank. This happened in the early hours of 24 February. This convoy, OB288, also lost one ship to *U-69* (Metzler). From the positions where these sinkings occurred, Schultze saw that he was too far south and too near land to have any chance of reaching the convoy. Instead, on 24 February, south west of Fastnet on the 60-metre contour in very rough seas, he came across a lone steamer and missed with two torpedoes before a third hit from 450 metres at 2143 hrs. The victim was the British *Nailsea Lass*, 4,289 gross tons. Badly damaged by the torpedo, the storm did the rest.

Over the next few days *U-47* (Prien) fired at five ships of which four sank, while *U-48* was forced to put back to France with storm damage, confirmation being received on 25 February. *U-46*, *U-69*, *U-96*, *U-107* and *U-123* followed. On 28 February *U-48* entered Lorient after her most difficult war patrol. When Schultze made his report next morning to the Great Lion, Dönitz saw that the patrol had taken a lot out of him. He asked him whether he would not prefer to take over as chief of a training flotilla in the Baltic now that this voyage had proved that 'he was his old self'. Schultze was decisive in declining. 'I would like to make a few more voyages, Herr Admiral,' he said, and added after a brief pause, 'the next will be better.'

'I am sure it will be,' Dönitz replied, 'but I would not want you to run yourself down again. Your knowledge and experience are needed for the younger commanders. You have the gift of making the command of a boat comprehensible for them, and mould them into good captains. You could also be head of a Front flotilla. Think it over carefully! We shall talk again after your next patrol.' The two men knew each other well after many years of training and U-boat warfare, and they left it at that.

CHAPTER 14

The Eleventh War Patrol – Rapid Fire

After a fast turnaround, re-equipping, reprovisioning and loading new torpedoes, *U-48* sailed from Lorient on 17 March 1941. Nearby were *U-46*, *U-69*, *U-98* and *U-551*. On 20 March Schultze reported by burst-signal that he had reached his operational area in grid squares AE74-75 to AE77-78 and was on the lookout for victims. On the way out he had had to dive on numerous occasions when attacked by aircraft. This proved that Herbert Schultze was the 'Vaddi' of old, had lost none of his sure instinct for danger and still reacted lightning fast. The new watchkeepers had worked in well and all was going like clockwork.

At 1201 hrs on 21 March while outward bound, *U-69* (Metzler) reported a convoy heading for Britain in grid square AL8822. Being in reasonable proximity, *U-48* was ordered to attack this convoy together with the Italian boats *Emo* (Rosselli-Lorenzini) and *Veniero* (Petroni), but *U-69* was forced to submerge by an escorting destroyer and lost contact. On 22 March *U-69* and *U-48* received orders to continue their patrols in AE78, arriving there on 25 March. This same day the BdU divided his available Atlantic boats into two groups: *Nordboote* (*U-46*, *U-48*, *U-69*, *U-74*, *U-98* and *U-551*), and *Südboote* (*U-105*, *U-106* and *U-124*). A short sentence in the KTB by Dönitz on this date reported that *U-47* (Prien), *U-70* (Matz), *U-99* (Kretschmer) and *U-100* (Schepke) had all ceased to send signals. What could be responsible for this – had they all been sunk, or was there some other explanation for their silence?

The 5th Escort Group at Work
From Captain Donald Macintyre's book *U-boat Killer* we know the events of 24 and 25 March 1941 affecting the four missing U-boats. He wrote:

> On 14 March we put out for our rendezvous with Convoy HX112. Atlantic meetings were always a special navigational experience, for

The Eleventh War Patrol – Rapid Fire

in the usually indifferent weather there it was difficult to find even a large convoy. Together with my own ship *Walker* my escort group consisted of the destroyers *Vanoc, Volunteer, Sardonyx* and *Scimitar*, and the corvettes *Bluebell* and *Hydrangea*.

We met the convoy and steamed eastwards for home. At dusk on 15 March I warned my escorts to be ready for an attack by German U-boats after night fell. We had not long to wait. Shortly before midnight on 15 March the first U-boat showed itself on the starboard side of the convoy. It attacked and fired a fan of four at a long row of overlapping steamers. Two minutes later the tanker *Erodona* was hit and burst at once into bright flames. Never before had I seen this ghastly sight. On the *Walker*'s bridge a horrified silence reigned. Then the alarm bells shrilled and sent the men to their stations. Nothing was to be seen of the enemy, and our Asdic also gave no sign of him.

It was Lemp in *U-110* who had torpedoed the *Erodona*. Macintyre ordered the corvette *Bluebell* to the sinking tanker and he was happy enough that only one ship was lost that night. *U-110* was forced to make an alarm dive by the escorts and driven off. Meanwhile *U-100* (Schepke) had closed in. The boat was sighted by *Scimitar* and reported. Captain Macintyre took *Walker* and *Vanoc* at once to the reported position, but *U-100* had dived.

Late on the morning of 16 March, *U-99* (Kretschmer) penetrated between the outer escorts to the middle of the convoy and torpedoed the Norwegian tanker *Ferm*, 6,593 gross tons. Seconds after the hit she was burning fiercely. A destroyer approached and forced *U-99* to submerge. As *Walker* made a turn after the torpedo hit, a U-boat was seen. This was *U-100*, which had found the convoy again and dived. *Walker* went at full ahead to the location and dropped a pattern of ten depth charges into the bright phosphorescence marking the spot where *U-100* had submerged. *U-100* survived to be hunted by escorts of Convoy HX112.

This gave Kretschmer the chance to surface for a fresh attack on another tanker, *Bedouin*, 8,136 gross tons, which was turned into a conflagration by his torpedo. Fifteen minutes later the steely-nerved U-boat commander sighted a third tanker, *Franche Comté*, which also erupted in flames and lay burning after the torpedo hit. *U-99* moved through Convoy HX112. Night had fallen. Depth charges exploded underwater in all directions. Star shell lit the night, distress rockets flared. Kretschmer reached the leading ships of the convoy. These were valuable freighters. All three went under with well-aimed aimed torpedoes, although the *J.B. White* survived long enough to merit a second torpedo to finish her off. Now out of torpedoes, *U-99*

U-48

allowed the convoy to pass by and headed for *Lousy Bank* between two escorts. *U-100*, seriously damaged in *Walker*'s counter-attack, could no longer remain submerged and in the early hours of 17 March was forced to surface. The U-boat came up very close to *Vanoc* which rammed her at full speed. Schepke was crushed on the bridge by the destroyer's bow and lost both legs. As *Vanoc* reversed at full speed to tear free of the wreck of *U-100*, Shepke was hurled overboard, arms flailing wildly, and sank. Soon afterwards *U-100* followed him down. Only five members of the U-boat crew could be fished out by *Vanoc*.

In this critical situation the Asdic operator aboard *Walker* detected another submerged U-boat. Macintyre would not believe this report at first but gave the Depth Charge Officer, Lt Langton, the order to drop a pattern of six. As *Walker* turned to make a second attack, *Vanoc* signalled: 'U-boat surfaced behind you.' *U-99* had come up after receiving severe damage from *Walker*'s depth charges, leaving Kretschmer with no choice. The guns of *Walker* opened fire, a lamp on the U-boat tower flashed: 'We are sinking', and the crew began to abandon the submarine. *Walker* created a lee for the Germans and began taking them aboard. Kretschmer was the last to be saved. A third boat to be lost was *U-70* (Matz), sunk on 7 March 1941 south east of Iceland by the corvettes *Camellia* and *Arbutus*. There were 25 survivors. *U-47* (Prien) was sunk with all hands on 8 March by the destroyer *Wolverine* running escort for Convoy OB293.[*] The loss of *U-47* was not announced until 23 May 1941 when it was certain that the boat could no longer return. The Wehrmacht report of this day stated: 'The U-boat commanded by Korvettenkapitän Prien has failed to return from its latest operation.' In his Order of the Day, the BdU praised this brave commander, 'The Hero of Scapa Flow', with an impressive eulogy and closed: 'The struggle goes on in his spirit!'

U-48, which had sailed later with the boats of its group, sighted Convoy HX115 early on the morning of 29 March and reported it, followed by homing signals. The boat attacked soon after 0600 hrs. The first torpedo was fired at 0619 hrs supplemented by three more in the hour, and a fifth was loosed at 0807 hrs. Convoy HX115 was in uproar. The steamers *Germanic*, *Limbourg* and *Eastlea* sank, although the big motor tanker *Athelprince*, 8,900 gross tons, though seriously damaged, stayed afloat for a tow home.

---

[*] It was believed originally that HMS *Wolverine* was responsible for sinking *U-47*. Recent research has identified the boat attacked, which survived and reported the incident. Therefore the cause of the loss of *U-47*, and the whereabouts of the wreck, remain unknown. See Clay Blair, *Hitler's U-boat War*, Vol 1, London: Weidenfeld & Nicolson, 2000, pp 249–53. Tr

The Eleventh War Patrol – Rapid Fire

A furious depth charge attack by all convoy escorts ensued, and were concentrated on the only U-boat present, *U-48*.

Schultze demonstrated his great ability by escaping all attacks with constant changes of speed, bearing and depth. The eight commanders of the escort ships were no novices themselves. Schultze exceeded his previous best in this situation. Had he not done so, the BdU would have had to add another successful U-boat commander to the grievous losses of his aces. The whole crew paid tribute to their commander. Now he could ask anything of them, and even the new intake to the boat knew that this was a man to whose hands they could entrust their lives. Meanwhile *U-48* had made desperate attempts to escape but had been forced below after being bombed by aircraft.

Finally the enemy lost the scent, and on the evening of 1 April 1941 Schultze took the boat to square AD87. Here he received orders from the BdU to progress to AK23-33, but before he got there a large, fast tanker was seen.

'Boat will attack!'

Despite the rough conditions the boat came up on the enemy ship. Schultze took a long look at her through binoculars. 'She is a giant, we shall fire a fan of two.'

IWO Schrewe stood at the UZO. When the tanker entered the field of the optic, he fired from tubes I and II. The torpedoes hit in the forecastle and amidships. The tanker lost momentum, afire in the interior.

'This is a fat one, Herr Kaleunt,' Schrewe said, 'he is stopping.'

'Steamer sending distress message. Name is *Beaverdale*, British, 9,957 gross tons in *Lloyd's Register*,' came the report from the radio room.

'Destroyer behind the tanker's stern is coming up!' a lookout shouted.

'He doesn't see us, he is intent on saving the crew. IWO, fire another torpedo.'

The third torpedo set off and after hitting astern directly forward of the stern structure, giant flames rose up through the gaps in the decking. It was just after midnight on 2 April. 'The whole ship is aflame. She is done for!' *U-48* left the scene, and it was as well that she did so, for suddenly a pair of escorts came in sight, approaching the boat at a threatening speed, forcing *U-48* to dive with both E-motors at full ahead. Depth charges were dropped as a deterrent but presented no danger to the boat, which headed for safety. A calculation of the trim weight a few hours later showed that *U-48* was light on fuel and that it was time to turn for home. Schultze had sunk five ships of 27,256 gross tons and seriously damaged a sixth. The *Athelprince*

U-48

had been incorrectly assumed sunk but needed extensive repairs after reaching a British shipyard. Another torpedo had been fired and no hit recorded, although the bridge watch heard a torpedo explode.

U-48 entered St Nazaire on 8 April; next morning Herbert Schultze made his report to the Great Lion and his Staff from the *U-48* war diary. Dönitz was much impressed by Schultze' cool-headedness upon hearing his description of how he attacked Convoy HX115 and its eight escorts alone yet obtained successes.

'So how do things look for you now, Schultze?' Dönitz enquired.

'I should like to make one more voyage, Herr Admiral, in the hope of a 200 with three zeros.' By this he meant the Oak Leaves to his Knight's Cross by reaching the magic figure of 200,000 gross tons of shipping sunk.

'This worries me, Schultze; Old Prien said the same and now he is no longer with us.'

'I am confident, Herr Admiral.'

'Very well, one more voyage, and then you will go to a Front flotilla and the boat to the Baltic, agreed?'

'Agreed, Herr Admiral!'

That was an end to the matter, an end to war patrols after the next patrol for one of the most successful commanders and the most successful U-boat.

In his KTB Dönitz wrote: 'The old commander has made another outstanding voyage which resulted in six ships of 40,350 gross tons sunk.' (The difference between claimed tonnage and the actual tonnage sunk was the survival of the *Athelprince*: the *Hylton,* 5,197 gross tons, was later credited to *U-48*, this being the torpedo explosion heard by the lookouts in Convoy HX115.)

CHAPTER 15

The Last Tanker Attacks: The Loss of the *Bismarck*

After a full overhaul and change of watchkeeping officers, on 22 May 1941 *U-48* sailed from St Nazaire on her twelfth and last war patrol. IWO Oberleutnant-zur-See Peter Schrewe had left the boat as a 'commander-apprentice' aboard another, and in his place Oberleutnant-zur-See Atzinger the former IIWO became IWO; Leutnant-zur-See Knackfuss arrived as IIWO. Kapitänleutnant (Ing) Zürn remained chief engineer.

At the request of Naval Group West the boat was sent to Biscay squares BE 6420 to 6620 together with *U-97* and *U-98*. They were joined by *U-556* (without torpedoes but to be employed as a scout) and *U-73*, these both making their way to the assembly area. The reason for holding this group of U-boats, reinforced later by *U-108* and *U-552*, in reserve was to offer distant cover to the battleship *Bismarck* and the heavy cruiser *Prinz Eugen*.

On 25 May the BdU signalled, '*U-73, U-97, U-98, U-48* form patrol line from BE 6155 to BF 7155, twenty nautical miles in length. All boats are to hold themselves in readiness to support the *Bismarck*.'

'This looks as though she is in trouble,' Schultze said when he was given the signal.

'I think it is just a precaution,' the IWO suggested.

'Let us hope so, Atzinger!' Schultze replied before returning to his compartment to write up the KTB.

Bismarck was in the North Atlantic as part of a major operation codenamed *Rheinübung,* in which she was to 'impede the enemy traffic passing through this region by her intervention'. In support she had the heavy cruiser *Prinz Eugen*, and at different rendezvous two scout ships, two fleet tankers and five auxiliary tankers, and the U-boat group and 6.Destroyer Flotilla as the distant escort should she need it.

In an encounter in the Denmark Strait with the capital ships *Hood* and *Prince of Wales* early on 24 May 1941, a serious fire had been started aboard

U-48

the battlecruiser *Hood* by shelling from the *Prinz Eugen*, and *Hood* blew up after being straddled by *Bismarck*'s fifth salvo. The battleship *Prince of Wales* was also hit, but the extent of the damage was not known to the Germans. *Bismarck*'s captain, Kapitän-zur-See Lindemann, suggested to the Fleet Commander, Vizeadmiral Lütjens, aboard the battleship that *Prince of Wales* should be pursued and sunk, but Lütjens dismissed this idea, probably fearing that he might run foul of other heavy units which might be in the area. *Prince of Wales* had 60 per cent of her guns out of action, a fact which might have changed Lütjens' mind had he known it. While *Prinz Eugen* was the only ship of the four to escape damage in the battle, *Bismarck* had been hit three times, these shells causing a series of problems. One of these allowed seawater to enter the forepeak at high speed, giving *Bismarck* a 2 per cent bow heaviness. Neither the SKL Chief of Staff nor Admiral Raeder could decide whether to recall *Bismarck* because she did not report the damage. Another of the problems was a leakage of oil which was noticed and brought to Lütjens' attention by *Prinz Eugen*.

Bismarck entered the North Atlantic followed by the British cruisers *Norfolk* and *Suffolk*. Lütjens detached *Prinz Eugen* by ordering her to continue on the planned course while *Bismarck* made a detour to the west at 24 knots, the best she could make with her damage. This loss of speed was critical, for now she could not outrun the enemy shadowers and this ruled out the idea of escaping back to Germany. As a result of her shortage of fuel, Lütjens decided finally to make for Brest, and after enemy forces lost contact early on 25 May, the way seemed clear. However, at 1000 hrs on 26 May a British reconnaissance aircraft found *Bismarck* again. Three attacks by Swordfish torpedo aircraft ensued, and the second wave obtained a hit on the battleship's port rudder. The third wave torpedoed her twice. Because of the rudder damage, she was unable to manoeuvre satisfactorily. *U-556* (Wohlfahrt) had sighted *Ark Royal*, the aircraft carrier from which the Swordfish attacks were being launched. A hit on this ship might have helped save *Bismarck*, but Wohlfahrt had no torpedoes.

On the night of 26 May in skirmishes with enemy destroyers attempting to torpedo the battleship, *Bismarck* scored a number of hits with her gunnery, but by 0710 hrs on 27 May it was clear that the game was up, and in her last signal but one she requested: 'Send a U-boat to collect the KTB.' After hundreds of hits from enemy heavy guns and numerous torpedoes, the cruiser *Dorsetshire* fired the last three torpedoes into *Bismarck*'s hull. The engineers then scuttled the wreck to prevent her capture, and *Bismarck* went down at 1040 hrs on 27 May 1941.

The Last Tanker Attacks: The Loss of the Bismarck

The Effort to Save the *Bismarck* Survivors

On the evening of 27 May, *U-74* (Kentrat) picked up three *Bismarck* ratings from a drifting rubber dinghy. This was the signal for the U-boats to broaden their search in the region. At 1400 hrs that day the BBC had announced the sinking of *Bismarck*. At 1416 hrs the BdU ordered U-boats to search for survivors north west of square BE 6150. After no success had been reported by 1954 hrs, the BdU sent a new order: '*U-48* search BE 6120.'

'Everybody 100 per cent alertness, this is about our comrades!' Schultze told the watch. It was unnecessary: everyone knew the score. After *U-74* reported her find with the position, Dönitz ordered, 'All boats *U-48*, *U-108*, *U-97*, *U-73* go to vicinity *U-74* and search there towards BE 5330.' The search was taken up anew. On 28 May at 1320 hrs *U-48* came into a field of wreckage in the southern half of square BE 6141.

'Now look, men! Everything depends on it!'

This search yielded nothing, however, and when another field of debris was found in BE 6142, more hope grew that *Bismarck* survivors might be found, but this hope was misplaced. 'Vaddi' Schultze took off his cap in tears. His bridge watch were also shaken at the extent of the disaster. One hundred and three officers and 1,962 men of the battleship, twenty-seven men of the Fleet Staff and the merchant captains of the prize commando were missing. Later it was established that four officers and around 112 men had survived the sinking, the majority picked up by the British.

As night fell on 28 May the search for survivors was abandoned on the orders of Naval High Command (OKM) following talks with Group West, and all boats resumed their normal patrols. There was fresh hope at midnight next day when the weather trawler *Sachsenwald* found two more survivors in square BE 6150 (which was the square from where the search had spread out to the north-west after the sinking). On the orders of OKM, Group West asked Dönitz to return U-boats to square BE 61 to continue the search, and they returned in high spirits. 'Even if we only find one, it will be worth it, comrades!' Schultze said to fire up his crew, and *U-48* spent the next 72 hours looking for survivors. Boats such as *U-48* and *U-73*, which had spent some time at sea now began to run low on fuel, and for these Dönitz requested a rendezvous with a fleet tanker to top up.

'We had no luck, but we did all we could,' Schultze told a reporter attached to Naval War Correspondents Corps West afterwards, 'for a single comrade we would all have willingly allowed any ship coming in front of our tubes to go free.'

On 1 June 1941 *U-48* headed for the newly-ordered patrol line running

U-48

from square BE to BD. The boat was moving at slow speed through a slight swell. She dived once to avoid a destroyer. On the evening of 2 June the bridge watch heard a dull torpedo explosion far to the west. This was *U-108* (Scholtz) sinking the British steamer *Michael E*. A little later Schultze was called to the bridge. Leutnant-zur-See Knackfuss reported. The commander whistled. 'That looks an inviting tanker.' After confirmation the boat made a surfaced approach, firing a fan of two from a textbook shooting position. They struck the tanker *Inversuir*, 9,456 gross tons, which came to a stop and transmitted the submarine warning 'SSS'. Flames began to escape from the innards of the stricken tanker. 'She is not sinking, Herr Kaleunt,' Knackfuss advised.

'Prepare the gun!'

The gunners came to the foredeck. Fire was opened exactly 120 seconds after the order was given. Shell after shell struck the tanker below the waterline. As she began to settle the oil surrounding her caught fire to form a dancing, flickering, blazing carpet. Her crew had taken to the boats immediately the torpedo hit, had got well clear of the wreck and were in no danger. *Inversuir* sank at 48°34'N 31°34'W, after which *U-48* headed west and found another tanker, the British *Wellfield*, 6,054 gross tons, two days later. This tanker went down at 48°34'N 31°34'W. It was noticed over subsequent hours that a large number of independent vessels frequented the region. This fact was reported to the BdU that same morning when Schultze notified Dönitz of the two tankers of an aggregate 15,000 gross tons he had sunk, and as a result more U-boats were sent to the area.

U-48 next chased after a fast freighter with destroyer escort for several hundred nautical miles but gave up eventually because the run home from the west would be that much longer and fuel was short. On 6 June a fast lone ship was sighted. 'This one is ours!' Schultze promised after being shown the freighter and working out her estimated course and speed. The boat turned 10° south and was favourably placed to attack by evening. Suddenly the steamer appeared to get wind of the danger, for she changed course, showing the lurking U-boat her stern.

'New attack run. He is not going to escape!'

U-48 ran to the correct position to intercept and Atzinger at the UZO fired a single torpedo bringing the brand-new British steamer *Tregarthen*, 5,201 gross tons, to a stop. A second torpedo sealed her fate after the crew had taken to the boats. Meanwhile *U-108* (Scholtz) had gone far to the west where at 0006 hrs on 8 June he sank the British freighter *Baron Nairn* in latitude 39°02'W, and six hours later the Greek steamer *Dirphys*. After *U-*

The Last Tanker Attacks: The Loss of the Bismarck

46 (Endrass) had torpedoed a tanker and sunk a freighter in the vicinity of *U-48* in the early afternoon of 8 June, *U-48* came across Convoy OB329 outward bound from Liverpool, and after reporting it and transmitting homing signals, prepared to attack one of its large tankers. From the limits of the range of vision Schultze began his attack run submerged then went to periscope depth. He had the instrument raised carefully and observed the target. He noticed a destroyer steaming up from the rear at high speed to reach the head of the convoy. A fan of two torpedoes was ready in the flooded tubes. The bow caps were open. Schultze gave the order to fire and Atzinger, leaning on the chart table in the control room, started the stopwatch. Seconds ticked by. The silence created tension throughout the boat.

'Hit amidships and astern.' A great liberating shout broke out from everyone. Schultze raised his hand and silence fell.

'Steamer is lying stopped. Steam is escaping through the two gaping holes in her side. There are flames amidships. The tanker is beginning to burn.'

Schultze passed these snippets of information to the crew to give them an impression of the event.

'Go to 70 metres.'

A destroyer had turned towards *U-48*. The boat went deep and a touch to the rudders changed her heading. The noise of the destroyer's propellers grew fainter. Schultze had come down from the tower to the control room and had the reports from the hydrophone compartment relayed to him. He ordered a fresh course change.

'Propeller noise becoming fainter – has died away!'

'Go to periscope depth.'

Schultze swept the horizon through the attack lens. The flames of the burning tanker licked as high as a church. Otherwise the sea was deserted. After putting some distance between the boat and the convoy, Schultze surfaced.

'Tanker sending distress message. She is the Dutchman *Pendrecht*, 10,746 gross tons in *Lloyd's Register*.'

'That is the Oak Leaves for the commander,' the 'mixer' informed his colleagues in the bow room. According to his calculations, Schultze had now sunk over 200,000 gross tons of shipping, but it was apparently not the case, for even after the sinking was reported the BdU did not react.

U-48 headed for France, for the fuel situation was critical and did not allow another day of searching for ships. 'The boat is returning to port,'

U-48

came Schultze's voice through the loudspeaker system. Jubilation broke out. The men knew it was a long way home, but they were sure 'Vaddi' Schultze would get them there safely.

'With a bit of luck we can get rid of the two torpedoes still in the tubes,' IWO Atzinger said to the chief engineer in the control room.

'Yes, something is bound to cross our path,' Zürn replied confidently.

On the night of 12 June the British steamer *Empire Dew*, 7,005 gross tons, sailing alone and overestimated by Schultze as a 10,000-tonner, came towards them. At 0252 hrs a fan of two was fired with a five-second interval. The boat's nose jerked up, the control room petty officer flooded the forward tanks to compensate and restored the boat to trim.

'Hit amidships and astern!' Schultze exclaimed in surprise, for the running time of the torpedoes should not have been up for another 15 seconds. This miscalculation was caused by his thinking the steamer would be farther away as a result of overestimating her tonnage. *Empire Dew* sank at 51°09'N 30°16'W. With this last victim, *U-48* had sunk five ships in ten days, including three valuable tankers.

'To BdU. On run-in sank independent freighter 7005 gross tons. Schultze.'

'Bravo *U-48*!' the Great Lion replied, and a little later morsed:

'To Commander *U-48*. The Führer has awarded you the Oak Leaves to the Knight's Cross of the Iron Cross as the 15th German serviceman to receive it. I congratulate you. BdU.'

As the boat arrived at the end of this twelfth patrol, five sinkings pennants fluttered from her extended periscope. She had returned safely from her last war patrol and brought the crew home. Since Schultze had promised to retire from service at the Front, he had no choice but to agree when Admiral Dönitz told him that his abilities were required to lead a fighting flotilla and that his boat *U-48* was to be preserved as the most successful U-boat of the Second World War. Herbert Schultze took leave of his charge and crew. *U-48* went into the yards and was withdrawn from active duty at the Front. On 1 August 1941 she joined 26.U-Flotilla under Korvettenkäpitan von Stockhausen. For a long period Oberleutnant-zur-See Atzinger, who survived the war, was her commander.

After the ballyhoo of the receptions in the Germania Werft at Kiel and elsewhere, and well-earned leave, on 1 September Schultze returned to take over as chief of 3.U-Flotilla. This was a joyous appointment, for the Great Lion had acceded to his request that he remain with a Front flotilla. In 3.U-flotilla there were commanders who had taken part in convoy battles and

The Last Tanker Attacks: The Loss of the Bismarck

the pursuit of independent ships, his old colleagues Reschke and Rollmann and namesake Oberleutnant-zur-See Heinz-Otto Schultze, to whom he presented the Knight's Cross on 9 July 1942.

It only remains to mention that his chief engineer, Oberleutnant-zur-See (Ing) Erich Zürn was awarded the Knight's' Cross on 23 April 1941. Schultze had requested it twice from the Great Lion for this deserving *U-48* officer. Knowing that a less experienced chief engineer would probably not have been able to save *U-48* from a series of critical situations, Dönitz gave his approval for the award.

In June 1942 Schultze was succeeded as chief of 3.U-Flotilla by Korvettenkäpitan Zapp, and in the rank of Korvettenkapitän took up his last wartime position as commander, II Division, Naval Academy Schleswig, where he passed on his knowledge to young U-boat officers and midshipmen. He visited his *U-48*, now a training boat, frequently. She was eventually scuttled in Neustadt Bay on 3 May 1945 by her last commander, Oberleutnant-zur-See Todenhagen.

Appendices

Type VIIB U-boats
All boats of the series *U-45* to *U-55* inclusive were of Type VIIB and built at Germania Werft, Kiel. This 'medium high seas type' had a single pressure hull.

Displacement: 517 tonnes
Length: overall 66.5 metres/waterline 48.8 metres
Diameter: 6.2 metres outer hull/4.70 metres pressure hull
Draught: 4.74 metres standard/9.5 metres submerged
Engine performance: 2,800–3,200/700shp
Speed: 17.2–17.9 knots surfaced/9 knots submerged
Depth: recommended maximum operating, 100 metres/maximum safe 200 metres
Bunkers: 108.3/99.7 tonnes
Armament: Four bow torpedo tubes, one stern tube, 14 torpedoes or 39 mines
Guns: One 88mm deck gun, one 20mm FlaMW, one 37mm FlaMW/two 20mm FlaMW (1195/4380)
Complement: Four officers and 40, later up to 56, ratings.

List of Successes
First war patrol (Schultze)
5 Sep 1939 1225 hrs BE 6473 *Royal Sceptre* 4,853 grt
8 Sep 1939 0830 hrs BE 2888 *Winkleigh* 5,055 grt
11 Sep 1939 1335 hrs AM 1366 *Firby* 4,869 grt

Second war patrol (Schultze)
12 Oct 1939 1808 hrs BE 3246 *Emile Miguet* 14,115 grt
12 Oct 1939 2024 hrs BE 3194 *Heronspool* 5,202 grt
13 Oct 1939 0814 hrs BE 3544 *Louisiane* 6,903 grt
14 Oct 1939 1213 hrs BE 3836 *Sneaton* 3,677 grt
17 Oct 1939 2035 hrs BE 3835 *Clan Chisholm* 7,256 grt

Third war patrol (Schultze)
26 Nov 1939 2332 hrs AN 1400 *Gustav E Reuter* 6,336 grt

Appendices

8 Dec 1939 1155 hrs BF 1532 *Brandon* 6,668 grt
9 Dec 1939 0644 hrs BE 3933 *San Alberto* 7,397 grt
15 Dec 1939 1740 hrs BE 3334 *Germaine* 5,217 grt

Fourth war patrol (Schultze)
After minelaying mission in English Channel:
10 Feb 1940 0845 hrs BE 2400 *Burgerdijk* 6,853 grt
14 Feb 1940 1655 hrs BE 1800 *Sultan Star* 12,306 grt
15 Feb 1940 1400 hrs BF 4300 *Den Haag* 8,971 grt
17 Feb 1940 2040 hrs BF 1600 *Wilja* 3,396 grt

Fifth war patrol (Schultze)
Norwegian campaign, no successes.

Sixth war patrol (Rösing)
6 Jun 1940 .... hrs AM 3338 *Stancor* 798 grt
7 Jun 1940 0213 hrs AM 5299 *Frances Massey* 4,219 grt
7 Jun 1940 0322 hrs AM 5296 *Eros* 5,888 grt (torp.)
11 Jun 1940 0110 hrs BE 9397 *Violando N Goulandris* 3,598 grt
19 Jun 1940 0125 hrs BE 9369 *Tudor* 6,607 grt
19 Jun 1940 0256 hrs BE 9369 *Baron Loudoun* 3,164 grt
19 Jun 1940 0346 hrs BE 7171 *British Monarch* 5,661 grt
20 Jun 1940 1730 hrs BE 9574 *Moerdrecht* 7,493 grt

Seventh war patrol (Rösing)
16 Aug 1940 1203 hrs AL 3888 *Hedrun* 2,325 grt
19 Aug 1940 0005 hrs AM 4424 *Ville de Gand* 7,590 grt
21 Aug 1940 0026 hrs AM 4621 Unidentified ship (torp.)
21 Aug 1940 0027 hrs AM 4621 Unidentified ship (torp.)
24 Aug 1940 1424 hrs AM 2743 *La Brea* 6,666 grt
25 Aug 1940 0245 hrs AM 2583 *Athelcrest* 6,825 grt
25 Aug 1940 0246 hrs AM 2583 *Empire Merlin* 5,763 grt

Eighth war patrol (Bleichrodt)
15 Sep 1940 0024 hrs AM 1998 *Alexandros* 4,343 grt
15 Sep 1940 0025 hrs AM 1998 HMS *Dundee*, 1,060 tons displacement.
15 Sep 1940 0123 hrs AM 1998 *Empire Volunteer* 5,318 grt
15 Sep 1940 0300 hrs AM 1998 *Kenordoc* 1,780 grt
18 Sep 1940 0001 hrs AL 2966 *City of Benares* 11,081 grt

U-48

18 Sep 1940 0007 hrs AL 2966 *Marina* 5,088 grt
18 Sep 1940 1849 hrs AL 2881 *Magdalena* 3,118 grt
21 Sep 1940 0614 hrs AL 5436 *Blairangus* 4,409 grt
21 Sep 1940 2338 hrs AL 6554 *Broompark* 5,136 grt (torp.)

Ninth war patrol (Bleichrodt)
11 Oct 1940 2150 hrs AL 0378 *Brandanger* 4,624 grt
11 Oct 1940 2209 hrs AL 0378 *Port Gisborne* 8,390 grt
12 Oct 1940 0014 hrs AL 0381 *Davanger* 7,102 grt
17 Oct 1940 0553 hrs AL 3388 *Languedoc* 9,512 grt
17 Oct 1940 0553 hrs AL 3388 *Scoresby* 3,843 grt
17 Oct 1940 0553 hrs AL 3388 *Haspender* 4,678 grt (torp.)
18 Oct 1940 1025 hrs AL 2593 *Sandsend* 3,612 grt
20 Oct 1940 0024 hrs AL 0355 *Shirak* 6,023 grt

Tenth war patrol (Schultze)
1 Feb 1941 2125 hrs AL 3616 *Nicolais Angelos* 4,351 grt
24 Feb 1941 2143 hrs BF 1185 *Nailsea Lass* 4,289 grt

Eleventh war patrol (Schultze)
29 Mar 1941 0619 hrs AE 7844 *Germanic* 5,352 grt
29 Mar 1941 0624 hrs AE 7844 *Limbourg* 2,483 grt
29 Mar 1941 0627 hrs AE 7844 *Athelprince* (torp.)
29 Mar 1941 0655 hrs AE 7844 *Eastlea* 4,267 grt
29 Mar 1941 0806 hrs AE 7844 *Hylton* 5,197 grt
2 Apr 1941 0100 hrs AD 8789 *Beaverdale* 9,957 grt

Twelfth war patrol (Schultze)
3 Jun 1941 0101 hrs BD 6131 *Inversuir* 9,456 grt
5 Jun 1941 0131 hrs BD 5185 *Wellfield* 6,054 grt
6 Jun 1941 2325 hrs BD 4827 *Tregarthen* 5,201 grt
8 Jun 1941 1545 hrs BD 7212 *Pendrecht* 10,746 grt
12 Jun 1941 0252 hrs AK 9784 *Empire Dew* 7,005 grt

Total number of ships sunk: 56 merchant vessels and one naval sloop
Tonnage: 322,478 gross register tons and 1,060 tons displacement
Torpedoed and damaged: six ships of approx. 35,000 grt

Appendices

U-boat Tactical Organisations
Tactical Organisation of 7.U-Flotilla from 1 Sep 1939
Flotilla Chief: Korvettenkäpitan Sobe
U-45 (Gelhaar), *U-46* (Sohler), *U-47* (Prien), *U-48* (Schultze), *U-49* (von Gossler), *U-51* (Knorr), *U-52* (Barten), *U-53* (Heinicke), *U-54* (from 15 Sep 1939 Michel), *U-A* (from 1 Oct 1939 Cohausz)

Tactical Organisation of BdU Group from 1 Nov 1939
BdU: Konteradmiral Dönitz
BdU Organisations Div. (Kiel): Kapitän-zur-See von Friedeburg
BdU Operational Div. (Wilhelmshaven) Korvettenkäpitan Godt
(7.U-Flotilla)
Flotilla Chief: Korvettenkäpitan Sobe
U-45 (Gelhaar), *U-46* (Sohler), *U-47* (Prien), *U-48* (Schultze), *U-49* (von Gossler) ,*U-51* (Knorr), *U-52* (Barten), *U-53* (Heinicke), *U-54* (Michel), *U-A* (Cohausz)

7.U-Flotilla – Status as at 15 Apr 1940
Flotilla Chief: Korvettenkäpitan Sobe: acting Flotilla Chief (from 1 Oct 1940) Korvettenkäpitan Eckermann
U-46 (Endrass), *U-47* (Prien), *U-48* (Rösing, later Bleichrodt), *U-51* (Knorr), *U-52* (Salman), *U-93* (Korth), *U-95* (from 1 Sep 1940 Schreiber), *U-96* (from 1 Oct 1940 Lehmann), *U-97* (from 1 Oct 1940 Heilmann), *U-73* (from 15 Oct 1940 Rosenbaum), *U-98* (from 15 Oct 1940 Gysae), *U-74* (from 1 Nov 1940 Kentrat), *U-69* (from 15 Nov 1940 Metzler), *U-551* (from 15 Nov 1940 Schrott), *U-A* (from 15 Nov 1940 Eckermann), *U-70* (from 1 Dec 1940 Matz), *U-96* (from 1 Dec 1940 Lehmann-Willenbrock), *U-71* (from 15 Dec 1940 Flachsenberg), *U-76* (from 15 Dec 1940 von Hippel), *U-552* (from 15 Dec 1940 Topp).

7.U-Flotilla – Status as at 1 Jan 1941
Flotilla Chief: Kapitänleutnant Sohler
U-46 (Endrass), *U-47* (Prien), *U-48* (Schultze), *U-52* (Salman), *U-69* (Metzler), *U-70* (Matz), *U-71* (Flachsenberg), *U-73* (Rosenbaum), *U-74* (Kentrat), *U-75* (Ringelmann), *U-76* (von Hippel), *U-93* (Korth), *U-94* (Kuppisch), *U-95* (Schreiber), *U-96* (Lehmann), *U-97* (Heilmann), *U-98* (Gysae), *U-99* (Kretschmer,) *U-100* (Schepke), *U-101* (Mengersen), *U-551* (Schrott), *U-552* (Topp), *U-553* (Thurmann), *U-A* (Eckermann), torpedo recovery vessel, Stabsobersteuermann Etterich.

U-48

The Commanders of *U-48*
Korvettenkapitän Herbert Schultze (b. Kiel 24 Jul 1909, d. Kiel 3 Jun 1987)
Knight's Cross 1 Mar 1940, Oak Leaves (15th recipient) 12 Jun 1941
Last Appointment: Cdr II.Div. Naval Academy Schleswig

Kapitän-zur-See Hans-Rudolf Rösing (b. Wilhelmshaven 28 Sep 1905, d. Kiel 16 Dec 2004)
Knight's Cross 29 Aug 1940
Last Appointment: FdU West/North

Korvettenkapitän Heinrich Bleichrodt (b. Berga/Kyffhäuser 21 Sep 1909, d. 9 Jan 1977 Munich)
Knight's Cross 24 Oct 1940, Oak Leaves (125th recipient) 23 Sep 1942
Last Appointment: Flotilla Chief, 22.U-Flotilla

Convoy SC7 – Ships Sunk and Torpedoed
16 Oct 1940
U-124 (Schulz) *Trevisa* 1,813 grt

17 Oct 1940
U-48 (Bleichrodt) *Languedoc* 9,512 grt
U-48 (Bleichrodt) *Scoresby* 3,843 grt
U-38 (Liebe) *Aenos* 3,554 grt

18 Oct 1940
U-38 (Liebe) *Carsbreck* 3,670 grt (torp.)
U-123 (Moehle) *Beatus* 4,885 grt
U-46 (Endrass) *Convallaria* 1,996 grt
U-101 (Frauenheim) *Shekatika* 5,458 grt (torp.)
U-99 (Kretschmer) *Empire Miniver* 6,055 grt
U-46 (Endrass) *Creekirk* 3,917 grt
U-101 (Frauenheim) *Blairspey* 5,458 grt (torp.)
U-100 (Schepke) *Sjekatika* 5,458 grt (torp.)
U-99 (Kretschmer) *Niritos* 3,854 grt

19 Oct 1940
U-101 (Frauenheim *Assyrian* 2,962 grt
U-101 (Frauenheim) *Soesterberg* 1,904 grt

Appendices

U-123 (Moehle) *Snefjeld* 1,643 grt
U-123 (Moehle) *Boekolo* 2,118 grt
U-99 (Kretschmer) *Empire Brigade* 5,154 grt
U-100 (Schepke) *Blairspey* 4,155 grt (torp.)
U-99 (Kretschmer) *Thalia* 5,875 grt
U-123 (Moehle) *Shekatika* 5,458 grt
U-99 (Kretschmer) *Clintonia* 3,106 grt (torp.)
U-123 (Moehle) *Clintonia* 3,106 grt

Total number of ships attacked: 24, of which *Shekatika* three times, *Blairspey* and *Clintonia* twice.
Total number of ships sunk: 20
Total tonnage sunk, Convoy SC7: 82,030 grt

Successes against Convoy HX 79 (19/20 October 1940)
19 Oct 1940
U-38 (Liebe) *Matheran* 7,653 grt
U-38 (Liebe) *Uganda* 4,966 grt
U-47 (Prien) *Bilderdijk* 6,856 grt
U-47 (Prien) *Shirak* 6,023 grt (torp.)
U-48 (Bleichrodt) *Shirak* 6,023 grt
U-47 (Prien) 'Wandby' 4,947 grt (torp.)
U-46 (Endrass) *Wandby* 4,947 grt
[*Wandby* was attacked by *U-47* and *U-46* simultaneously]
U-46 (Endrass) *Ruperra* 4,548 grt

20 Oct 1940
U-100 (Schepke) *Caprella* 8,230 grt
U-100 (Schepke) *Sitala* 6,218 grt
U-47 (Prien) *La Estancia* 5,185 grt
U-47 (Prien) *Whitford Point* 5,026 grt
U-47 (Prien) *Athelmonarch* 8,995 grt (torp.)
U-46 (Endrass) *Janus* 9,965 grt
U-100 (Schepke) *Loch Lomond* 5,452 grt

Total number of ships torpedoes: 15 (of which two twice)
Total number of ships sunk: 12 of 75,069 grt
Damaged: 1 ship, 8,995 grt (the torpedoed ships *Shirak* and *Wandby* are included under the ships sunk).

U-48

Allied Merchant Tonnage Lost in the Second World War
Total sinkings: 5,150 merchant ships of 21,570,720 grt by:
German U-boats: 2,828 ships of 14,687,231 grt
Aircraft: 820 ships of 2,889,883 grt
Mines: 534 ships of 1,406,037 grt
Regular warships: 104 ships of 498,447 grt
Raiders: 133 ships of 829,644 grt
E-boats: 99 ships of 229,676 grt
Other causes (prizes, scuttled after torpedo or mine damage): 632 ships of 1,029,802 grt

U-boat Successes against Warships 1939–45
Battleships/Battlecruisers: 2 sunk, 3 damaged
Aircraft carriers (escort and auxiliary): 5 sunk, 2 damaged
Cruisers: 6 sunk, 7 damaged
Destroyers: 34 sunk, 11 damaged
Escort destroyers: 18 sunk, 13 damaged
Frigates: 2 sunk, 4 damaged
Corvettes: 26 sunk, 3 damaged
Sloops: 13 sunk, 4 damaged
Minesweepers: 10 sunk
Motor minesweepers: 3 sunk, 1 damaged
Submarines: 9 sunk
Anti-submarine vessels: 3 sunk
Gunboats: 1 sunk
Landing craft: 13 sunk
Depot ships: 2 sunk
Aircraft tenders: 1 sunk

German U-boat Losses in the Second World War
British Listing
Total destroyed: 785
By enemy warships: 246
By land aircraft (no bombing): 245
By naval aircraft and aircraft from carriers: 43
By submarines: 21
By bombing attacks on ports: 61
By mines: 26
By accident and scuttling: 57

Appendices

By Soviet involvement of all kinds: 7 (9)
By causes unknown: 29 (27)

German Statistics on U-boat Losses
U-boats Commissioned: 1,170 (including 10 confiscated foreign boats)
Served at Front: 863
Lost to enemy action: 603
Lost to causes unknown: 20
Lost through accidents: 7
Lost to mines and bombs in German-controlled waters: 81
Lost to accident in German-controlled waters: 42
Scuttled or blown up at war's end when evacuating bases: 215
Decommissioned: 38
Transferred to foreign navies: 11
Surrendered in Allied ports at war's end: 153

Notes

Chapter 1: The German U-boat Arm: Development and Command
1. Karl Alman, *Grossadmiral Karl Dönitz*.
2. Franz Kurowski, *Krieg unter Wasser*.
3. See RM 7/891 Seekrieg 1939 Vol. 4-1 BdU: Befehle und Absichten ('Orders and Intentions') August 1939 to July 1940.
4. RM 87/1 KTB FdU Ost from 22 August to 19 September 1939.

Chapter 2: The U-boat War Begins: The First War Patrol of *U-48*
1. *U-48* KTB.
2. Jochen Brennecke, *Jäger-Gejagte*.
3. Captain SW Roskill, *The War at Sea*, London: PUBLISHER, 1954–6.
4. Winston S Churchill, *Der Zweite Weltkrieg*, Vol 1, PLACE: PUBLISHER, DATE, pp 362–3.

Chapter 3: The Second War Patrol of *U-48*: Five Days – Five Sinkings
1. FdU KTB.
2. Leon Peillard, *Die Schlacht im Atlantik*, Vienna/Berlin: PUBLISHER, 1974.
3. Gerhard Wagner, *Lagevorträge des Oberbefehlshabers der Kriegsmarine vor Hitler, 1939-1945*, Munich: PUBLISHER, 1972.
4. Wagner, *Lagevorträge des Oberbefehlshabers der Kriegsmarine vor Hitler, 1939-1945*.

Chapter 4: The Third War Patrol of *U-48*: Cruiser in Sight!
RM 98/50 and 51, pp 59–69.

Chapter 5: The Fourth War Patrol of *U-48*: General Observations
1. Wagner, *Lagevorträge des Oberbefehlshabers der Kriegsmarine vor Hitler*.
2. BdU KTB.

Chapter 6: Wooden Swords: The Fifth War Patrol of *U-48*: Preparations for *Hartmut*
1. SKL I op 226/40 Chefsache.
2. Karl Dönitz, *Zehn Jahre und Zwanzig Tage*, Bonn: PUBLISHER, 1958.

Notes

3. Dönitz, *Zehn Jahre und Zwanzig Tage*.
4. Fritz Brustat-Naval, and Teddy Suhren, *Nasses Eichenlaub – Als Kommandant und FdU im Ubootkrieg*, Herford: PUBLISHER, 1983.
5. BdU KTB, 15 May 1940.

Chapter 7: The Battle of the Atlantic: *U-48* under New Command – Sixth War Patrol
1. Dönitz, *Zehn Jahre und Zwanzig Tage*.
2. *U-48* KTB.
3. BdU KTB.

Chapter 8: The Seventh War Patrol: Summer Duel
1. Dönitz, *Zehn Jahre und Zwanzig Tage*.

Chapter 10: *U-48* and Her New Commander: Convoy SC3
1. Brustat-Naval and Suhren, *Nasses Eichenlaub*.
2. HMS *Dundee* (L84) was a *Shoreham* class sloop built in 1932 commanded by Captain O. Stokes. The ship's company was around ninety-five officers and men of which twelve, six officers and six ratings, died in the sinking. The captain survived.
3. Terence Robertson, *Der Wolf im Atlantik*, Wells: PUBLISHER, 1961.

Chapter 11: The Duel with Convoy SC7 – 'The Night of the Long Knives'
1. See Appendix for list of ships sunk from Convoys SC7 and HX79.

Chapter 12: British Anti-Submarine Developments
1. Roskill, Capt. S.W. Royal Navy, Oldenburg, 1962

Chapter 13: The Grand Finale – *U-48*'s Tenth War Patrol
1. Brustat-Naval and Suhren, *Nasses Eichenlaub*.
2. Brustat-Naval and Suhren, *Nasses Eichenlaub*.

Bibliography

Alman, Karl, *Ritter der sieben Meere*, Rastatt: Pabel-Moewig, 1964.
_____, *Angriff, ran, versenken!*, Rastatt: Pabel-Moewig 1965.
_____, *Günther Prien – der Wolf und sein Admiral*, Leoni am Stamberger See, Druffel, 1981.
_____, *U-boot Asse*, Vienna: Prisma, 1981.
_____, *Grossadmiral Karl Dönitz, Vom U-boat Kommandant zum Staatsoberhaupt*, Leoni am Stamberger See, Druffel, 1983.
_____, *Graue Wölfe in blauer See*, Herrsching: Pawlak, 1985.
Antier, Jean-Jacques, *Histoire mondiale du sous-marin*, Paris: Laffont, 1968.
Auphan, Admiral Paul, and Mordal Jacques, *La marine française dans la seconde Guerre mondiale*, Paris: Editions France-Empire, 1959. (In English as *The French Navy in World War II* Annapolis: US Naval Institute, 1959)
Bekker, Cajus, *Kampf und Untergang der Kriegsmarine*, Hanover: Sponholz, 1953. (In English as *Swatsika at Sea: The Struggle and Destruction of the German Navy, 1939-1945* London: Kimber, 1953)
Brandi, Albrecht, *Meine U-boot Einsätze* (manuscript).
Brennecke, Jochen, *Jäger-Gejagte*, Biberach/Riss: Koehler, 1956. (In |English as *The Hunters and the Hunted: German U-boats 1939-1945* Annapolis: US Naval Institute, 2003)
Brustat-Naval, Fritz and Suhren, Teddy, *Nasses Eichenlaub – Als Kommandant und FdU im Uboot-krieg*, Herford: Koehler, 1983 (in English as *Teddy Suhren, Ace of Aces:Memoirs of a U-boat Rebel* Annapolis, US Naval Institute, 2006 and Barnsley: Frontline, 2011).
Buchheit, Gerd, *Der U-bootkrieg in der deutschen Strategie, 1939-1945*, ZS, 1972.
Busch, Dr Harald, *So war der U-bootkrieg*, Bielefeld: Deutscher Heimat, 1952.
Chatterton, Edward Keble: *Fighting the U-boats*, London: Hurst & Blackett, 1942.
Cocchia, Aldo, *Sommergibili all' attacco*, Milan: Rizzoli, 1955.(in English as *Submarines Attacking: Adventures of the Italian Naval Forces* London, Kimber, 1956)
Cope, H F, and Karig, Walter, *Battle Submerged*, New York: Norton, 1951.
Creswell, John, *Sea Warfare 1939-1945*, London: Longmans Green, 1950.
Cunningham, Admiral Lord Andrew B, *A Sailor's Odyssey*, London: Hutchinson, 1951.

Bibliography

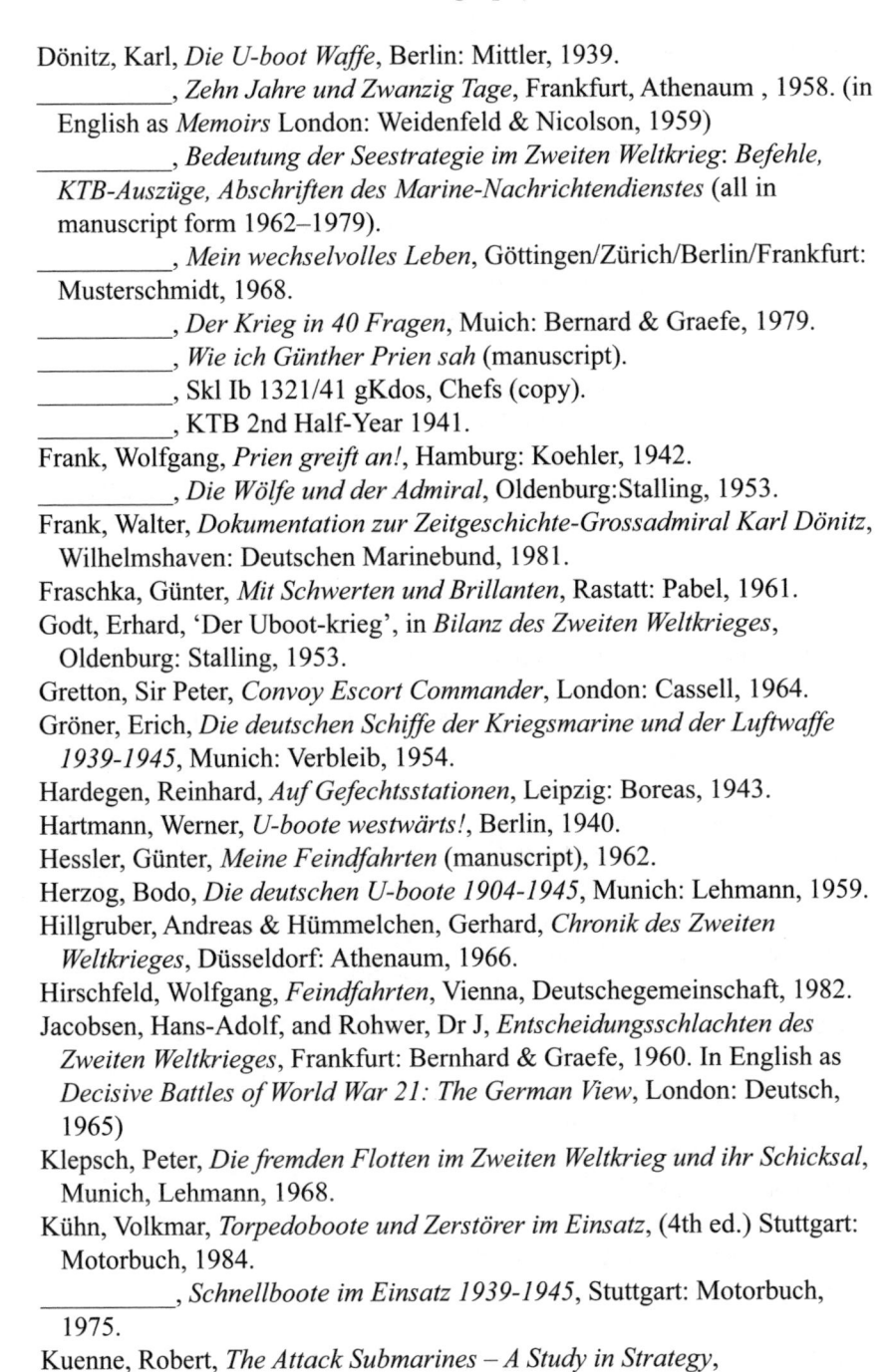

Dönitz, Karl, *Die U-boot Waffe*, Berlin: Mittler, 1939.
_____, *Zehn Jahre und Zwanzig Tage*, Frankfurt, Athenaum , 1958. (in English as *Memoirs* London: Weidenfeld & Nicolson, 1959)
_____, *Bedeutung der Seestrategie im Zweiten Weltkrieg: Befehle, KTB-Auszüge, Abschriften des Marine-Nachrichtendienstes* (all in manuscript form 1962–1979).
_____, *Mein wechselvolles Leben*, Göttingen/Zürich/Berlin/Frankfurt: Musterschmidt, 1968.
_____, *Der Krieg in 40 Fragen*, Muich: Bernard & Graefe, 1979.
_____, *Wie ich Günther Prien sah* (manuscript).
_____, Skl Ib 1321/41 gKdos, Chefs (copy).
_____, KTB 2nd Half-Year 1941.
Frank, Wolfgang, *Prien greift an!*, Hamburg: Koehler, 1942.
_____, *Die Wölfe und der Admiral*, Oldenburg:Stalling, 1953.
Frank, Walter, *Dokumentation zur Zeitgeschichte-Grossadmiral Karl Dönitz*, Wilhelmshaven: Deutschen Marinebund, 1981.
Fraschka, Günter, *Mit Schwerten und Brillanten*, Rastatt: Pabel, 1961.
Godt, Erhard, 'Der Uboot-krieg', in *Bilanz des Zweiten Weltkrieges*, Oldenburg: Stalling, 1953.
Gretton, Sir Peter, *Convoy Escort Commander*, London: Cassell, 1964.
Gröner, Erich, *Die deutschen Schiffe der Kriegsmarine und der Luftwaffe 1939-1945*, Munich: Verbleib, 1954.
Hardegen, Reinhard, *Auf Gefechtsstationen*, Leipzig: Boreas, 1943.
Hartmann, Werner, *U-boote westwärts!*, Berlin, 1940.
Hessler, Günter, *Meine Feindfahrten* (manuscript), 1962.
Herzog, Bodo, *Die deutschen U-boote 1904-1945*, Munich: Lehmann, 1959.
Hillgruber, Andreas & Hümmelchen, Gerhard, *Chronik des Zweiten Weltkrieges*, Düsseldorf: Athenaum, 1966.
Hirschfeld, Wolfgang, *Feindfahrten*, Vienna, Deutschegemeinschaft, 1982.
Jacobsen, Hans-Adolf, and Rohwer, Dr J, *Entscheidungsschlachten des Zweiten Weltkrieges*, Frankfurt: Bernhard & Graefe, 1960. In English as *Decisive Battles of World War 21: The German View*, London: Deutsch, 1965)
Klepsch, Peter, *Die fremden Flotten im Zweiten Weltkrieg und ihr Schicksal*, Munich, Lehmann, 1968.
Kühn, Volkmar, *Torpedoboote und Zerstörer im Einsatz*, (4th ed.) Stuttgart: Motorbuch, 1984.
_____, *Schnellboote im Einsatz 1939-1945*, Stuttgart: Motorbuch, 1975.
Kuenne, Robert, *The Attack Submarines – A Study in Strategy*,

Newhaven/London: Yale University Press, 1965.

Kurowski, Franz, *Zu Lande zu Wasser in der Luft*, Bochum: Poppinghaus, 1969.

_____, *Krieg unter Wasser*, Düsseldorf: Econ, 1979.

_____, *Mit Eichenlaub und Schwertern*, Herrsching: Pawlak, 1985.

_____, *Ton dokumente – Gespräche mit U-boot-Kommandanten* 1962-1985.

Lenton, H T, *Navies of the Second World War*, London: Macdonald, 1966.

Lüth, Wolfgang, and Korth, Klaus, *Boot greift wieder an!*, Berlin: Klinghammer, 1944.

Lusar, Rudolf, *Die deutschen Waffen und Geheimwaffen des Zweiten Weltkrieges*, Munich: Lehmann, 1960. (In English as *German Secret Weapons of World War 2* London: Spearman, 1959)

MacIntyre, Donald, *U-boat Killer*, London: Weidenfeld & Nicolson, 1956.

Mars, Alastair, *Unbroken, The true story of a Submarine*, London: Muller, 1953

Metzler, Jost, *Sehrohr südwärts!*, Berlin: Limpert, 1943.

_____, *U-69, die lachende Kuh*, Ravensburg: Heyne, 1954 (in English as *The Laughing Cow: A U-boat Captain's Story*, London, Kimber, 1955)

Mielke, Otto, *Die deutschen U-boote 1939-1945*, Munich: Moewig, 1959.

_____, *Paukenschlag vor Kapstadt*, Munich: Moewig, 1954.

Murawski, Dr Erich, *Der deutsche Wehrmachtsbericht 1939-1945*, Boppard: Bolt, 1962.

Morrison, Samuel E, *United States Naval Operations in World War II*, Vol I–XV, Boston: Little Brown, 1950-7.

_____, *The Two Ocean War*, Boston-Toronto: Little Brown, 1963.

Murat, S, *La guerre sous-marin en atlantique*, Paris, 1946.

OKM 3.Skl: Marine Dienstvorschrift Nr. 135: *Die Handelsflotten der Welt*, Munich-Berlin: Reichskriegsmarine, 1942.

Peillard, Leonce, *Geschichte des U-bootkrieges, 1939-1945*, Klagenfurt: Wilt, 1970.

_____, *Die Schlacht im Atlantik*, Klagenfurt, Wilt, 1974.

Pollina, Paolo, *I sommergibili italiani*, Rome: USMM, 1963.

Prien, Günther: *Mein Weg nach Scapa Flow*, Berlin: Volk und Reich, 1940. (in English as *I Sank the Royal Oak* London: Grays Inn Press, 1954)

Raeder, Erich, *Mein Leben*, Vol II, Tübingen: Schlichtenmayer, 1957. (in English as *My Life* Annapolis: US Naval Institute, 1960)

Range, Clemens, *Die Ritterkreuzträger der Kriegsmarine*, Stuttgart: Motorbuch, 1974.

Robertson, Terence, *Jagd auf die Wölfe*, Oldenburg: Stalling, 1960. (in English as *Night Raider of the Atlantic* New York: Dutton, 1956)

Bibliography

_____, *Wolf im Atlantik*, Munich: Welsermuhl, 1961. (in English as *The Golden Horseshoe* London, Evans Bros, 1956)

Rohwer, Dr Jürgen, _____, *Der Ubootkrieg und sein Zusammenbruch 1943*, Frankfurt/Main, Bernhard & Graefe, 1960.

_____, *U-boote*, Oldenburg: Stalling,1962.

_____, *Die U-boot-Erfolge der Achsenmächte 1939-1945*, Munich: Lehmann,1968.

_____, and Hümmelchen, G, *Chronik des Seekrieges, 1939-1945*, Oldenburg: Bernhard & Graefe, 1968. (in English as *Chronology of the War at Sea* Shepperton, Ian Allan, 1976)

Roskill, Captain S W, *The War at Sea*, Vols I, III, IV, London: HMSO, 1954–6.

_____, *Royal Navy*, Oldenburg: HMSO, 1961.

Ruge, Friedrich, *Der Seekrieg 1939-1945*, Stuttgart: Koehler, 1954.

Schramm, Percy E (ed), *KTB des OKW 1940-1945*,Munich, Bernhard & Graefe, 1982.

Schulz, Joh, *Tödlicher Atlantik*, Munich, Moewig, 1962.

Turner, John Frayn, *Periscope Patrol*, London: Harrap, 1957.

Wagner, Gerhard (ed), *Lagevorträge des Oberbefehlshabers der Kriegsmarine vor Hitler, 1939-1945*, Munich: Lehmann, 1972.

Warlimont, Walter, *Im Hauptquartier der Deutschen Wehrmacht, 1939-1945*, Frankfurt/Main: Athenaum, 1962. (in English as *Inside Hitler's Headquarters, 1939-1945*, London: Weidenfeld & Nicolson, 1964)

Files Consulted at BA/MA Freiburg/Breisgau

RM 7/84: Survey of Situation in the Atlantic 15 Aug 39–5 Sep 39.

RM 87/3: FdU/BdU War Diary, 15 Aug 39–31 Jan 40.

RM 87/13: BdU War Diary 15 Aug 39–31 Dec 39.

RM 87/2: FdU West War Diary, 23 Aug 39–31 Jul 40

RM 87/1: FdU East War Diary, 22 Aug 39–19 Sep 39

RM 7/891: 'Seekrieg' 1939, Issue 4 – 1 BdU, Orders and Intentions, Aug 39–Jul 40.

RM 7/91: 1.Skl Teil B.V.: Files of general contents to Part A, Sep 39– Dec 39.

RM 98/51: *U-48* War Diary, Cdr Kptlt Schultze: begun 21 Dec 39, ends 26 Feb 1940.

RM 87/14: BdU War Diary 1 Jan 40–31 Mar 40.

RM 87/13, 14,15: BdU War Diary 1 Jan 40–30 Jun 40.

RM 7/84/85: 1.Abt.Skl War Diary, Part B Vol I: Atlantic – Survey of the Atlantic Situation: Survey of Foreign War Policy, 31 Dec 40–31 Mar 44.

RM 98/50: Schultze; Herbert: Experiences and Reflections following Three War Patrols at the Request of the BdU.

U-48

RM 87/50: Tactical Organisation of the U-boat Flotillas from 1 Sep 1939–1942: Tactical Organisation of the U-boat Training Flotillas from 1 Oct 1939: Tactical Organisation of the BdU Group, Starting Date 1 Nov 1939: The U-boat Training Flotilla: The U-boat Further-Training Flotilla: The 7. U-boat Flotilla, Status as at 15 Aug 1940: The 7.U-boat Flotilla, Status as at 1 Jan 1941: Organisation of U-boat Command, 15 Jan 1941: Officers aboard *U-48* on 1 May 1941.

The Author extends his thanks to all institutions and offices and to all former U-boat seafarers who contributed to this work.

Winter 1985
Karl Alman

Index

Abadan 9
Abo 2
Alaunia 134
Albatros 3, 40
Alexandros 116
Allen, Commander 132
Amsterdam 29, 70
Angle 134
Anglo-German Naval Treaty 1
Anna 67
Anvil Point 68–9
Arabis 134
Arbuthnot, Rear Admiral 138
Arbutus 150
Ark Royal 19, 38, 72–74, 143, 154
Athelcrest 106
Athelmonarch 135
Athelprince 94, 150–2,
Athenia 12–5
Atlantic Group 7, 21
Attlee, Clement 138
Atzinger, Oberleutnant-zur-See 145, 153, 156–8
Aurora 142
Australia 141
Azores 113
B-Dienst 80–1, 98, 100, 113, 121, 146
Bailey Bank 8
Bandon, Captain Charles 25–8
Baron Blythswood 123–4
Baron Loudon 95
Baron Nairn 156
Barsch, Kapitänleutnant 3
Barten 109, 163
Batory 84
Battle of the Atlantic 89–91, 93, 95, 97, 126, 137

Bauer 110
Bay of Biscay 7, 99, 127
BBC 118, 155
BdU 32–4, 37, 39, 41, 45, 47, 51–6, 65–6, 72–4, 76–8, 80–1, 84–5, 89–90, 93–4, 96–8, 100, 104, 106–9, 112, 114, 117, 122, 126, 130–2, 134–5, 144, 146, 148, 150–1, 153, 155–8
Beatty, Lord, Admiral of the Fleet 1
Beatus 133
Beaverdale 151
Bedouin 149
Beduhn 3, 110
Belfast 142
Bergen 67, 80, 82, 90
Berlin 37, 114
Bertel 144
Berwick 84
Bilderdijk 135, 165
Biscay 7, 99, 107–8, 110, 112–3, 127, 153
Bismarck 153–5, 157, 159
Blackfly 134
Blairangus 124
Bleichrodt, Heinrich 113–33, 135–6, 144–5
Bluebell 131, 149
Bombay 141
Bordeaux 112
Bosun Dzillas 36
Brandanger 128
Brandon 52
Bräutigam, Korvettenkäpitan 2–3
Brazen 85
Brazza 89
Bremen 142

Brest 15, 114, 154
Bretagne 27
Bristol Channel 55, 59
British Monarch 96
Broompark 125–6, 144
Browning 11–2
Brunsbüttel 47, 56, 65, 77, 90, 97, 103
Brunsbüttel Lock 47, 56, 65, 77, 97
Burgerdijk 70, 161
Cadiz 2
Camellia 150
Canada 141
Canonesa 125
Cape Finisterre 33, 39, 52, 89
Cape Town 141
Carsbreck 132
Casablanca, 21
Ceramic 99
Chamberlain, Neville 138
Churchill, Winston 16, 18, 39, 138–40
City of Benares 118–9
City of Mandalay 33
City of Simla 123, 126
Clan Chisholm 33
Cockburn Bank 74
Cocos Islands 61
Confidential Orders 45
Convallaria 133
Convoy HG3 33
Convoy HX112 148–9
Convoy HX115 150, 152
Convoy HX65A 106
Convoy HX72 122, 125–6
Convoy HX75 129–30
Convoy HX79 133, 135
Convoy HX79 134
Convoy OB17 26
Convoy OB202 102
Convoy OB216 123

Convoy OB228 134, 147
Convoy OB229 134
Convoy OB288 147
Convoy OB293 150
Convoy OB329 157
Convoy SC3 115–7, 119, 121, 123, 125
Convoy SC7 127, 129, 131–5, 137
Convoy SC7 127, 129, 131, 133, 135, 137
Convoy U-73 146
Cook, Captain James 12–3
Coreopsis 134
Cork 55, 65
Courageous 16, 18–9
Crispin 146
Cumberland 102
Dau, Kapitänleutnant Rudolf 3, 28, 109
Davanger 129, 162
Deecke 110
Delcain 125
Den Haag 76
Denmark 80, 153
Denmark Strait 153
Denning, Vice-Admiral Norman 140
Deutsche Werke 64
Devonshire 84
Dietl, Generalmajor 83
Dirphys 156
Donau 66
Dönitz, Admiral 3–4, 12–4, 16, 21, 34–5, 37–43, 54, 56, 77–8, 80–2, 85–7, 89, 90, 97, 107, 108–10, 112–4, 121-22, 126, 132–6, 143–8, 152, 155–6, 158–9
Dorsetshire 154
Dover 110
Downs 70
Dublin 22
Dundee 116, 144

Index

Dunster Grange 89
East Africa 88
Eastlea 150
Eckermann 3
Eckernförde 39
Edam 70
Edinburgh 142
Egersund 80
Elbe 65, 90, 142
Elmbank 124
Emden 3, 61
Emile Miguet 23, 26, 30
Emo 148
Empire Citizen 146
Empire Dew 158
Empire Merlin 106
Empire Volunteer 117
Endrass, Oberleutnant-zur-See Engelbert 35–6, 94, 113, 133, 135–6, 144, 157
Engel, Obersteuermann Herbert 127
England 21, 27–8, 112, 121, 131, 133, 136
English Channel 53, 59, 67–9, 75, 78, 80, 82, 109
Erodona 149
Eros 92–3, 96
Erwin Wassner 145
Ettore 70
Ewerth, Kapitänleutnant 3
Exeter 72, 74
Fair Isle 47–8, 51, 55, 66, 77
Falke 146
Falklands 61
Faroes Narrows 142
Faulknor 19
FdU (Führer der U-boote) 3, 6, 8, 14, 21–2, 30, 32, 34, 37–8, 113
Fearless 85
Ferm 149

Firby 16
Firedrake 19
Firth of Clyde 110
Forbes, Sir Charles, Commander-in-Chief Home Fleet 39
Fowey 131
Foxhound 19, 39
Frahm 110
France 2, 7–8, 11, 42, 46, 108, 135, 147, 157
Frances Massey 92
Franche Comté 149
Fraser, Rear Admiral 138
Frauenheim, Fritz 94, 109, 133, 136,
Frederick S. Fales 126
Freetown 72, 141
Freiwald, Kapitänleutnant 3
Fresdorf, Kapitänleutnant Werner 3
Friedeburg, Kapitän-zur-See 108
Frohavet 90–1
Fröhlich 110
Funksonne 76
G7a 38–9, 41, 85, 87
G7e 39, 41, 87
Gelhaar 27, 110, 163
Germaine 55, 161
German Bight 20, 47, 55, 57, 66, 77
Germania Werft 2, 57, 64, 77, 107, 145, 158
Germanic 150, 162
Germany 1–2, 4, 7–8, 13, 15, 33, 38, 42–3, 45, 55, 63, 77, 80–2, 103, 115, 138, 142–3, 154
Gibraltar 21, 33, 141
Glasgow 84, 142
Glattes, Kapitänleutnant 19, 38, 109
Godt, Fregattenkapitän 6, 86, 108
Götting, Vizeadmiral 40–1
Graigwen 127
Great Lion 49, 56, 74, 77–9, 85, 97,

108, 112, 122, 137, 146–7, 152, 158–9
Great War 2–3, 37, 43, 45, 88, 136
Greenwood, Arthur 138
Greif 146
Grille, (State Yacht) 4
Grosse, Kapitänleutnant 3, 110
Group Hartmann 21, 33
Halifax 122, 134, 141
Halifax, Lord 138
Hänig, Oberleutnant-zur-See 3
Hardegen, Oberleutnant-zur-See Reinhard 106
Hartlepool 16
Hartmann, Korvettenkapitän Werner 21, 89, 113
Hartmut, Operation 80, 82–3
Harwich 64
Hauptmann, Korvettenkäpitan Werner 109
Havildar 102
He115 floatplane 91
Hebrides 22, 34, 66, 77, 98–9, 104, 109, 145
Hedrun 98, 161
Heidel 110
Heligoland 65–6, 77, 145–6
Heliotrope 134
Henke, Kapitänleutnant Werner 99
Hero of Scapa Flow, The 150
Heronspool 23, 25–6
Hessen 77
Hessler, Kapitänleutnant Günther 145–6
Hibiscus 134
Hitler 4, 8, 14–5, 37–8, 41–4, 46, 64–5, 88, 136, 143–4, 150
Hitler's Reichstag speech 8, 88
Högel, Funkmaat Georg 13

Holm Sound 35
Holtenau Lock 90
Hood 39, 142, 153–4
Horns Reef 142
House of Commons 16
House of Lords 1
Huber, Oberleutnant-zur-See 3
Humber Estuary 64
Huntingdon 146
Husöy 90
HX72 122, 125–6
HX79 133–5
Hydrangea 149
Hylton 152
Iberian Peninsula 22
Iceland 7, 142, 145, 150
Ilex 27
Imogen 27
Indian Ocean 63
Invershannon 123–4
Inversuir 156, 162
Ireland 21–2, 30, 34, 54, 57, 67, 72, 74, 76–7, 109–10, 115
Iron Cross 78, 107, 126, 136, 158
Ites, Oberleutnant-zur-See Otto 20, 23, 115
J.B. White 149
Jade 66, 110, 142
Jade Bay 110
Jamaica 27
Japan 44, 139
Jason 134
Jenisch, Kapitänleutnant Karl Heinrich 110, 122
Junker, Kapitän-zur-See Rudolf 40
Jürst, Kapitänleutnant Harald 127
Karamea 28
Kattentidt, Korvettenkäpitan 40
Keitel, Generaloberst 37
Kenordoc 117, 161

Index

Kerneval 114
Kiel 2–4, 7, 16, 20, 34, 47, 56, 64–5, 77, 79, 83, 90, 97–8, 107, 113, 145, 158
Kiel Canal 20, 47, 56, 64–5, 90, 145
Kiel-Wik 2
Kingfisher 75
Kingston 27
Kinnaird Head 65
Kirk Sound 35
Kirkwall 142
Klot-Heydenfeld 110
Knackfuss, Leutnant-zur-See 153, 156
Knight of the Long Knives 114
Knight's Cross 37, 78–9, 90, 107, 109, 113, 126, 131, 136, 144–5, 152, 158–9
Knorr 84, 110, 163
Königsberg 61, 88
Korth, Korvettenkapitän Claus 130, 134, 163
Kretschmer, Fregattenkapitän Otto 86, 109, 117, 122–4, 133, 136, 148–50
Kriegsmarine, Generaladmiral Raeder 4
Kristiansand 80
Kruse, Oberfunkmaat Wilhelm 10
Kuhnke, Günther 113, 134
Kuhnt, Leutnant-zur-See 6
Kummetz, Konteradmiral Oskar 86
Kutschmann 110
La Brea 105
La Estancia 135
Lacklan 105
Lady Elsa 134
Lamb Holm 36
Lands End 70
Langton, Lt 150
Languedoc 132

Lassen, Georg 17
Le Havre 9
Lebrun, Jean 26
Lehmann-Willenbrock 146, 163
Lemp, Fritz-Julius 13–4, 16, 109, 149
Lerdam 30–1
Lerwick Bay 48–9
Lerwick Bight 48
Lido 22–3
Liebe, Fregattenkapitän, Heinrich 15, 84, 105, 109, 132, 134, 136
Limbach, Leutnant-sur-See Johann 145
Limbourg 150
Lindemann, Kapitän-zur-See 154
Lindesnes 82
Little, Sir Charles 138
Liverpool 13, 157
Lloyd's Register 13, 33, 92, 105, 118, 122–3, 132, 135, 151, 157
Lochavon 27
London 1, 8, 15, 45, 75, 94, 138, 142, 150
Looff, Kapitänleutnant 3, 88, 110
Lorentz 110
Lorient 99, 106–8, 114–5, 126–7, 135, 147–8
Lotos 118
Lott, Korvettenkapitän Werner 109
Louisiane 25–7
Lousy Bank 150
Löwe 65
Loycke, Kapitän-zur-See 3
Luftwaffe 36, 44, 62, 122
Luth, Wolfgang 86, 123, 127, 130, 136
Lütjens, Vizeadmiral 154
Macintyre, Captain Donald 148–50
Madeira 72

Magdalena 121–2
Makeig-Jones, Captain 18
Manaar 15
Marina 119
Matheran 135
Mathes, Korvettenkapitän Ludwig 3, 110
Matz, Korvettenkapitän Joachim 148, 150, 163
Meckel, Oberleutnant-zur-See 3
Mecklenburg Bight 60
Meldung 72
Memel 64
Metzler, Korvettenkapitän Jost 147–8
Mexico, Gulf of 9, 25
Michael E 156
Michahelles, Oberleutnant-zur-See 3
Mobilisation-Armament Plan 42
Moehle 127, 133
Moerdrecht 96
Mohr, Oberingenieur 39
Mondorf 110
Monsun 77
Montclare 134
Montevideo 61
Montreal 13
Mugler, Korvettenkapitän (posthumous) Gustav Adolf 110
Murmansk 45, 142
Nailsea Lass 147
Nantes 8
Narvik 80–5
Narvik Fjord 84–5
Nasses Eichenlaub 116
Naval Operations Command (SKL) 42
Naval Treaty 1–2
Neger 40
Nelson 39, 142
Neustadt Bay 159
New Sevilla 123

New Zealand 141
Newcastle 110
Nicolaos Angelos 146
Nord 40, 142
Nordboote 148
Norderney 56
Norfolk 154
North Africa 141
North Atlantic 63, 110, 143, 153–4
North Sea 7–8, 20, 34, 47, 55, 57, 63, 66, 77, 110, 115, 143, 145
Northern Passage 48, 66, 145–6
Norway 63, 67, 80–1, 83, 85, 87, 89, 113, 142–3
Nova Scotia 122, 131
O-21 134
Oak Leaves 107, 123, 131, 136, 152, 157–8, 164
Oehrn, Kapitänleutnant 3, 6, 89, 137
Ofotfjord 110
OKM 14, 44, 108, 155
Orion 83
Orkneys 7, 22 35, 47, 82, 110, 142
Oslo 9, 80
Oxley 142
P&O 75
Pacific 63
Papenberg 2
Paris 112, 114
Pauckstadt, Fregattenkapitän Hans 3
Pecton 102
Pendrecht 157
Pentland Firth 82
Perona, Admiral 107, 112
Petroni 148
Philipps, Rear Admiral 138
Popper Shipping Co. Ltd 16
Port Gisborne 128
Portland 68
Pound, Sir Dudley 39, 138

Index

Prellberg 110
Prien, Kapitänleutnant Günther 9, 15, 35–8, 51, 55, 79, 82, 85–7, 109, 122–4, 133–6, 147–8, 150, 152
Prince of Wales 153–4
Prinz Eugen 153–4
Prize Regulations 1, 12, 16, 44–5, 142
Prize Rules 9, 11, 45
Propaganda Ministry 13
Queen Elizabeth 141
Queen Mary 141
Raeder, Generaladmiral 4, 7, 37, 41–5, 64–5, 80, 86–7, 108–9, 154
Ramsay, Vice Admiral Sir Alexander 138
Regent Tiger 15
Reich Chancellery 37
Reich War Court 86–8
Reichsmarine 2, 4, 7, 20, 88
Reinhard Suhren 145
Renown 72, 74, 142
Repulse 36
Reschke, Korvettenkapitän Franz Georg 159
Reuter, Gustav E 48
Reykjavik 16
Rheinübung, Operation 153
Rockall 13, 117, 131, 133
Rockall Bank 117, 131
Rockepool 33–4
Rodney 39, 142
Rollmann, Wilhelm 15, 109, 159
Rose Ness 35
Rösing, Hans-Rudolf 3, 88, 90–101, 103–7, 109, 112–3, 144
Roskill, Captain 18, 37, 111, 143
Rosselli-Lorenzini 148
Rotterdam 30
Royal Oak 36, 50–1

Royal Sceptre 10–2
Rufiji 61, 88
Ruperra 135, 165
Russell, Lieutenant-Commander 134
Saar 3
Sachsenwald 155
Sagaing 32
Saint Dunstan 102
Salman, Korvettenkapitän Otto 85
Saltzwedel 4, 106
San Alberto 54
Sandsend 133
Sardonyx 149
Saunders, Rowe H 88
Scapa Flow 34–8, 87, 150
Scarborough 131
Scheer Building Programme 42
Scheer, Fregattenkapitän 4
Schepke, Kapitänleutnant Joachim 113, 122, 125–6, 133, 135–6, 148–50
Scherf, Kapitän-zur-See Albert 40
Scheringer, Oberleutnant-zur-See 3, 110
Scholtz, Fregattenkapitän Klaus 156
Schomburg, Fregattenkapitän 6
Schonder, Korvettenkapitän Heinrich 127
Schönermark, Korvettenkapitän 3
Schrewe, Oberleutnant-zur-See Peter 145, 151, 153
Schröter, Funkobergefreiter 17
Schuhart, Korvettenkapitän Otto 15–8, 94, 109
Schulte, Kapitänleutnant Max Martin 110
Schultz, Kapitänleutnant Karl Otto 107
Schultze, Korvettenkapitän Herbert 'Vaddi' 7–12, 15–6, 20, 27–34, 47–56, 65–8, 70–1, 73–9, 82–6,

181

88, 90, 97, 109, 127, 136, 144–8, 151–3, 155–8
Schultze, Oberleutnant-zur-See Heinz-Otto 159
Schulz, Korvettenkapitän Georg Wilhelm 106
Schütze, Kapitän zur See Viktor 3, 84, 127, 130
Scimitar 149
Scoresby 132
Second World War 14, 18, 45, 141, 158
Seelöwe 112, 114
Seelöwe, Operation 112, 114
Sengwarden 89, 107–8, 112
Sestini, Comandante 107
Shambles 69
Sheffield 84, 142
Shekatika 133
Shetlands 22, 34, 48, 66, 82–3, 98, 109–10, 142
Shirak 135, 144
Skagerrak 34
Skerry Sound 35
Slevogt, Fregattenkapitän 2
Sneaton 29–30, 160
Sohler, Korvettenkapitän Herbert 33, 39, 83, 163
South Atlantic 63
Southampton 84, 142
Spahr, Coxswain 35
Spearfish 143
Spee, Admiral Graf 61, 62
Sperrbrecher 65, 90, 97, 107
Spithead 26
SSS *Elmbank* 124
St Albans Head 65, 68
St George's Channel 59, 75
St Nazaire 152–3
St Villa 67

Stalin, Joseph 139
Stancor 91, 92, 161
Stavanger 80, 82, 110
Stephan, Oberleutnant-zur-See 134
Sturdy 134
Sturgeon 142
Stuttgart 49, 171, 173
Südboote 148
Süderau 16
Suffolk 154
Suhren, Oberleutnant-zur-See Reinhard Teddy 20–1, 23–4, 33, 48, 70, 80, 88, 90, 94–6, 99, 105–6, 114–7, 119, 128, 144–5
Sultan Star 75, 161
Sumburgh Head 48, 66, 77
Sumburgh light 48
Sunderland flying boats 33, 75, 127, 132, 141
Sweden 63, 80, 89
Swinemünde 6
Switzerland 141
Swordfish 142
Swordfish torpedo 154
Sydney 131
T-23 3
T-155 3
T-156 3
T-157 3
Tatem Steam Navigation Co 15
Terschelling 110, 142
Testing Group U-boats 3
Thames 64
The Battle of the Atlantic 89–91, 93, 95, 97
Thistlegarth 131
Tirpitz Mole 16, 34, 47, 56, 64, 79, 97
Todenhagen, Oberleutnant-zur-See 159

Index

Topp, Oberleutnant-zur-See Erich 99, 100–2
Torinia 125
Torpedo Inspectorate 34, 40–1, 54, 85
Trasyvoulus 33
Tregarthen 156
Triton 142
Trondheim 80, 82, 84, 90–1
Tudor 95, 161
TVA (Torpedo Research Institute) 23, 39–41, 87
U-1 2–3, 5, 83, 110
U-2 3, 5, 7, 83
U-3 3, 5, 86
U-4 3, 5, 83
U-5 3, 5, 83, 86
U-6 2–3, 5, 83, 86
U-7 3, 5, 82
U-8 3, 5
U-9 3, 5, 82, 86, 123
U-10 3, 5, 82
U-11 3
U-12 3, 5, 109
U-13 3, 5, 110
U-14 3, 5, 82
U-15 3, 5, 110
U-16 3, 5, 110
U-17 3, 5
U-18 3, 5
U-19 3, 5, 82
U-20 3, 5
U-21 3, 5, 109
U-22 3, 5, 110
U-23 3, 5
U-24 3, 5
U-25 4, 5, 39, 82, 84, 110
U-26 5, 16, 72–4, 110
U-27 5, 16, 109
U-28 5, 16, 41, 73, 134
U-29 5, 15–8, 73, 94, 109
U-30 5, 13–4, 16, 82, 98, 100, 108–9
U-31 5, 16, 47, 110
U-32 5, 16, 122
U-33 5, 15–6, 110
U-34 5, 15–6, 82, 109
U-35 5, 16, 47, 49, 109
U-37 5, 21, 31–3, 71–4, 84, 89–90, 109, 145
U-38 54, 84, 98, 100, 105, 109, 132, 134
U-39 16, 19, 38–9, 109
U-41 5, 66, 110
U-42 5, 28, 109
U-43 5, 94, 115
U-45 5, 27, 28, 71, 110, 160, 163
U-46 5, 31–3, 39, 83–4, 94, 97, 131, 133–5, 147–8
U-47 5, 9, 15, 35–7, 47, 51–5, 82, 85–6, 97, 109, 122–4, 133–6, 147–8, 150
U-48 passim
U-49 5, 41, 83–4, 110
U-51 5, 84, 97, 99, 110
U-52 5, 77, 85, 146
U-53 5, 16, 110
U-55 110, 141
U-56 5, 39, 82
U-57 5, 99–103
U-58 5, 127
U-59 5, 115, 127
U-60 5, 82
U-61 5, 82
U-64 83, 106
U-65 84–5, 98, 118
U-69 146–8
U-70 148, 150
U-73 146, 153, 155
U-74 148, 155
U-93 134, 146

U-48

U-94 146
U-95 146–7
U-96 146–7
U-97 153, 155
U-98 148, 153
U-99 109, 115, 117, 122–4, 131, 133, 135, 148–50
U-100 122, 125–6, 131, 133–5, 148–50
U-101 94, 109, 131, 133, 146
U-103 127, 130, 146
U-107 145–7
U-108 153, 155–6
U-110 149
U-123 127, 131, 133, 146–7
U-124 106, 131, 148
U-138 123, 127
U-181 123, 145
U-551 148
U-552 153
U-556 153–4
U-564 145
Uganda 135, 165
Ushant 75
Vaags Fjord 84–5
Valiant 84
Vanoc 149–50
Varendorff, Oberleutnant-zur-See 135
Veniero 148
Venland 55
Vestfjord 84–5
Ville de Gand 99–100
Violanda N Goulandis 93
Volunteer 117, 149, 161
von der Ropp, Kapitänleutnant Dietrich 109
von Dresky, Kapitänleutnant Hans Wilhelm 110
von Friedeburg, Hans-Georg 145

von Gossler, Korvettenkapitän Kurt 84, 110, 163
von Schmidt, Korvettenkapitän Werner 3
von Stockhausen, Korvettenkäpitan Hans Gerrit 3, 6, 84, 118, 158
von Varendorff, Oberleutnant-zur-See 135
Walker 149–150
Wandby 135
War at Sea, The 43, 111
Warspite 84–5
Washington naval treaties, 1921–2 2
Watson, Rear-Admiral 143
Weddigen 3
Wehr, Konteradmiral 39–40, 87
Weingärtner, Korvettenkapitän Hannes 3, 110
Wellfield 156
Weserübung, Operation 19, 80, 82, 88
Wessels, Korvettenkäpitan 36
Western Hebrides 34, 77
Whitehall 134, 138
Whitford Point 135, 165
Wilhelmshaven 7, 13, 14, 16, 37–8, 65–6, 73, 77, 89, 97, 113
Wilja 76, 161
Winkleigh 15, 160
Winn, Lord 140
Wohlfahrt, Oehrn 137, 154
Wolverine 150
Wotan 65
York 84, 170
Zahn 39
Zapp, Korvettenkäpitan 159
Zeesen 8
Zenker, Admiral 61
Zerpka, Kapitänleutnant 6
Zürn, Erich 10, 20, 22, 25, 49, 53, 64–5, 88, 119, 129, 153, 158–9